IMAGES
of America

Texas Citrus Fiesta

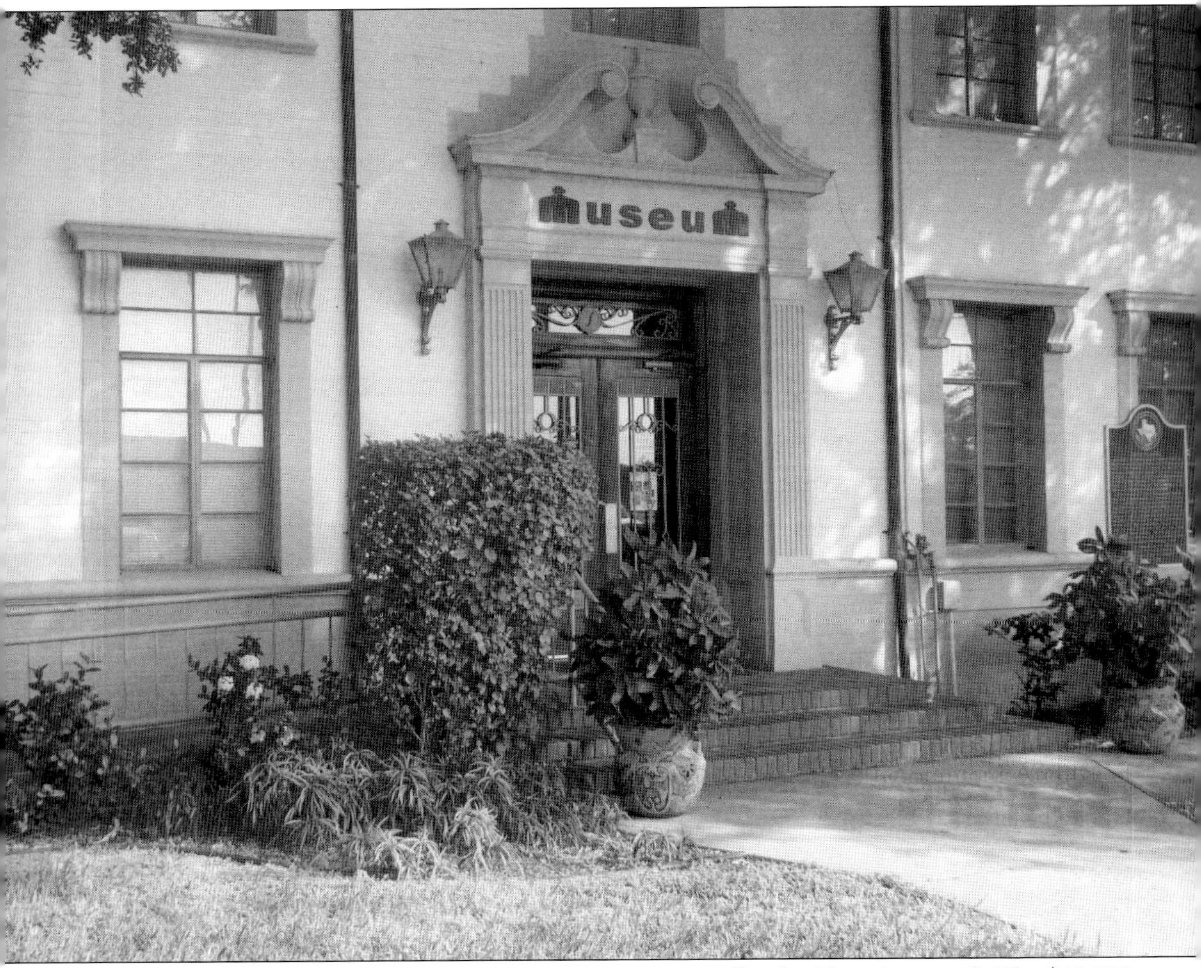

In 1939, John H. Shary broke ground for a new two-story office building (pictured). The $40,000 structure, completed that year, consisted of offices for his many business interests. Today, the historic office building is home to the Mission Historical Museum, Inc. (Courtesy Mission Historical Museum, Inc.)

On the Cover: In 1935, King Citrus III, Levi Walker, a Mission businessman, and Queen Citrianna III, Merble Parr of Raymondville, reigned over the Kingdom of Citrus, Court of Grapefruit. In addition, 18 duchesses represented Rio Grande Valley cities and Reynosa, Mexico. (Courtesy Mission Historical Museum, Inc.)

IMAGES
of America

Texas Citrus Fiesta

Karen Gerhardt Fort
and the Mission Historical Museum, Inc.

ARCADIA
PUBLISHING

ISBN 978-1-4671-3154-4

Published by Arcadia Publishing
Charleston, South Carolina

Printed in the United States of America

Library of Congress Control Number: 2013957657

For all general information, please contact Arcadia Publishing:
Telephone 843-853-2070
Fax 843-853-0044
E-mail sales@arcadiapublishing.com
For customer service and orders:
Toll-Free 1-888-313-2665

Visit us on the Internet at www.arcadiapublishing.com

Dedicated to the memory of Maurine Duncan Nickolaus, teacher, artist, costume designer, historian, author, city council member, businesswoman, wife, and mother

CONTENTS

ACKNOWLEDGMENTS

In the 1930s, the residents of Mission began celebrating the accomplishments of their young city with vision, imagination, ingenuity, and enterprise. They established the Texas Citrus Fiesta as the format for that celebration. Today, more than 80 years later, traditional and new events draw thousands of visitors to the city for the annual event. Fortunately, over the years, Maurine Duncan Nickolaus collected hundreds of photographs of the fiesta, now at the Mission Historical Museum Inc. Although images from a 1935 scrapbook have been used to illustrate some fiesta activities, the remaining photographs have come from the Duncan collection.

I wish to thank the Mission Historical Museum Inc. for permission to use these photographs, for support with research, and for technical assistance in reproducing the images. I extend deepest thanks to Luís Contreras, director of the museum; Vernon Weckbacher, archivist; Linda Castañeda, development officer; and María Picazo, office assistant, each of whom provided cheerful and generous encouragement.

Special thanks are due to Vernon Weckbacher, who kindly allowed me to use his desk and workspace numerous times for research and scanning. He provided many historical details about Mission and the fiesta.

I am deeply grateful to the late Berta Filut, former director of the Texas Citrus Fiesta, who answered many questions regarding details about the festivities.

I especially want to thank my husband, Tom A. Fort, for his help in acquiring research materials and for scanning images, offering valuable suggestions, and sharing the arduous process of creating a new book.

Finally, I wish to thank Arcadia Publishing for asking me to write this book about the Texas Citrus Fiesta.

All images appear courtesy of the Mission Historical Museum Inc. Historical details have come from the following newspapers: *Mission Times*, the *Monitor* (McAllen), and the *Upper Valley Progress* (Mission). Issues of the *Mission Times* are courtesy of the Museum of South Texas History (Edinburg).

Introduction

In 1912, John H. Shary (1872–1945), a registered pharmacist from Nebraska, arrived in the young city of Mission with big dreams. He had already enjoyed financial success as a salesman of redwood lumber in California, which allowed him to travel widely. Between 1904 and 1911, he and a partner bought and sold some 268,000 acres near Corpus Christi, Texas. With their land holdings depleted, in 1912, the partners went their separate ways, one to Colorado and the other to the Rio Grande Valley.

In 1913, Shary bought 16,000 acres at Mission and built an irrigation system, and he planted the first commercial grapefruit orchard in 1915. By 1922, he owned more than 49,000 acres, a development he named Sharyland. That year, he harvested the first commercial grapefruit crop. Workers sorted, cleaned, and graded the fruit by hand. In November 1922, he married longtime friend and business associate Mary E. O'Brien.

The next year, Shary visited California to study the more developed citrus industry there. He returned to Mission to build a large citrus-packing plant and to establish the Texas Citrus Fruit Growers Exchange for the marketing and distribution of citrus crops.

According to author Cleo Dawson Smith in a 1963 article that appears in the 26th Annual Citrus Fiesta Edition of the *Mission Times*, the idea for a festival to celebrate a successful crop and promote Mission and Hidalgo County was first suggested by Judge Dennis B. Chapin around 1910. Bermuda onions were his crop of choice. However, due to a hard-hitting freeze, the "Onion Fair" never materialized.

The highly successful crop of 1922 led to the celebration of the citrus industry with a fair and rodeo in early 1923. According to Dawson, fruit packers competed to see who was the quickest, and ladies from the area competed with their "special pastries, cakes, preserves and handwork" (decorative sewing) for first-, second-, and third-place prizes. The committee that was planning the event invited John Shary to be the Grapefruit King and Emogene (Mrs. A.Y.) Baker to be the queen.

Within a few years, the success of Mission's citrus industry had become well established. Conversations during a December 1930 party held at the Shary mansion inspired Mission leaders to promote the marketing and sale of citrus products by holding a community-wide event. Paul Ord, chairman of the Young Men's Business League, an affiliate of the Mission Chamber of Commerce, became general chairman of the event, and the league served as the committee in charge of events (and again in 1934), with the help of additional volunteer committees.

After a year of planning, the first Texas Citrus Fiesta took place on December 9, 1932, with Shary honored as the "father" of the Texas citrus industry. Since 1932, governance of the fiesta by a volunteer executive committee and apportionment of work to various committees of volunteers have remained essential parts of the fiesta's success. Several events of the first fiesta have become traditions: contests involving the entire community, citrus product exhibits, the coronation of Queen Citrianna and King Citrus, the Parade of Oranges with a float for fiesta royalty, printed programs, and the naming of Queen Citrianna for the following year. Also begun in 1932 was a program of entertainment during the coronation, followed by the Queen's Ball.

Some newspaper articles state that the first style show occurred in 1932, but it is not clear whether the garments were made from valley-grown products. Other articles from the 1930s are silent on the subject. It is definite, however, that in 1934, costumes made of fruits and vegetables were a prominent feature of the fiesta. In 1935, the style show became a well-publicized highlight.

Hispanic residents of Mission were represented in 1932 by dance director Carmen Barrera, numerous dancers, and high school band members. In future years, beautiful Hispanic girls and women participated as committee members, duchesses, princesses, queens, and style show models. Handsome Hispanic boys and men served on committees, escorted the duchesses, contributed musical fanfares at the coronation, placed citrus exhibits in their store windows, and performed many tasks. A few even served as models for the product costume shows.

The success of the first Texas Citrus Fiesta led to larger, more elaborate events and greater involvement of individuals and sponsors. The first local golf tournament took place in 1933 and became an official part of the Fiesta in 1934 as the Golden Grapefruit Golf Tournament. Duchesses representing cities throughout the Rio Grande Valley joined the queen's court. The governor of Texas announced Texas Citrus Week with an official proclamation. Newsreel cameramen, newspaper reporters, and radio newsmen provided coverage of the fiesta. Major periodicals and, later, television expanded that coverage. The lively and colorful Texas Citrus Fiesta lightened the dark days of the Great Depression across the country.

With the exception of 1933 (hurricane) and 1942–1946 (World War II), the fiesta has taken place each winter since 1932. Only images from the first 50 years (1932–1982) are presented here.

All of the photographs are from the Maureen Duncan Nickolaus Collection at the Mission Historical Museum, Inc. The reader is asked to remember that this was a personal collection of photographs. Neither all years and nor all events are represented. This is also an extensive collection, and information is not available about many of the images. Some could not be used because of damage or fading.

Many of the photographs appeared in the *Mission Times*, and details about the images between 1932 and 1972 come from that newspaper. Information about photographs dating between 1973 and 1982 come from the *Upper Valley Progress*, fiesta programs, and the Mission Historical Museum's archives.

In more recent times, some events have been dropped (the golf tournament, window and street decorations, and flower exhibits). But the fiesta continues to hold the Princess Anna contest (begun in 1951); the coronation of King Citrus and Queen Citrianna; the Queen's Ball; citrus exhibits by students in Future Farmers of America and 4-H organizations; the product costume style show; and the Parade of Oranges. Since the 1930s, the governor of Texas formally proclaims Texas Citrus Week each year.

Newer events include a one-day Fun Fair and Vaquero Cook-off Contest, a "fun run" marathon, activities designed for Winter Texans, and a carnival. A gala dinner for fiesta royalty and duchesses, their parents, dignitaries, sponsors, and the fiesta board of directors takes place prior to the coronation.

The Texas Citrus Fiesta now has a permanent office and staff, plus an active board of directors. Through grants and sponsorships, it is self-supporting. The Texas Citrus Fiesta will certainly continue for many years to come.

One

Creating Traditions

The goals of the first Texas Citrus Fiesta organizers were to promote the national marketing and sales of citrus fruit and to stimulate business by bringing visitors to Mission. The first fiesta, entitled "Coronation and Pageant of Citrus," established many of the traditions that continue today.

The first fiesta was a one-day celebration held on Saturday, December 9, 1932. A band concert preceded the first Parade of Oranges, featuring 27 floats. At noon, spectators watched an "aerial circus" at the flying field west of Mission. High school band concerts, a style show, fruit-packing and box-making contests, and a football game followed. A citrus and subtropical fruit exposition took place throughout the day. The Fox Film Corporation recorded fiesta events, footage of which was shown in movie theaters.

Decorations adorned buildings along the city's main streets. Live citrus trees lined the parade route and provided a setting for the coronation ceremony and pageant held at Lions Park that night. W.D. Toland of Mission was crowned King Grapefruit I (amended to King Citrus by 1936), and Marguerite Daniel became Queen Citrianna I. The Mission High School band provided music for vocal and dance performances, a "March of the Harvest," and the recessional. After the coronation and announcement of the next year's Queen Citrianna came the Queen's Ball (tickets cost $1.65 per couple), which took place at the Sprowl Fruit Packing Plant, the only building large enough to hold the crowd attending the ball.

A hurricane canceled the 1933 fiesta, but it returned in 1934 with new features, such as expansion to two days, a style show with garments made of citrus products, a rodeo, citrus displays in the windows of businesses, and the Golden Grapefruit Golf Tournament. The 1937 fiesta was moved to January 1938 in order to attract more winter visitors and to prevent conflicts with the Christmas holiday.

The fiesta offered new and bigger events, and it gained state and national attention through 1941. Plans were made for a 1942 fiesta, but it did not take place due to the nation's entry into World War II.

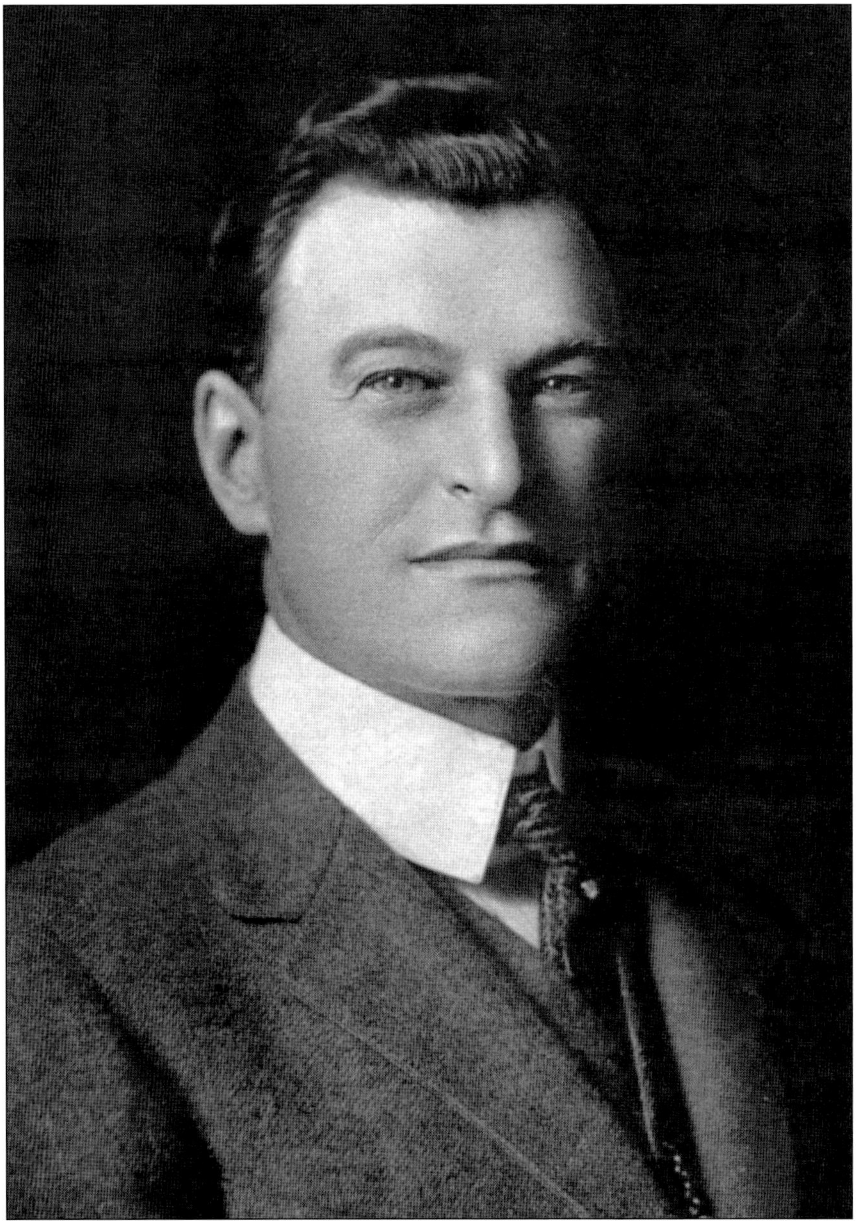

John H. Shary, seen here around 1910, arrived in Mission in 1912 and began buying large tracts of land in 1913. He named the property Sharyland, and by 1915, he had planted thousands of acres of grapefruit trees. The trees matured and produced the first crop in 1922. After a trip to California in 1923, Shary built the first commercial citrus-packing plant in Mission and founded the Texas Citrus Fruit Growers Exchange. Shary built a luxurious mansion (completed in 1917) to serve as a clubhouse for prospective land buyers, and it later became a home for his family and distinguished guests. He established the Sharyland Independent School District in 1921 and served as school board president until 1939. Shary built a yacht club at Port Isabel to entertain dignitaries such as Vice Pres. John Nance Garner, oilman Jesse H. Jones, and Mission developer Lloyd M. Bentsen Sr. In his later years, he was instrumental in the expansion of the intracoastal waterway between Corpus Christi and Brownsville.

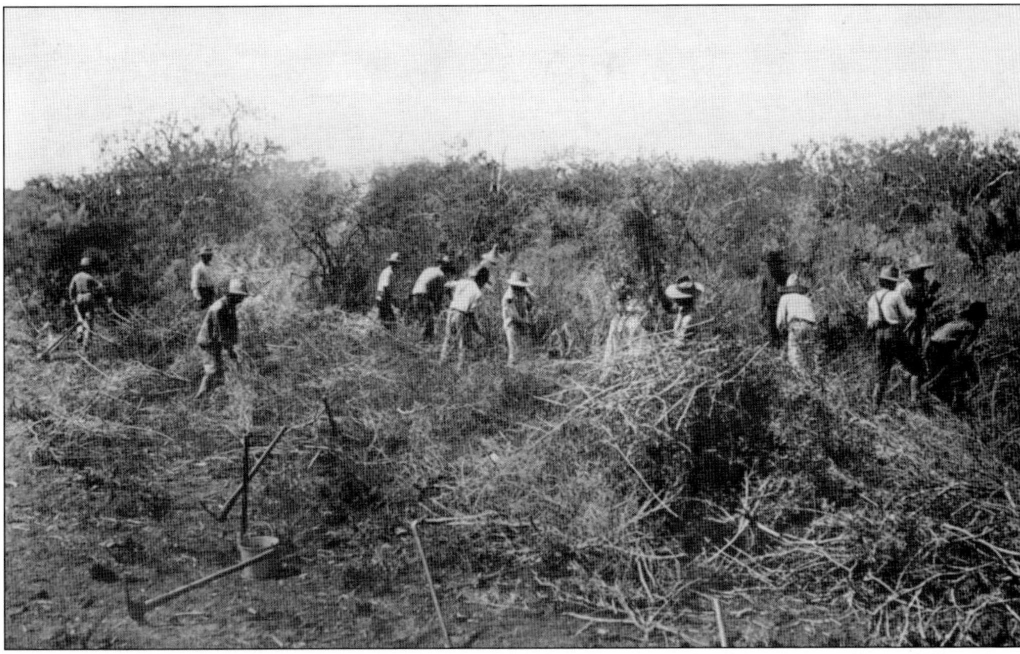

Before any improvements could be made, land had to be cleared. This image, from a Sharyland promotional booklet, shows workers using machetes to chop down thorny brush, cactus, and mesquite trees. They stacked the vegetation into large piles and set them on fire. Whether from Texas or Mexico, workers earned 25¢ per day, the usual rate for the time.

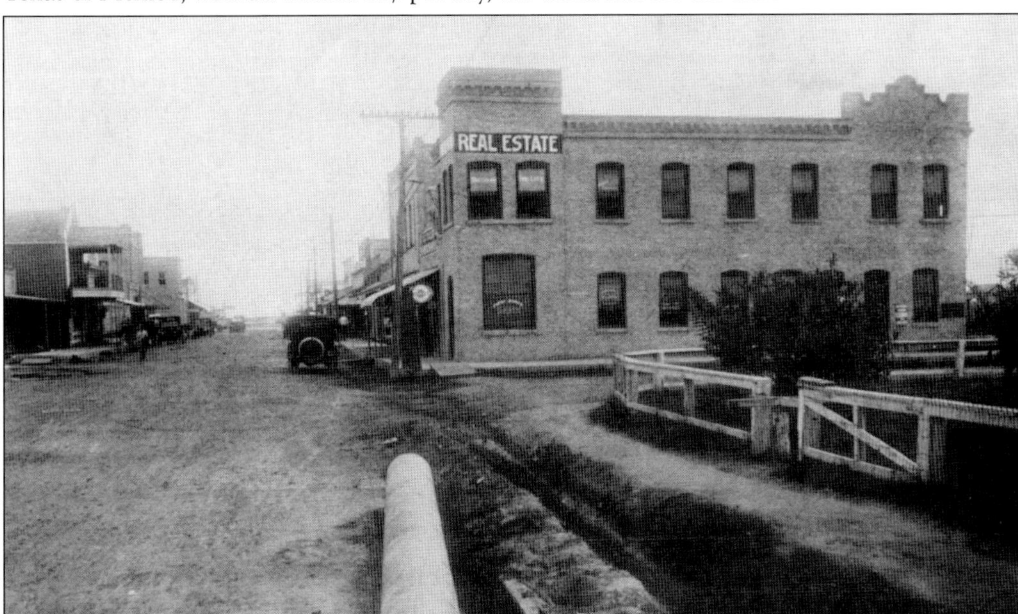

John J. Conway, a land developer from rural South Dakota, and James W. Hoit, a grain merchant from Minneapolis, Minnesota, traveled to the Rio Grande Valley in 1906. After buying land from the Oblate Fathers and others, the partners established Mission in 1909, named for the chapel near their townsite. The view in this undated street scene looks north along Lomita Boulevard (now Conway Avenue). A drainage pipe lies in the foreground.

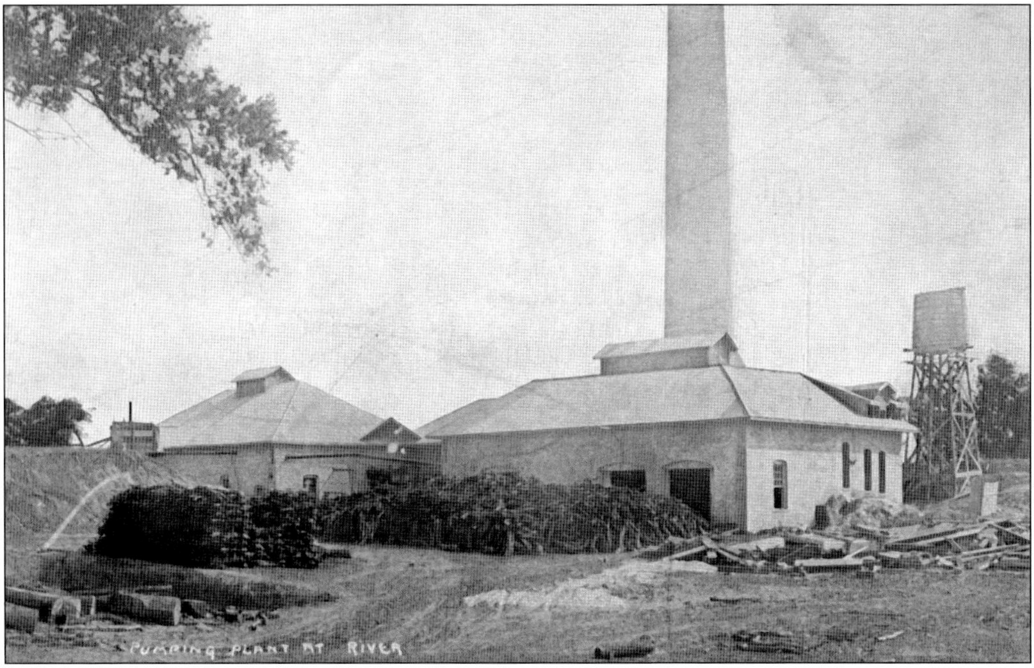

To provide water for thousands of new acres under cultivation, pumping stations were built along the Rio Grande to raise water above the banks and force it into a system of canals. The first of Shary's three lift stations, seen here, used centrifugal pumps, one measuring 48 inches and two at 36 inches. A timber pile to supply wood-fired boilers lies at center. The station had a capacity of 160,000 gallons per minute.

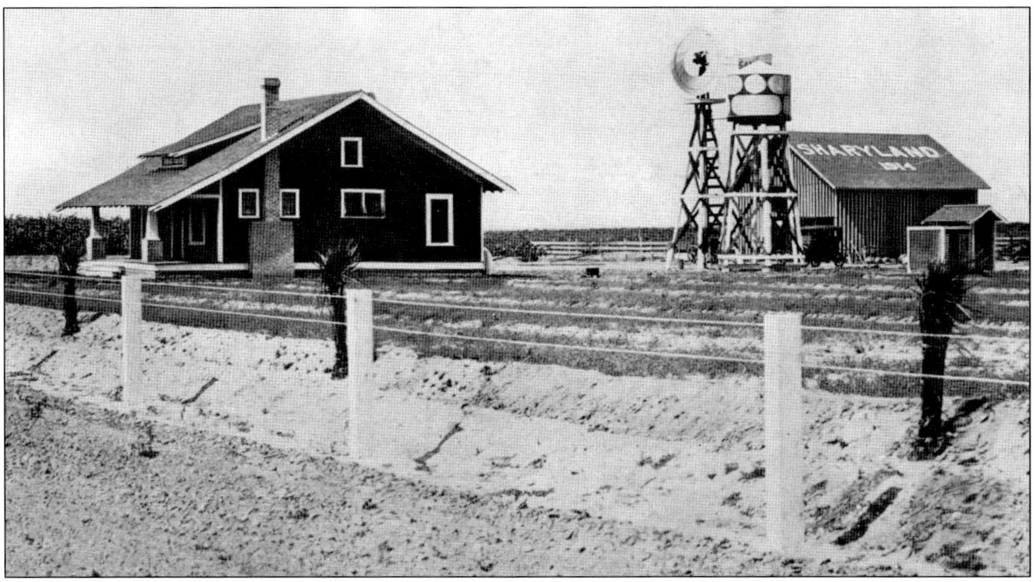

To sell land, developers like Shary brought prospective buyers on excursion trains from the Midwest to the Rio Grande Valley. They built model farms to show how productive the land could be. Shary owned this "Improved Farm in Sharyland," according to the promotional booklet, which states that the photograph had been taken less than five months after the land had been cleared. Note the date "1914" on the barn roof.

This young orange tree, photographed for Shary's promotional booklet, is heavily laden with fruit, indicating the success of citrus development in Sharyland. The caption beneath the image in the booklet reads, "No fertilization is necessary." The gentleman is unidentified. Although many citrus groves were damaged by freezes and droughts in later years, oranges, grapefruit, and lemons continue to thrive in the Rio Grande Valley.

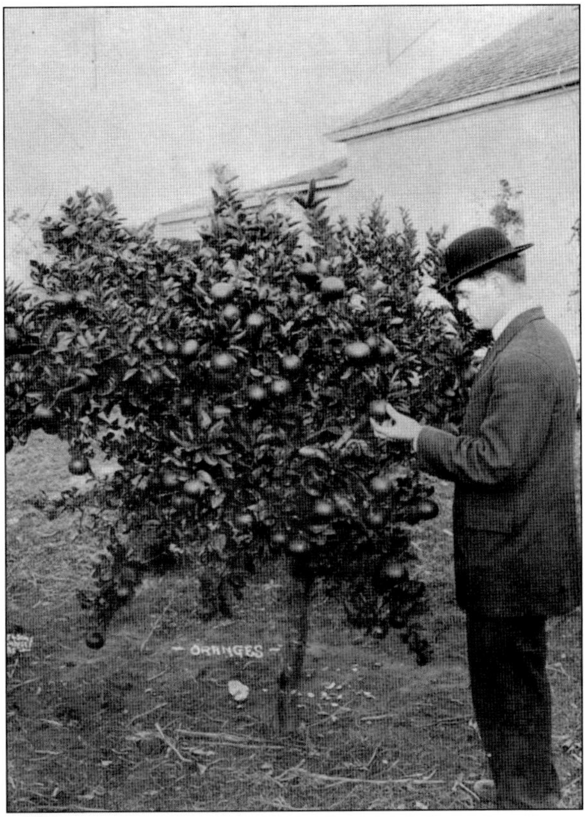

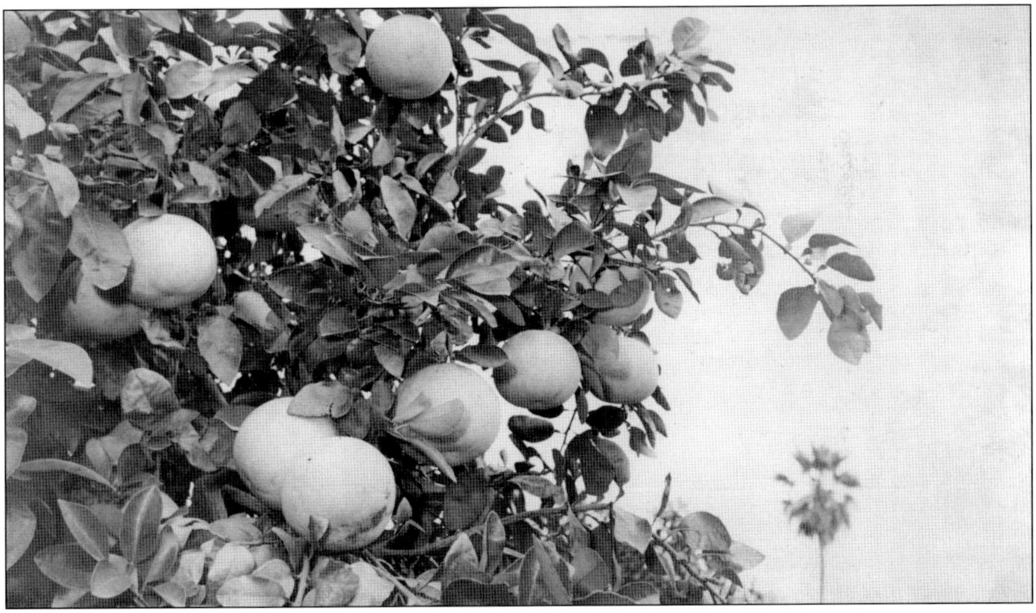

These bountiful branches show perfect clusters of grapefruit. Although this image does not appear in the promotional booklet, it is from the same time period (around 1920). Note the palm tree in the distance. Palm trees, except for the sabal palm, are not native to the valley, but they were planted here to make the flat terrain more attractive.

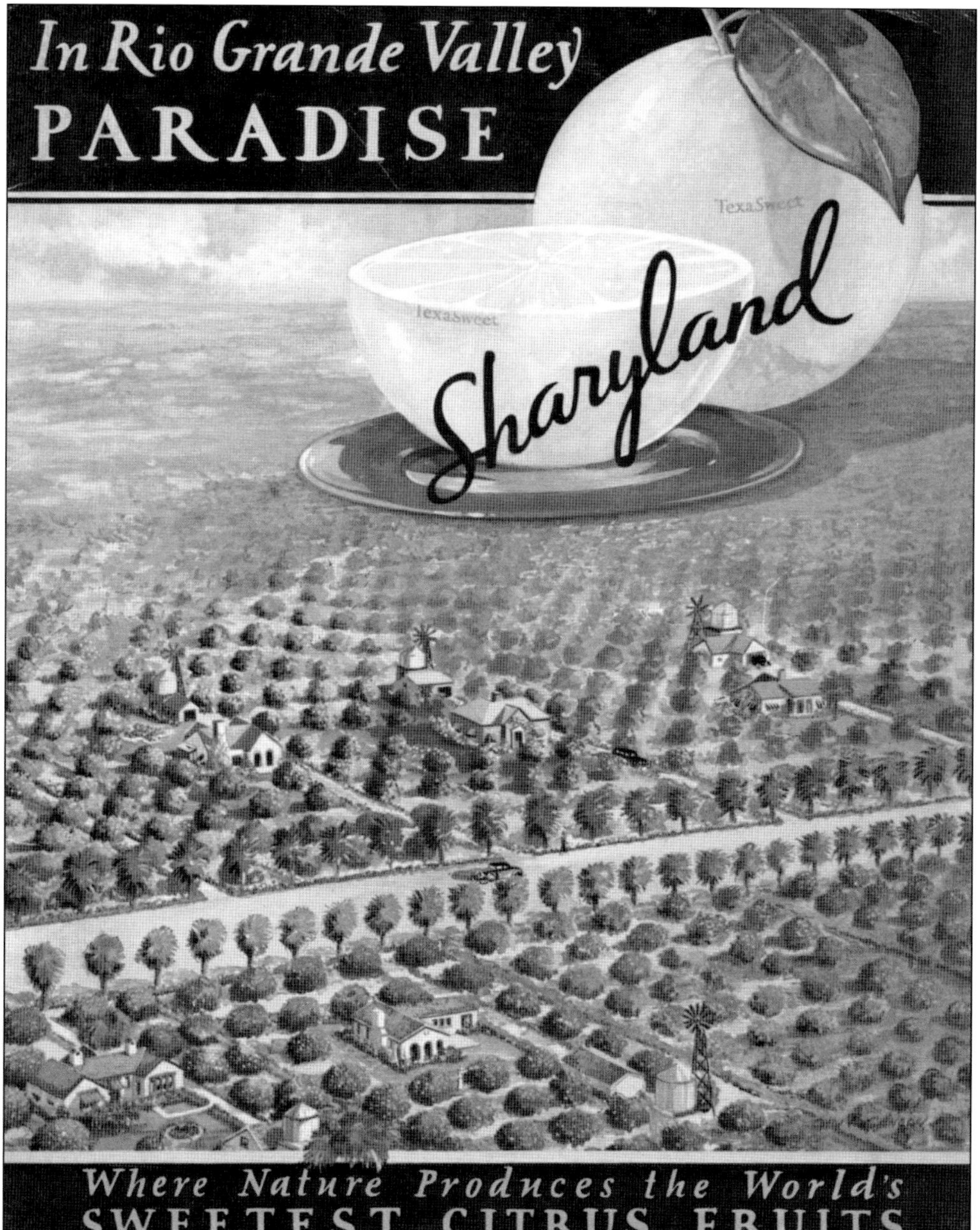

This promotional booklet, undated but from a later time than the previously mentioned booklet, indicates the influence of California on the citrus-growing region of the Rio Grande Valley. To advertise Sharyland, it emphasizes citrus groves, homes, and schools. Seen on the road are a school bus, an automobile, and horses. The full-color imagery spreads across the front and back covers. Along with his other interests, in 1930, John Shary founded the Shary Products Company to process, can, and bottle grapefruit juice, labeled Río Rey ("river king"). By the late 1930s, citrus had become a $125 million industry, and John Shary was recognized as the "Father of the Texas Citrus Industry." The citizens of Mission, "Home of the Grapefruit," had much to celebrate, and many of the Texas Citrus Fiesta events, especially the costumes made from fruit and vegetable parts, earned Mission national status.

Marguerite Daniel, Queen Citrianna I (1932), ruled over the Court of Citrus, which included two heralds, a prime minister (master of ceremonies), a maid of honor, four ladies-in-waiting, two train bearers, a crown bearer, a jester, and seven princesses from valley cities with their attendants and escorts. Daniel was the daughter of Sheriff and Mrs. R.T. Daniel. King Grapefruit I, William D. Toland, was a Mission produce shipper.

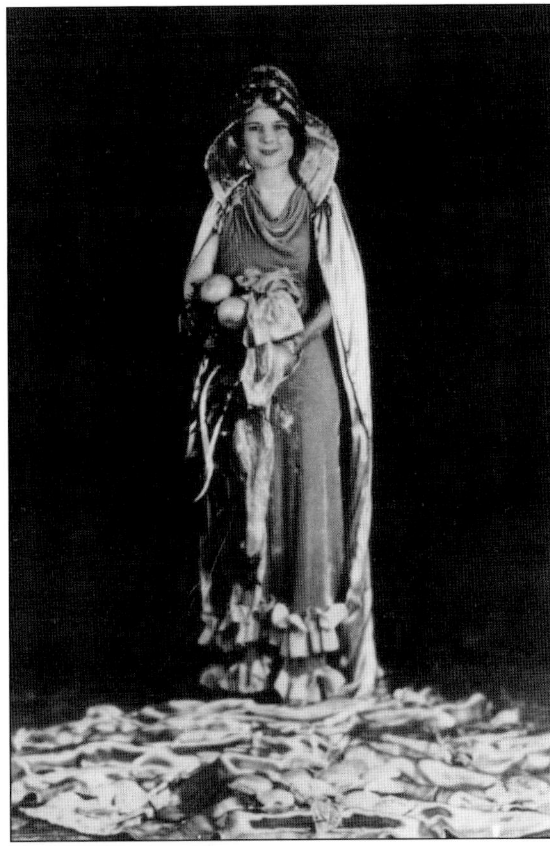

The first float designated for fiesta royalty is shown here during the rainy parade held on December 9, 1932. Seated in back is Marguerite Daniel. Her maid of honor, Jennie Page, sits nearby. Sharing the float are ladies-in-waiting Clyde Wilson (front, left), Annie Laurie Fontenot (behind Wilson), Melrose Stoops (front, right), and Ruth Duncan (almost unseen). The Fox Film Company recorded the Parade of Oranges, which featured 27 floats.

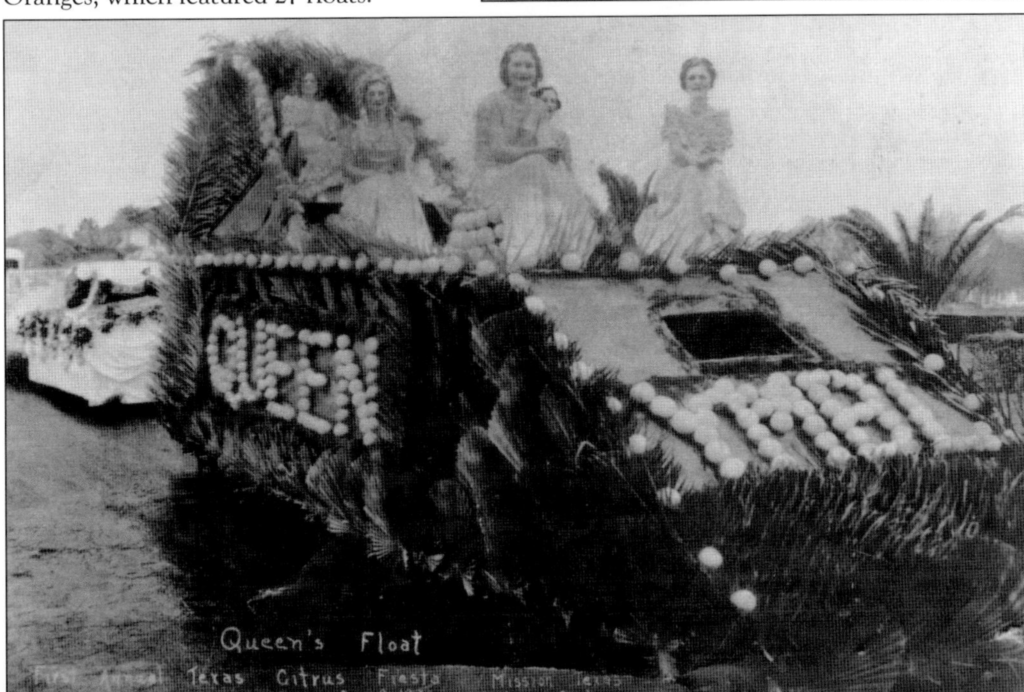

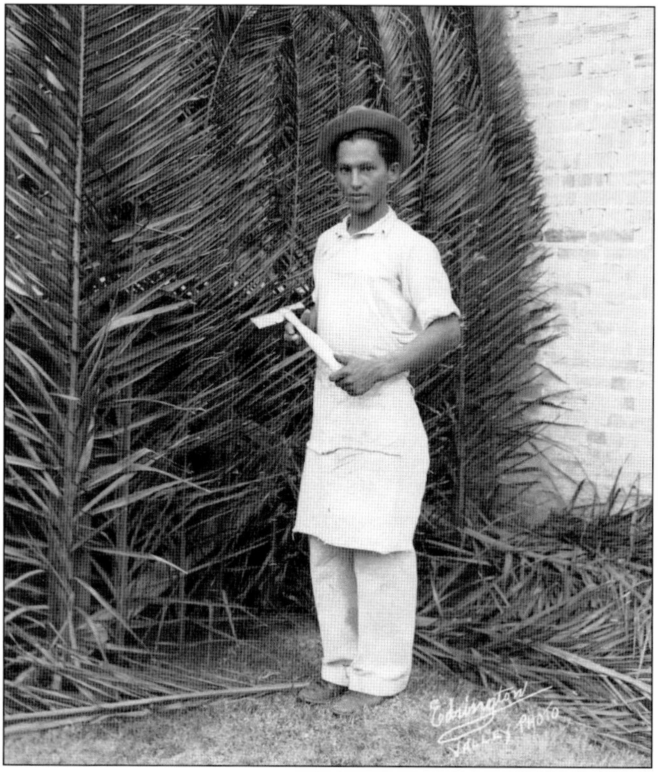

This unidentified worker is trimming palm branches to accent the speaker's platform in 1935. Street decorations for the Parade of Oranges included festoons of citrus leaves and fruit, arches covered with Spanish moss and citrus fruit, and streets lined with growing citrus trees. Palm branches were used in window decorations and formed a backdrop for the coronation festivities at night. In later years, they disguised parking meters.

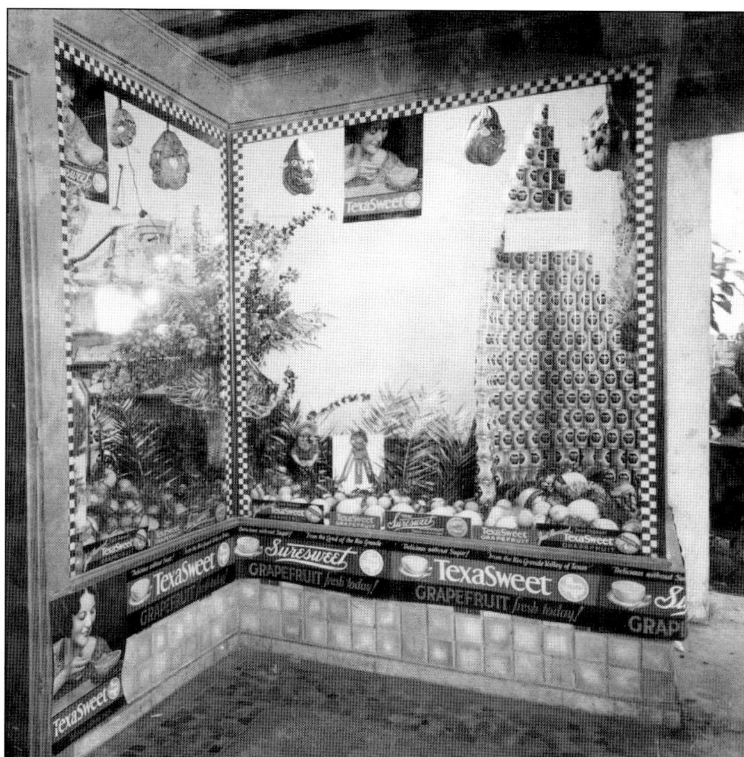

Merchants in 1934 did not create window displays, due to the loss of the 1933 citrus crop and the industry's need to recover those losses with the 1934 crop. However, in 1935, with plenty of fruit available, competition returned, and merchants again decorated their store windows. The Texas Citrus Fruit Growers Exchange won second place that year, using grapefruit from the Shary Products Company plant at Val Verde. Its entry is shown here.

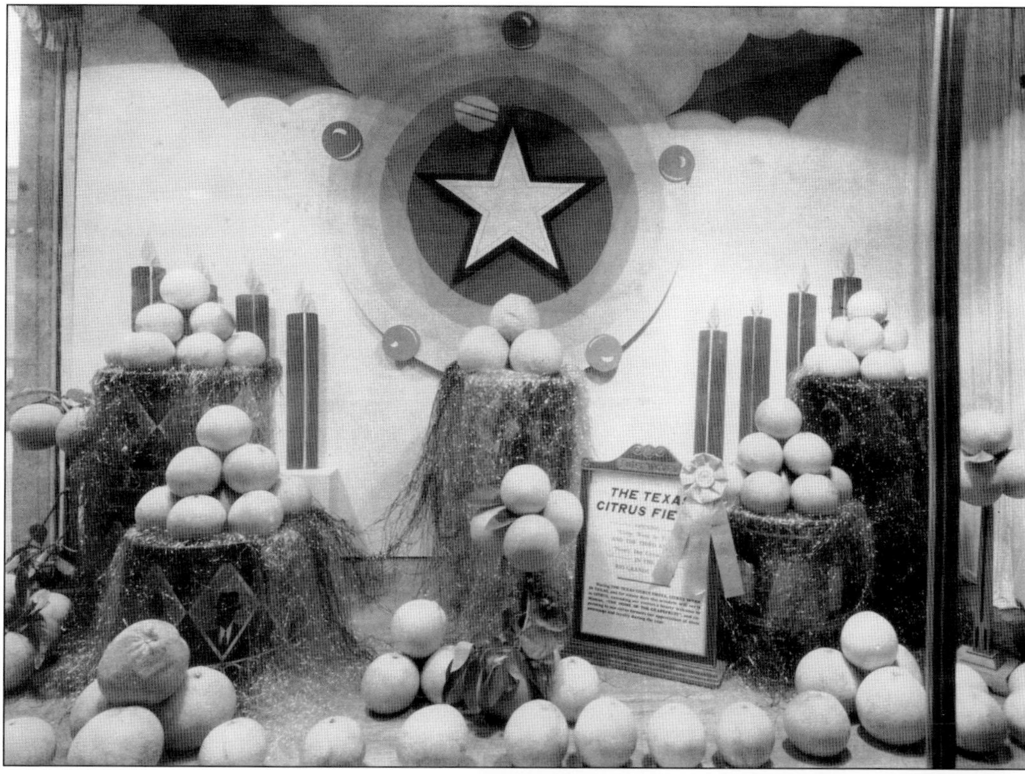

While most of the nation struggled with the hardships of the Great Depression, the Rio Grande Valley fared comparatively well. This was due to the development of rail transportation and concrete roads across the region, a plentiful labor force, and extensive advertising. Chambers of commerce throughout the valley joined the Texas Citrus Fiesta celebration. Baum's Men's Wear of Mission, shown here, won fourth place in the 1935 window display competition.

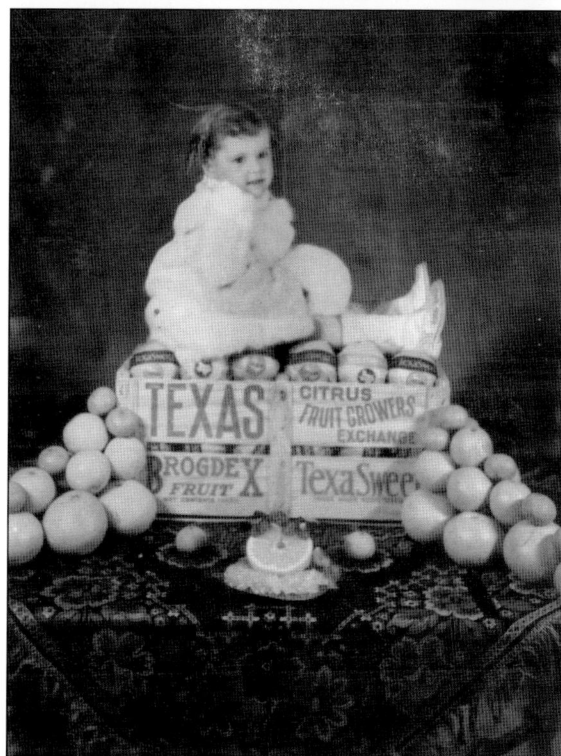

The 1935 exposition, held at the Caldwell Building, hosted over 50 displays of citrus and citrus by-products from 20 growers. The Texas Citrus Fruit Growers Exchange provided an exhibit on grading and packing fruit. The young lady perched on top of this display is believed to be Betty Bentsen (Winn). Contest winners received ribbons instead of monetary awards. The citrus exposition remains an important feature of the fiesta.

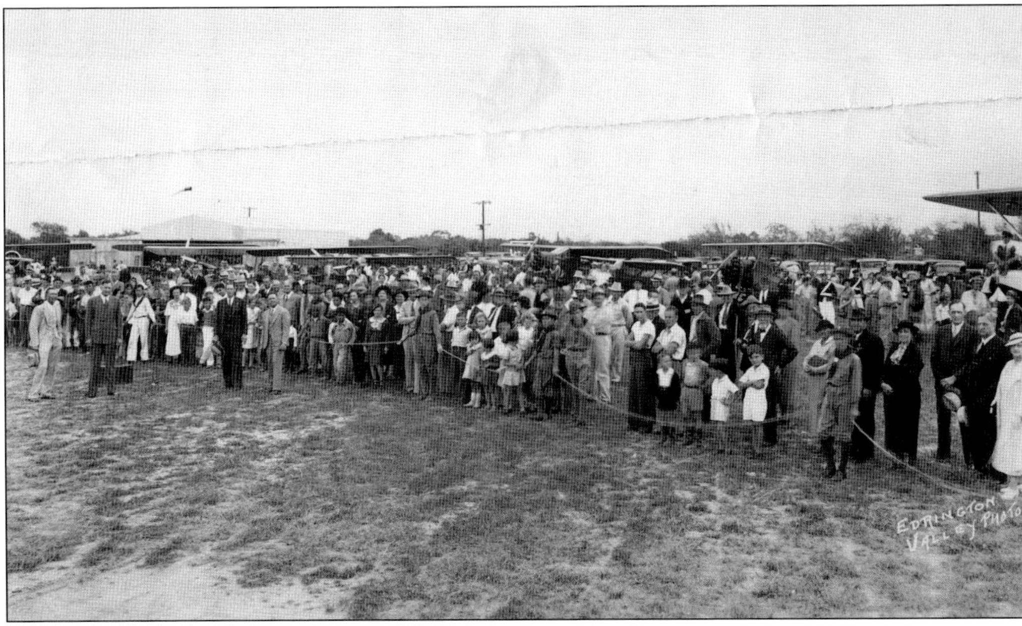

US congressman Milton H. West of Brownsville officially opened the 1935 celebration and dedicated the new Shary Municipal Airport. Spectators could view 12 airplanes parked at the airport (visible behind the crowd), watch an aerial circus, and visit a Boy Scouts model camp. O.K. Rumbel, father of rocket scientist Keith Rumbel, was chairman of the dedication committee. Aerial events remained an important part of the fiesta until 1940.

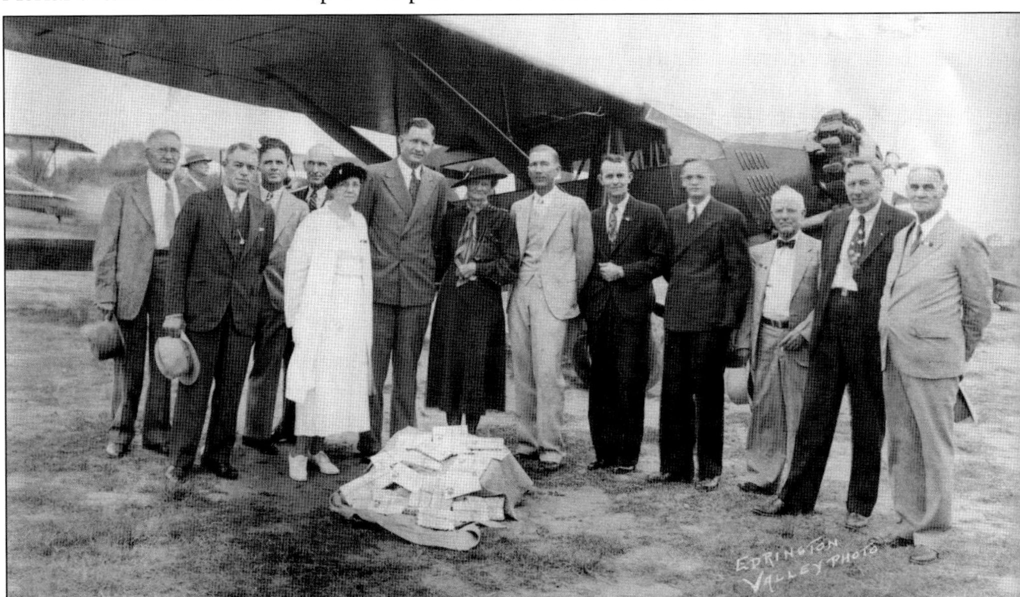

A Braniff Airways mail plane brought visitors from Brownsville to the new airport and collected bags filled with letters for the return to Brownsville and connection with other Braniff mail planes. The Mission Post Office offered a special two-color cancellation stamp, or cachet, for first-class and airmail letters on December 7 and 8, 1935. E.E. Marburger, general chairman of the Texas Citrus Fiesta, stands third from left.

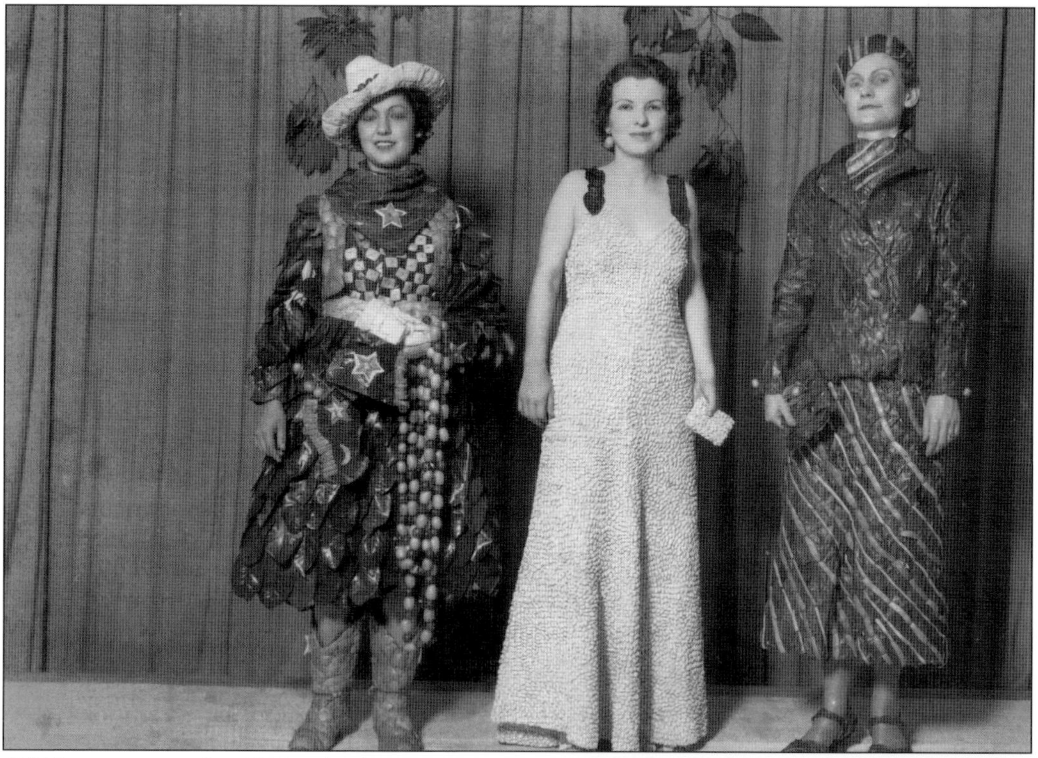

Of 19 entrants in the 1935 style show, the winners are, from left to right, Sara Femat (cowgirl costume of citrus peel and leaves), Mrs. Bob Euler (evening gown of citrus seed and peel), and Clyde Wilson (sports outfit of orange and grapefruit peel strips, citrus leaves, and kumquat trim). Gene Davis, sports writer for the *Mission Times*, designed the outfit for Wilson, his girlfriend, who received first prize ($25).

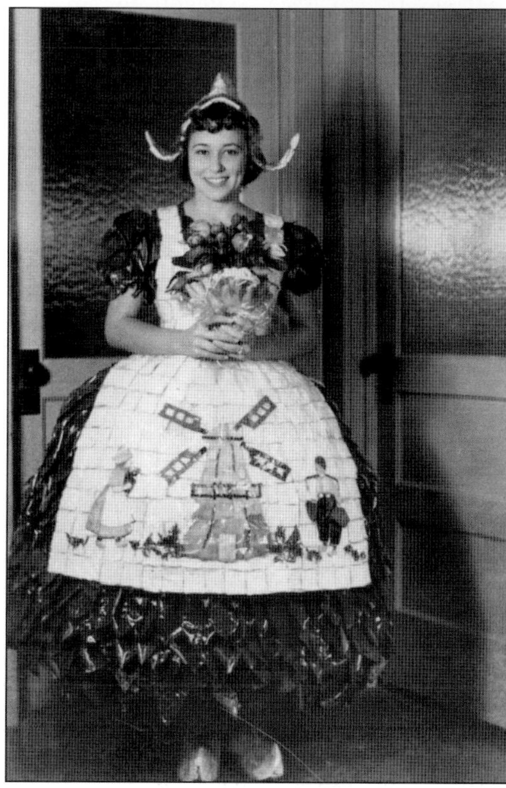

Elaborate costumes made from natural products have always been a highlight of the Texas Citrus Fiesta. Women from sponsoring organizations sewed on or wrapped the fresh materials in cellophane and glued them onto a foundation garment to make the costume in one day. In 1938, Mission High School sophomore Helen Miller wears a Dutch costume of tangerine peel and shoes covered with grapefruit rind. She holds a corsage made from cauliflower.

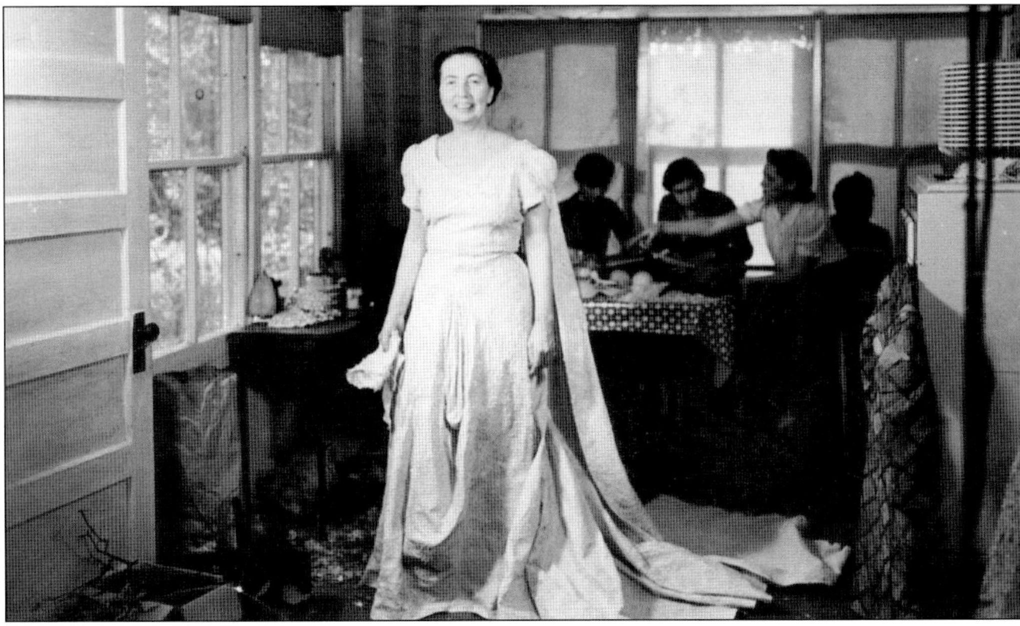

For the 1941 style show, John Shary's secretary, Lavinia Bourgeois, wears a dress that copied the inaugural ball gown soon to be worn by First Lady Eleanor Roosevelt. Instead of satin, this dress consists of a foundation covered with cornmeal bran. The "diamond" necklace was made from golden grapefruit peel. Mrs. Logan Duncan designed the costume, and newsreel cameramen filmed the progress of dress construction at the Duncan home.

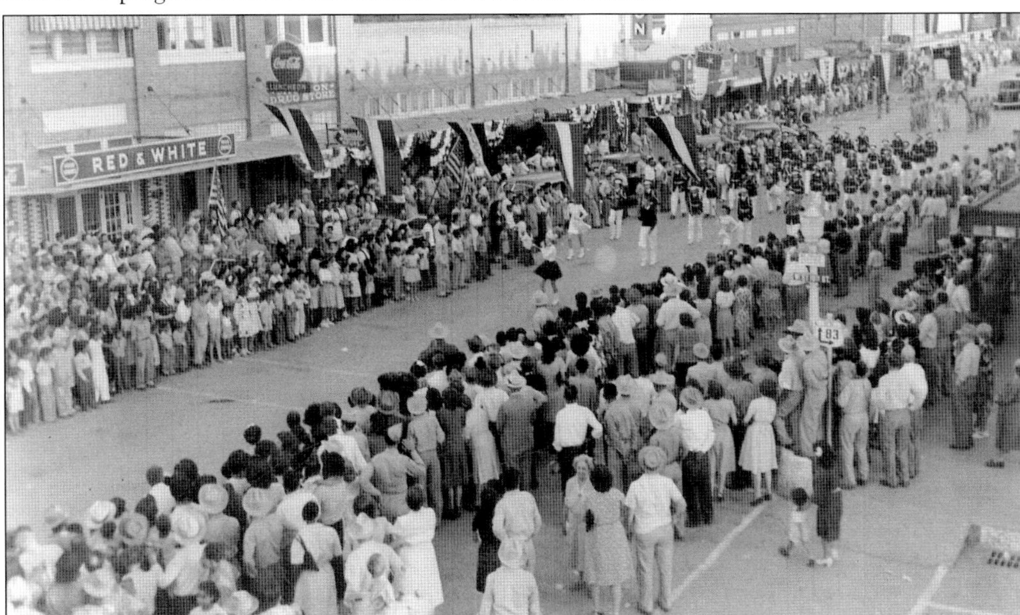

The theme for the January 1941 fiesta was patriotic: "The Rio Grande Valley Serves America." With thousands watching, the Parade of Oranges featured six bands and 21 floats, including two from Reynosa, Mexico. Bringing horses and mechanized units, 400 cavalrymen from Fort Ringgold set up camp at the Mission High School football field and marched in the parade. Note the many changes in downtown Mission since the early 1920s.

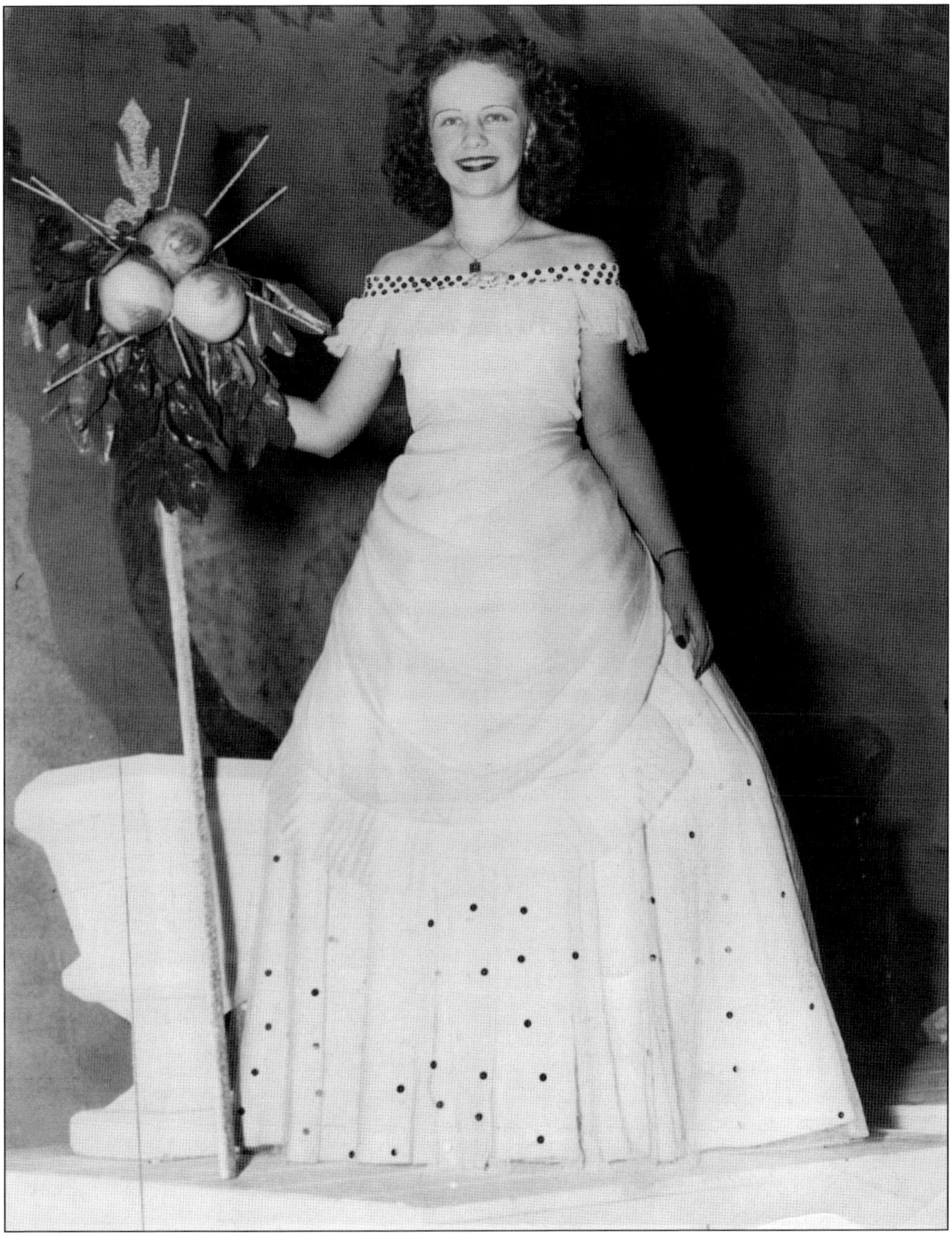

Dorothy Carlisle, Duchess of Harlingen and Princess of North America, is shown here at the 1941 coronation, which took place at the Tex-Sun juice canning plant. Each duchess, from 20 cities and Reynosa, Mexico, carried a staff decorated with citrus, other fruits, or vegetables that represented her hometown. Quita Sammons, who designed the all-white dresses worn by Queen Citrianna and her court, also designed the backdrop for the throne area. Built especially for the coronation, the stage rose in tiers up to the throne area, and single rows of grapefruit outlined each tier. A white background surrounded a large hemisphere, constructed in relief and painted in pastel colors. White urns held red and white gladiolas. Carlisle became an alternate for Queen Citrianna IX, but the 1942 fiesta was canceled due to the nation's entry into World War II.

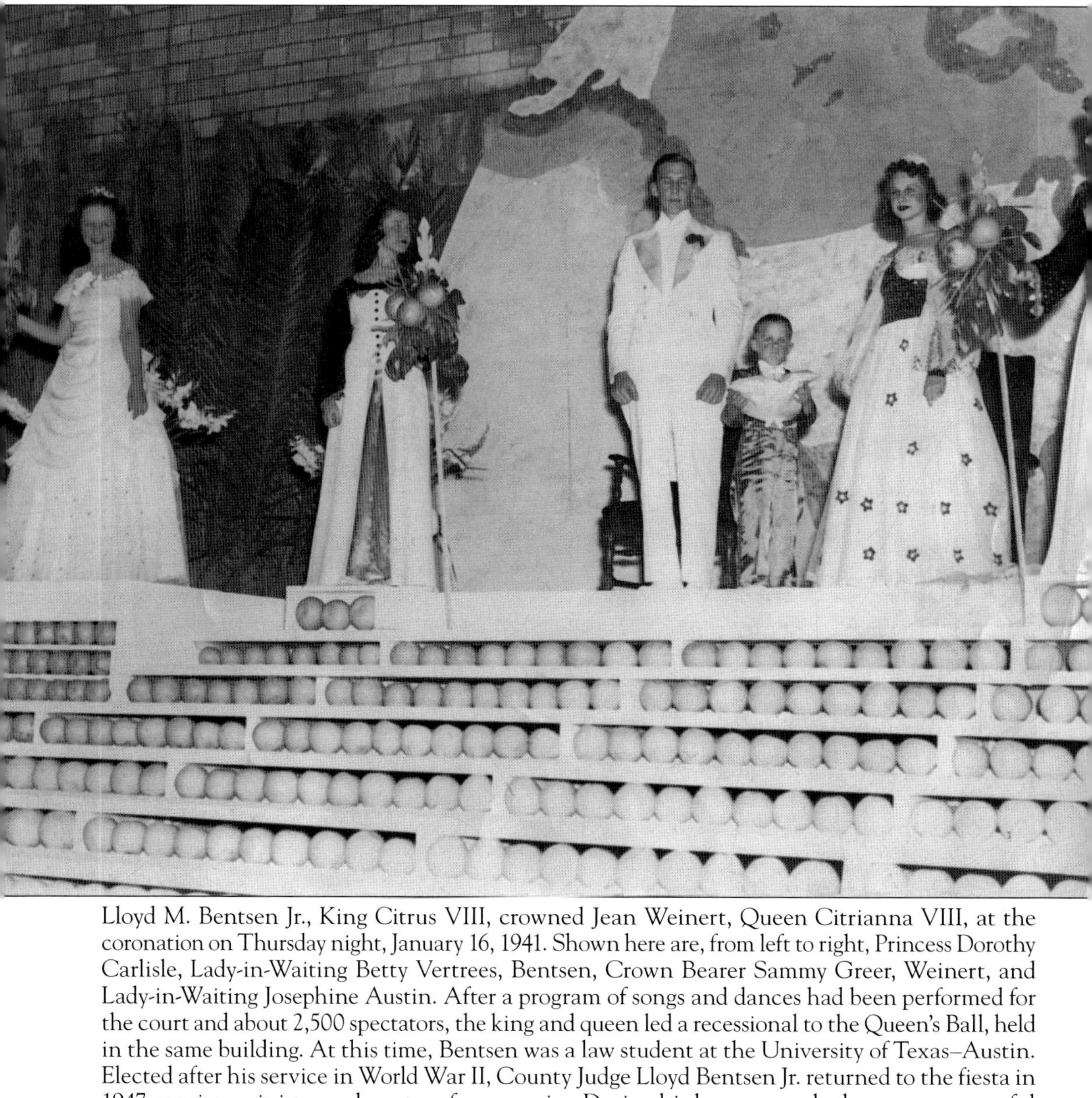

Lloyd M. Bentsen Jr., King Citrus VIII, crowned Jean Weinert, Queen Citrianna VIII, at the coronation on Thursday night, January 16, 1941. Shown here are, from left to right, Princess Dorothy Carlisle, Lady-in-Waiting Betty Vertrees, Bentsen, Crown Bearer Sammy Greer, Weinert, and Lady-in-Waiting Josephine Austin. After a program of songs and dances had been performed for the court and about 2,500 spectators, the king and queen led a recessional to the Queen's Ball, held in the same building. At this time, Bentsen was a law student at the University of Texas–Austin. Elected after his service in World War II, County Judge Lloyd Bentsen Jr. returned to the fiesta in 1947 as prime minister and master of ceremonies. During his long career, he became a successful businessman, a US representative, US senator, and US secretary of the treasury.

Two

Behind the Scenes

In 1932, committees were designated for music, dances, electrician and stage manager, art and design, and costumes. As the Texas Citrus Fiesta grew to four days and many more events, the executive committee created more committees and asked for more volunteers. For example, at a meeting called to organize the seventh fiesta (1940), citizens elected the executive committee and general chairman, E.E. Marburger, and called for volunteers to serve on the following committees: finance, parade, coronation, street decorations, window decorations, Queen's Ball, citrus exhibit, style show; junior parade (with divisions for pet, doll buggy, and bicycle parades), antique and hobby show; flower show; fruit-packing championship; Golden Grapefruit Golf Tournament; and Boy Scouts. Marguerite Daniel Jenkins served on the coronation committee, and her husband, Winston Jenkins, was a member of the street decorations committee.

Sponsoring organizations, prominent civic and social leaders, citrus growers, packers and shippers, and individuals from throughout the Rio Grande Valley joined those from Mission to create bigger and better fiesta events each year through 1941. After World War II, Mission citizens revived the fiesta in 1947 with great energy and imagination. Experienced committee members recruited new volunteers to help and to learn the traditions of the fiesta so that they could carry it forward.

Throughout the 1950s, the Texas Citrus Fiesta grew in organizational expertise, event planning, and community involvement. The opening of the Mission High School Memorial Gymnasium in January 1950 allowed the style shows and coronation to become identified with one location. Arrangements for the fiesta did not begin until November, when many of the volunteers were preparing for their holiday celebrations and travels. While the product costumes were often designed well ahead of time and constructed just before the fiesta, other events came together at the last minute. This was corrected in 1965, when year-round planning began. The following images from the 1950s present some of the volunteers, including one young lady whose volunteer "work" must have been great fun.

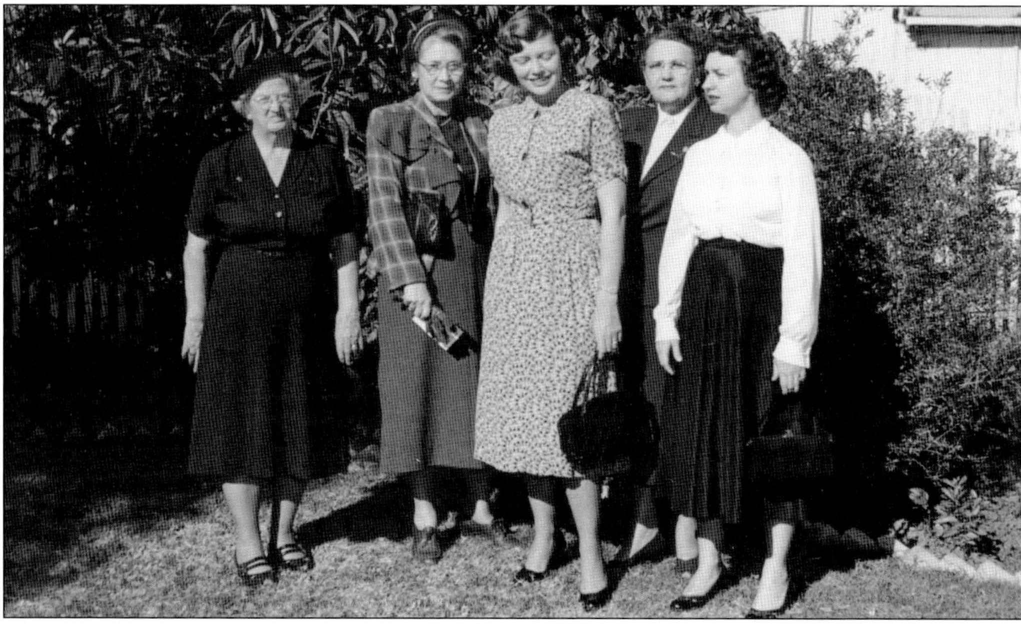

Members of the Mission Garden Club, founded in 1935, set up the flower exhibits for the 1953 fiesta in a showroom at Spikes Motor Company. Here, club members pose in the garden of Mrs. Vernon B. Hill. They are, from left to right, Mrs. W.L. Pearson, Mrs. Ray Goodwin, Mrs. James A. Blocklinger, Mrs. G.C. Williams, and Mrs. Paul Fankhauser.

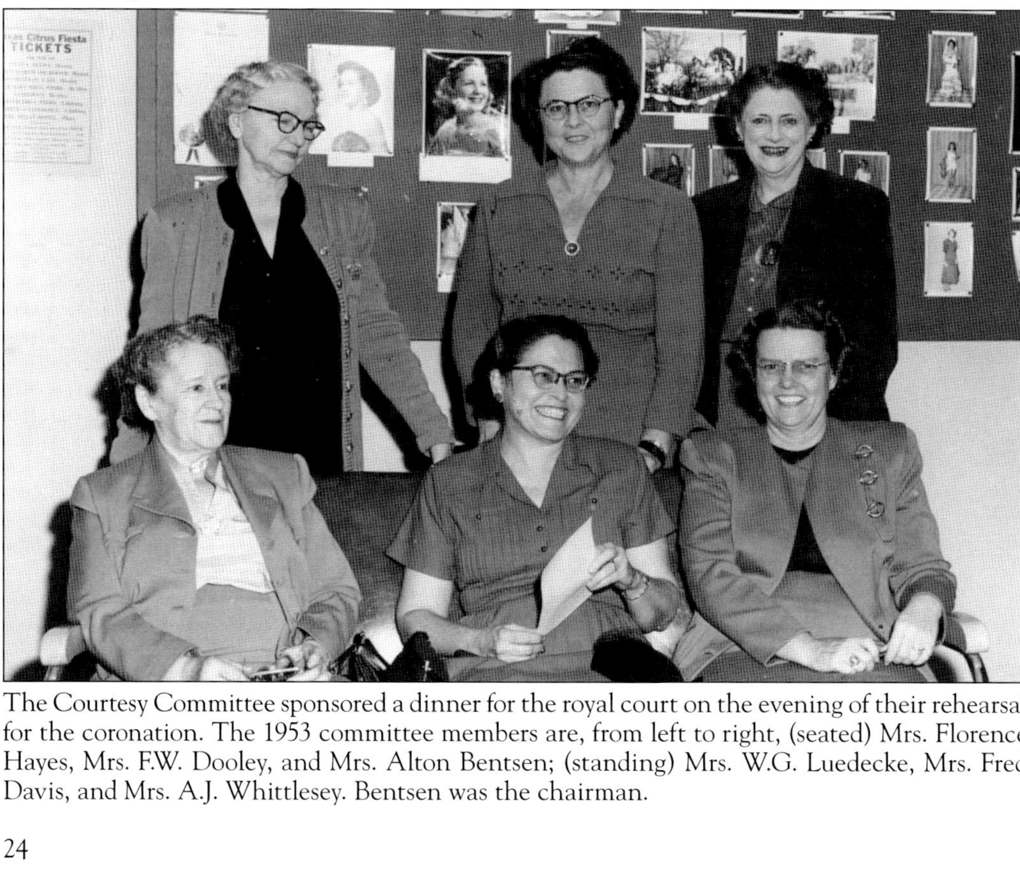

The Courtesy Committee sponsored a dinner for the royal court on the evening of their rehearsal for the coronation. The 1953 committee members are, from left to right, (seated) Mrs. Florence Hayes, Mrs. F.W. Dooley, and Mrs. Alton Bentsen; (standing) Mrs. W.G. Luedecke, Mrs. Fred Davis, and Mrs. A.J. Whittlesey. Bentsen was the chairman.

Members of the Mission Junior Service League took charge of ticket sales in 1953. Here Mrs. C.Y. Mills (left), committee chairman, gives a packet of tickets to Mrs. W.B. Thornton. Mrs. M.W. Held, Junior Service League president, looks on.

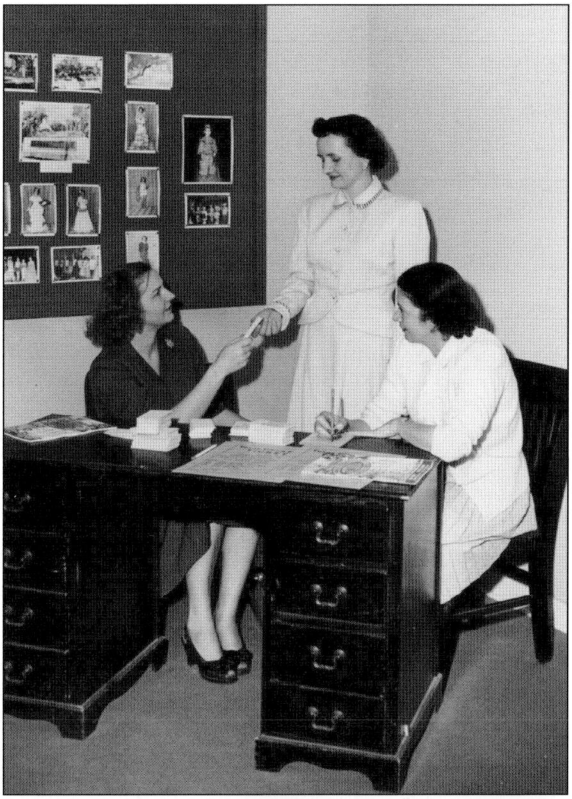

Ladies of the 1953 Junior Style Show Committee kept the event, featuring numerous children, well-organized and enjoyable. They are, from left to right, Mrs. Blaine Holcomb (committee chairman), Mrs. James A. Blocklinger, Mrs. Hugo Domínguez, Mrs. L.L. Riley, and Mrs. Sam Hornbeak.

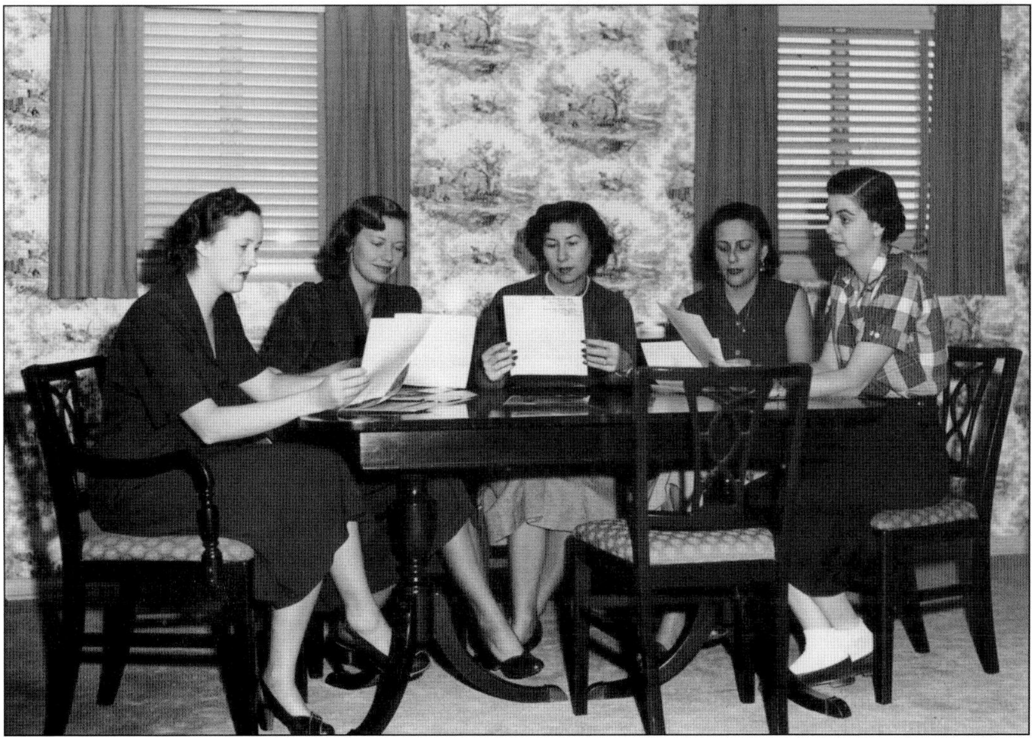

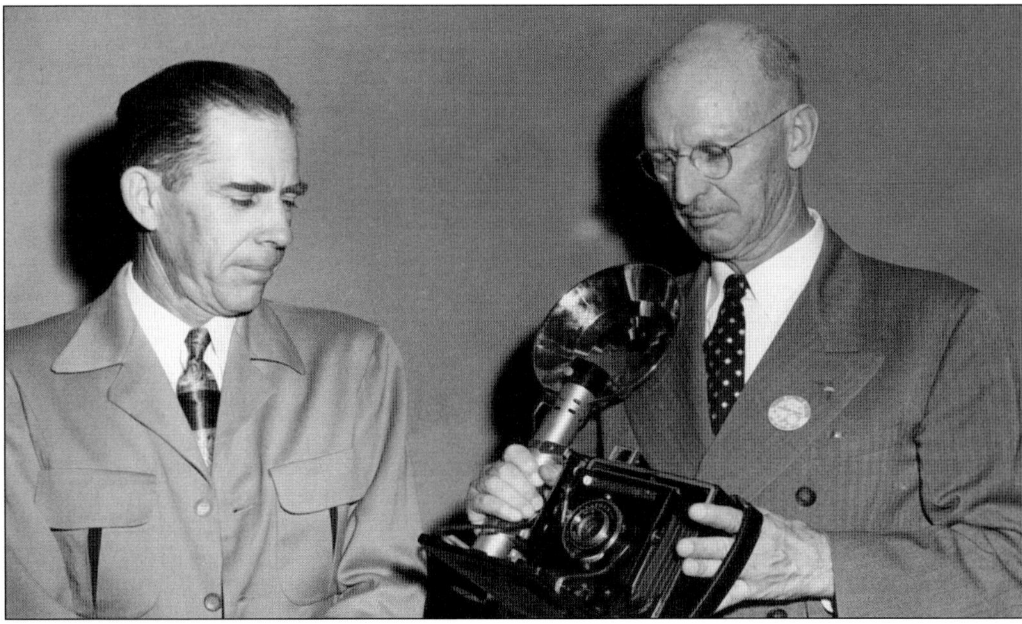

T.J. Johnson (left) and E.E. MacDonald fulfilled the duties of the 1953 Fiesta Photography Committee. Although Johnson and MacDonald were amateur photographers, the executive committee considered their work to be professional in quality. They photographed committees at work as well as activities throughout the fiesta. Many of their images were reproduced in the *Mission Times* and are shown in this chapter.

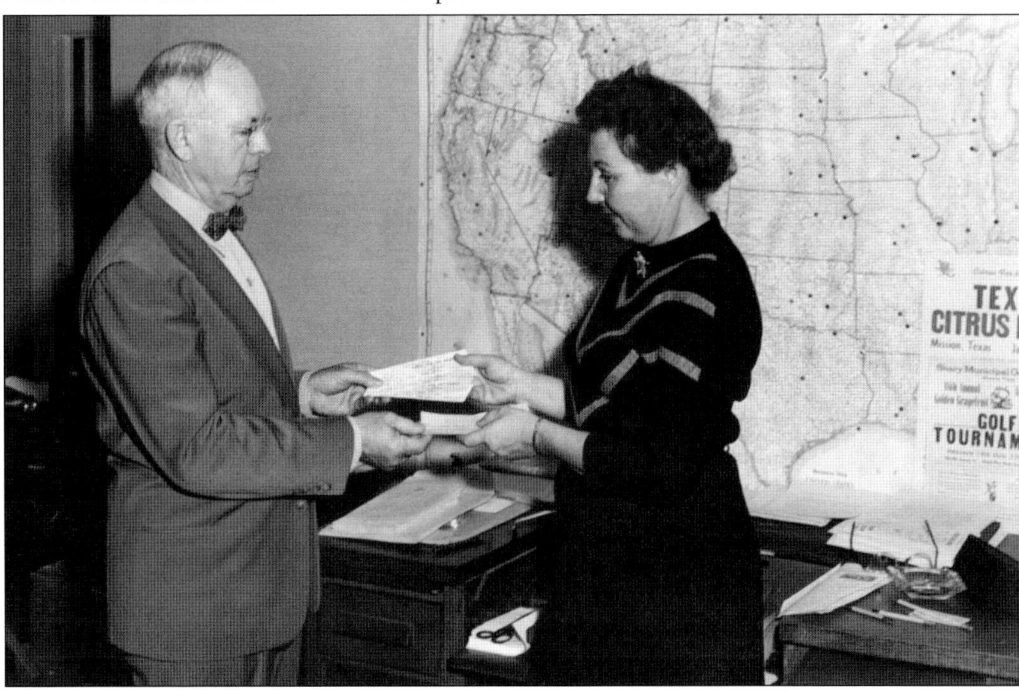

Earl Hunter (left) of Hastings, Nebraska, bought the first tickets sold in 1955. A frequent winter visitor, he created his own tradition of buying the first tickets to the fiesta each year. Mrs. O.C. Lindsey, fiesta executive secretary, accepts his check for four tickets.

C.B. de la Garza (left) and R.R. Howell, who made up the committee for the window decorations contest, had signed up 36 entries when this photograph was taken in 1955. Judging of the window decorations was based on two criteria: the use of citrus as an element in the design, and the relation of the design to the fiesta theme, "Citrus for the World."

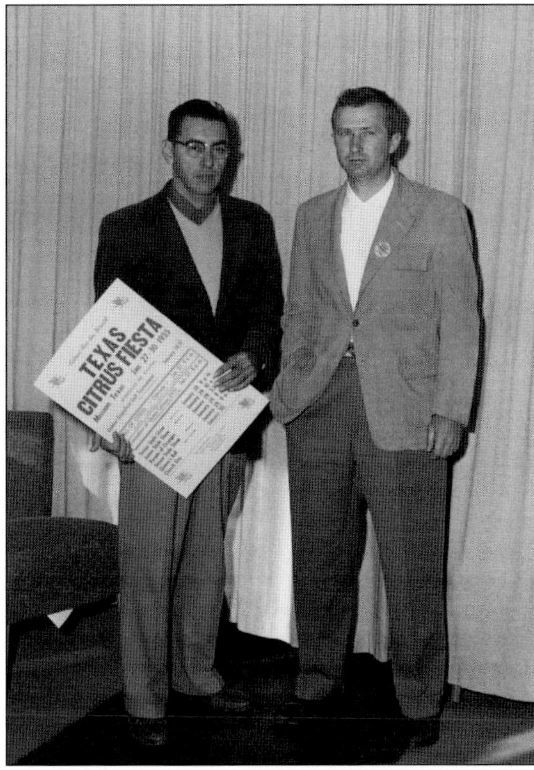

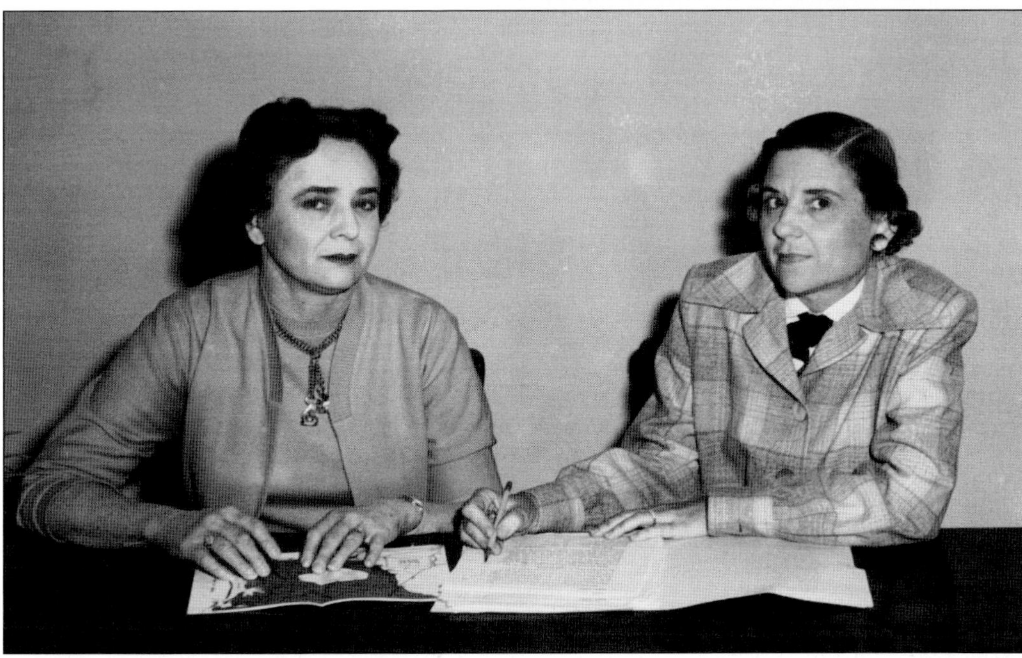

Each year, impartial judges had to be procured. They were charged with choosing winners in the contests held during the fiesta. Shown here in 1956 are Mrs. Parker Lampert (left) and Mrs. Winston Jenkins, members of the Judges Committee. Jenkins, committee chairman, was the former Marguerite Daniel and the first Queen Citrianna.

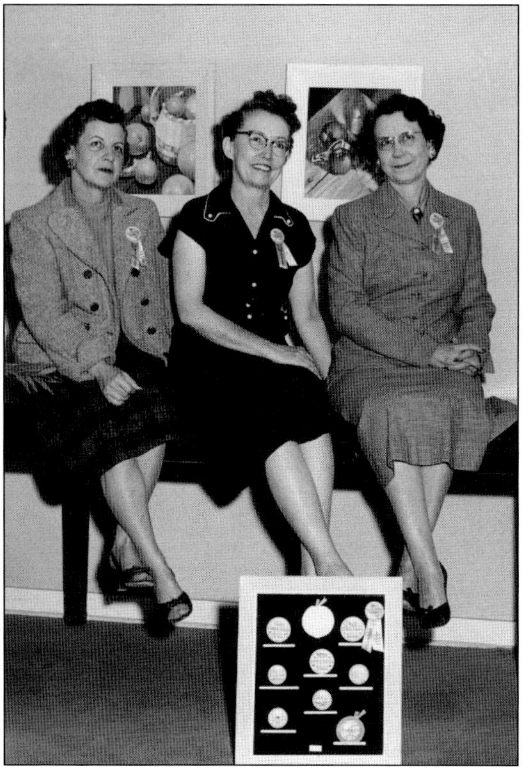

Committee members for the 1956 Citrus and Vegetable Style Show pose for a photograph. They are, from left to right, Mrs. Norton Boyd, Mrs. Ferguson Reynolds, and Mrs. L.R. Lehman. The Senior Style Show took place on Friday night, January 27, and Saturday night, January 28. The Junior Style Show began the day's festivities on Saturday morning, January 28. All were held at the Memorial Gymnasium.

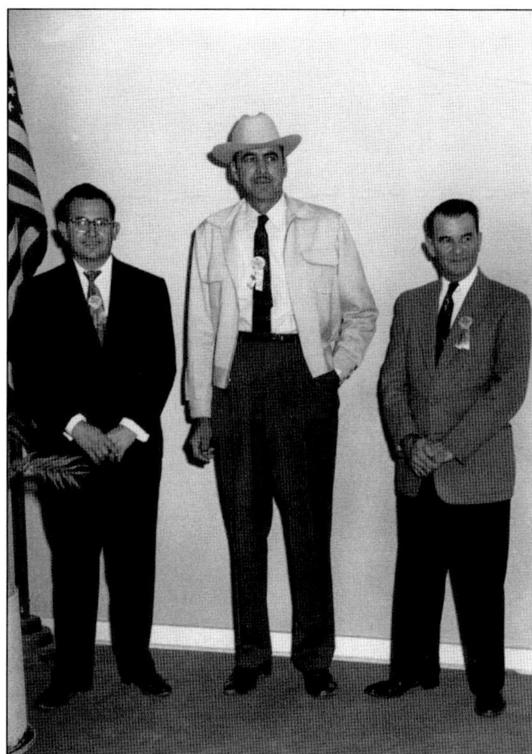

Committee chairmen for the 1956 fiesta were Luís Martínez (left), window decorations; Frank Pérez (center), rodeo arrangements; and Lein Bourgeois, art and photography show. New that year was the Triangle Bell Rodeo, held at 30-30 Park at 3:00 p.m. on Friday, Saturday, and Sunday, with only one performance each day. The Parade of Oranges began at noon to avoid a time conflict with the rodeo.

Scott Martin Jr. served as chairman of the concessions committee in 1956 and for many more years. His wife, Mary Alice Conway Martin, had been Duchess of Grapefruit and represented the South in the 1941 fiesta. She is the daughter of Roy Conway and the granddaughter of John J. Conway. Scott is known for his many civic and business interests.

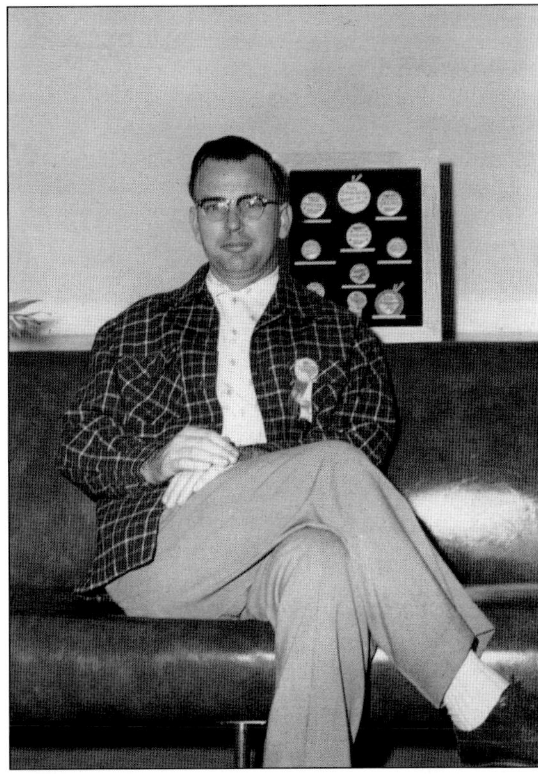

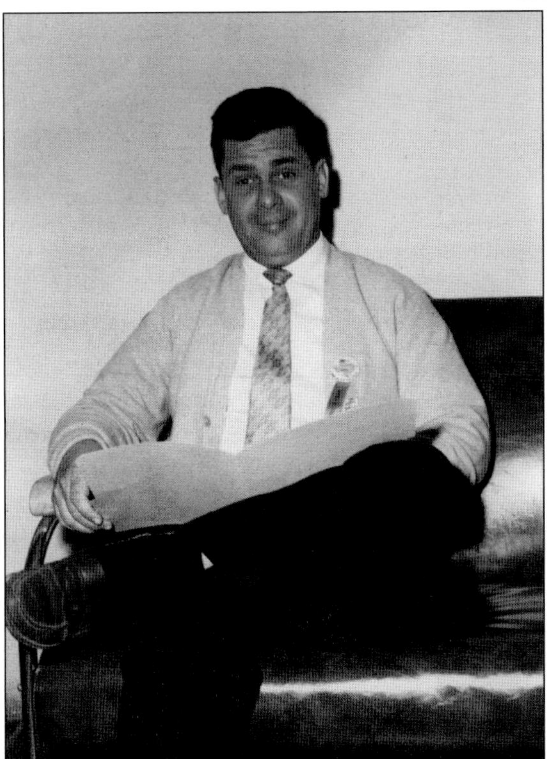

For several years, architect Warren Suter, seen here in 1956, designed and directed stage construction at the Memorial Gymnasium, drew maps, and provided other behind-the-scenes assistance. The style shows and the coronation required a ramp and a large throne area.

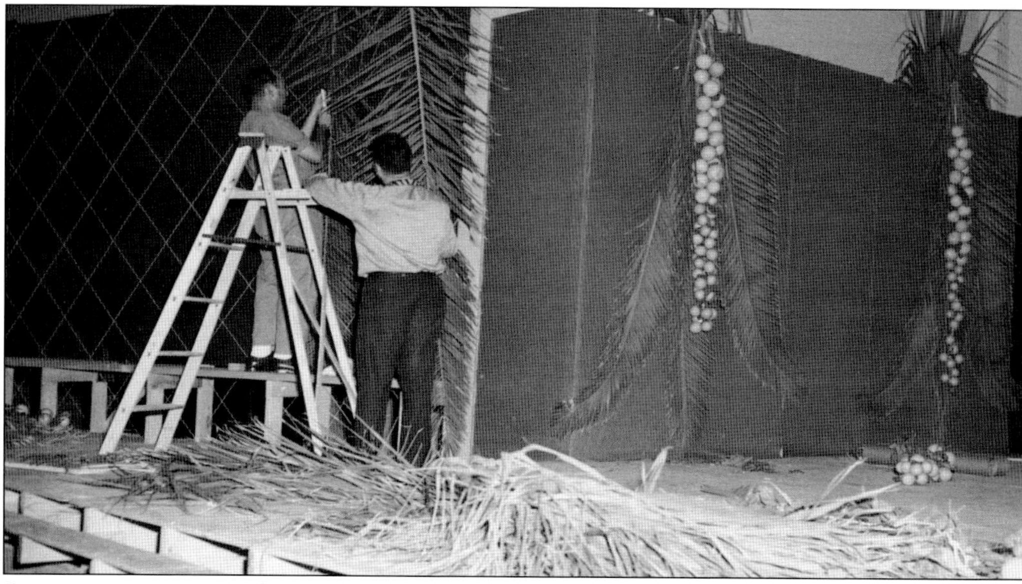

Stage preparations, such as these at the Memorial Gymnasium in 1956, were elaborate and required the help of many volunteers. The central figure may be Warren Suter. Due to full use of the Memorial Gymnasium, the Queen's Ball was held at the National Guard Armory/Fiesta Building (renovated in 1962 to become the Mission Community Center). Fiesta square dances with as many as 225 participants also took place at the armory.

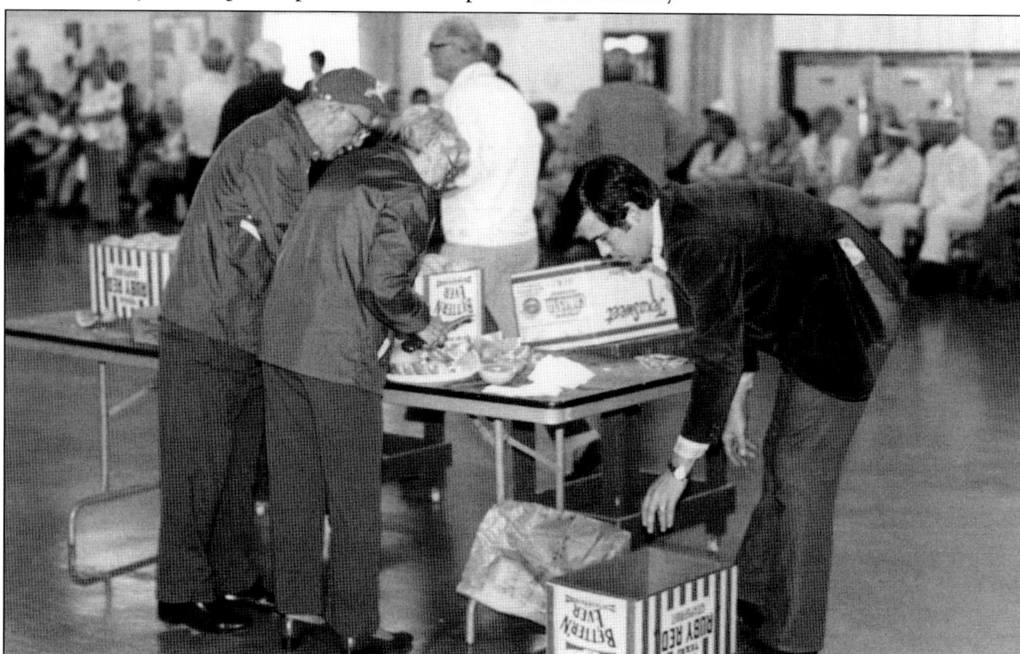

This citrus exhibit setup, although undated, reflects the importance of the event. The citrus exhibit used different locations, depending upon availability. Addresses such as the Saxet Building at Ninth Street and Conway Avenue, a former H-E-B grocery store at Tenth Street and Conway Avenue, 323 East Ninth Street, and the Bryan Park Shopping Plaza indicate the mobility of the contest.

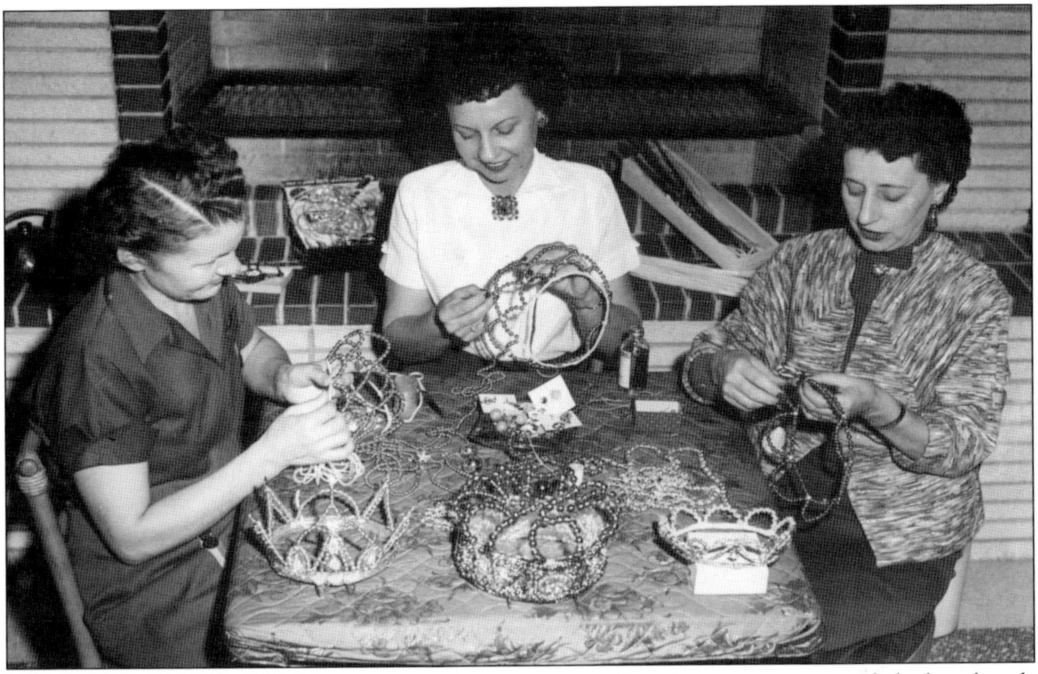

Crowns and jeweled accessories worn by fiesta royalty at all of the events were made by hand each year. Committee members making crowns for the 1953 fiesta are Mrs. Clarence Ashley (left), Mrs. Everett Bell (center), and Mrs. Ray Pfeiffer. Bell was the committee chairman.

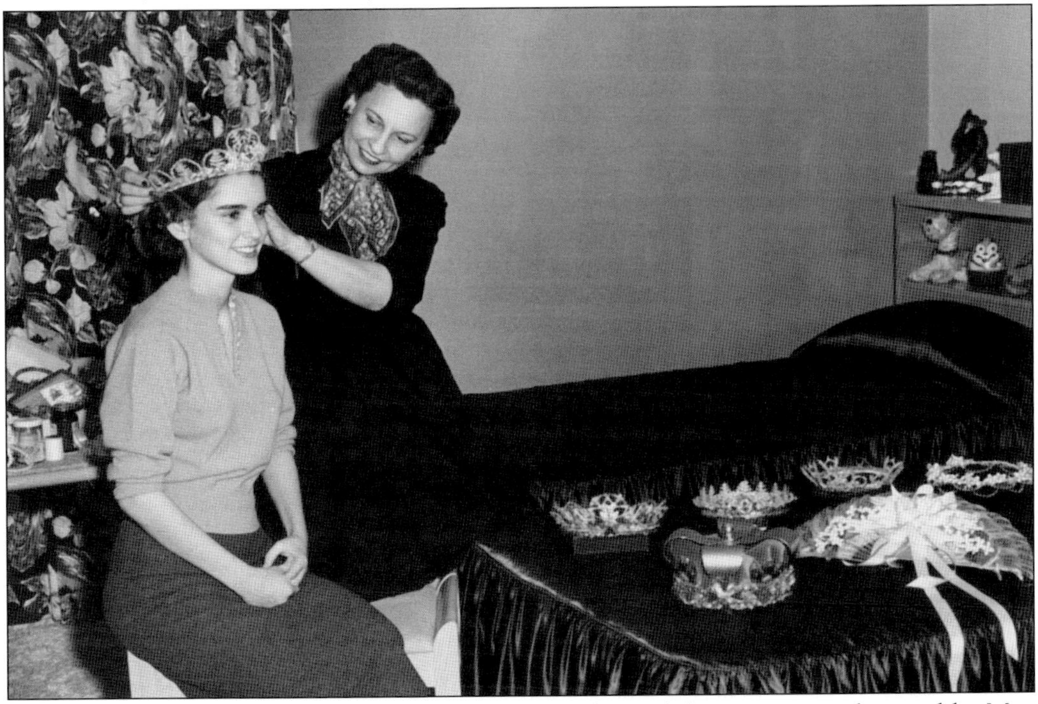

In the 1950s, many of the accessories worn by members of the court were designed by Mrs. Everett Bell (right) and made by her committee. Here, she fits the crown made for Sheridan Leigh Sammons, First Princess for 1956. Additional crowns and a fan lie on the bed.

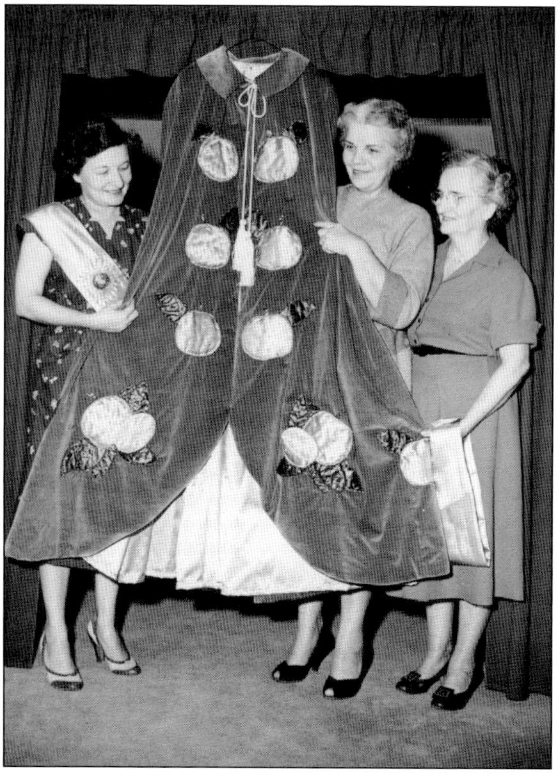

In 1955, King Citrus received a new robe of green velvet with a gold satin lining and ruby red grapefruit on the front. Mrs. F.A. Round, Mrs. L.E. Bridgewater, and Mrs. Everett Bell designed the robe. Shown here are, from left to right, Round, Bridgewater (chairman of the Robe Committee), and Mrs. D.G. de León, who made the robe.

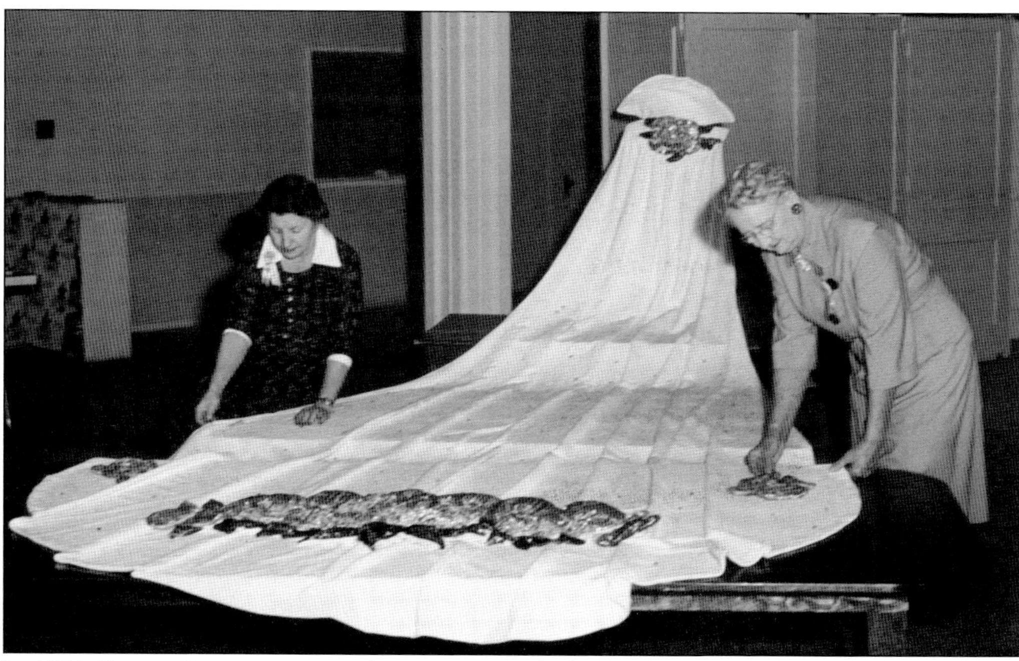

In 1956, Queen Citrianna received a new train, which was designed by Mrs. Glenn Fankhauser (left). Mrs. R.M. Winn (right) made it with the help of dozens of volunteers, who sewed on several thousand sequins by hand. Mrs. Woods Christian, not shown, was committee chairman. A new train replaced this one by 1966.

Pat Sohn, 13, representing Mission, modeled a swimsuit and accessories made of dehydrated bougainvillea, grapefruit peel, and sawdust in 1953. She and two other girls were invited to Houston, where they appeared on television and posed for photographs at a swimming pool for the *Houston Chronicle*. Sohn modeled at a Houston convention two years later (seen here). She became Lady-in-Waiting to Queen Citrianna XIX, Jeanette Waters, in 1956.

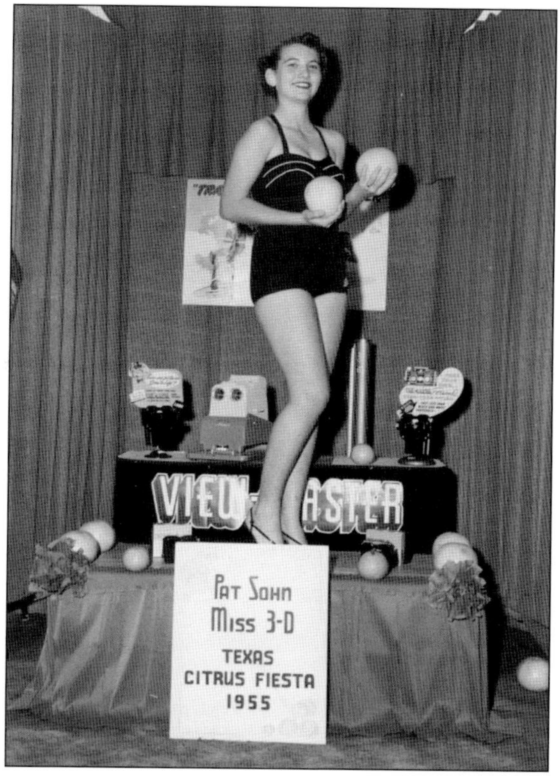

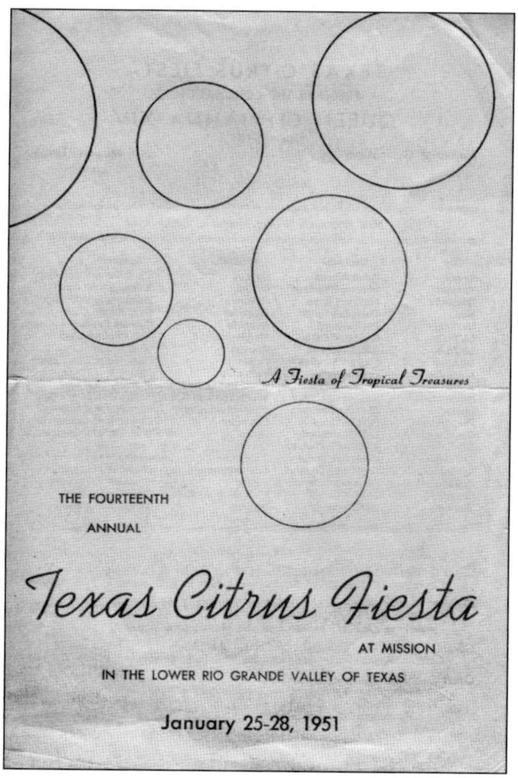

Besides published advertisements, photographs, articles, and even newspaper pullout sections relating to the Texas Citrus Fiesta, officials authorized the design and printing of souvenir programs. This one from 1951 lists the names of those in the coronation court as well as the duchesses, their sponsors, and the cities and products they represent. Fiesta events cover an entire page, and style show entries by name, sponsor, and division fill another.

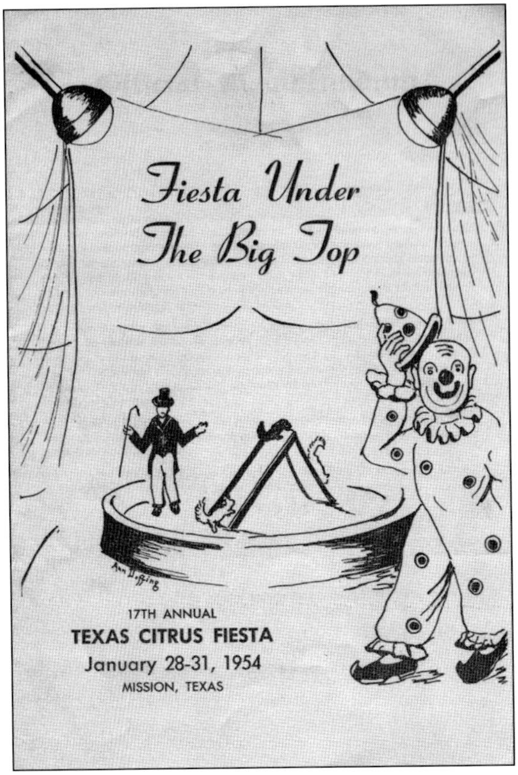

The 1954 Texas Citrus Fiesta program, illustrated with original artwork by Ann Doffing, announces the theme. The contents are similar to the 1951 program. A tent formed the stage backdrop for Queen Citrianna XVII, Sylvia Vela, and King Citrus XVII, Woods Christian. Vela was a descendant of Macedonio Vela, founder of the Laguna Seca Ranch, where the first citrus trees in the Rio Grande Valley were planted in 1871.

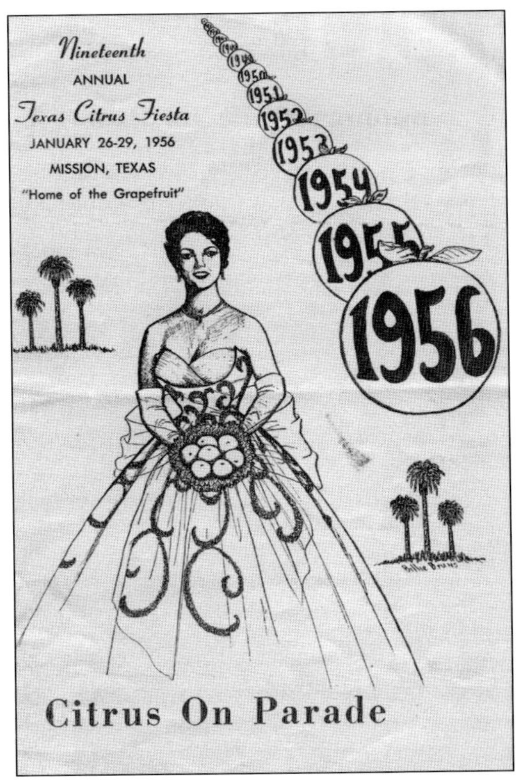

This 1956 program, with original artwork by Billie Bruns, features Queen Citrianna XIX, Jeanette Waters. Fiesta programs since 1956 have emphasized Queen Citrianna on the cover. The *Mission Times* published a special fiesta edition with green lettering and an image of Waters on the cover. A subtheme to the official "Citrus on Parade" that year was to "pay homage" to pioneers of the area.

Three

Windows on the Community

From the first Texas Citrus Fiesta, held in conjunction with a county fair, contests have been a popular part of the celebration. Cash, ribbons, medals, and trophies are examples of awards. Among the events and features garnering recognition have been citrus produce, street and window decorations, floats, flowers, costumes, children's events, golf, art and photography, antiques and hobbies, rocks and minerals, decorated hats, rodeos, midget auto races, sewing and cooking contests, and even a bullfight.

Winners in the Princess Anna event, who were entrants in the Junior Style Show, were initially chosen from photographs, which were sent to celebrities with Texas connections, such as actresses Greer Garson and Gale Storm, then to notable Texans who lived outside the Rio Grande Valley. Later, winners were chosen by local but unidentified judges. Now, with as many as 200 contestants in the Princess Anna contest, children are identified by number rather than name, and judges remain unknown to the contestants.

While the Ex-Kings Association chooses King Citrus each year, Queen Citrianna and other court members are selected by a panel of secret judges who are not from Mission or the Rio Grande Valley.

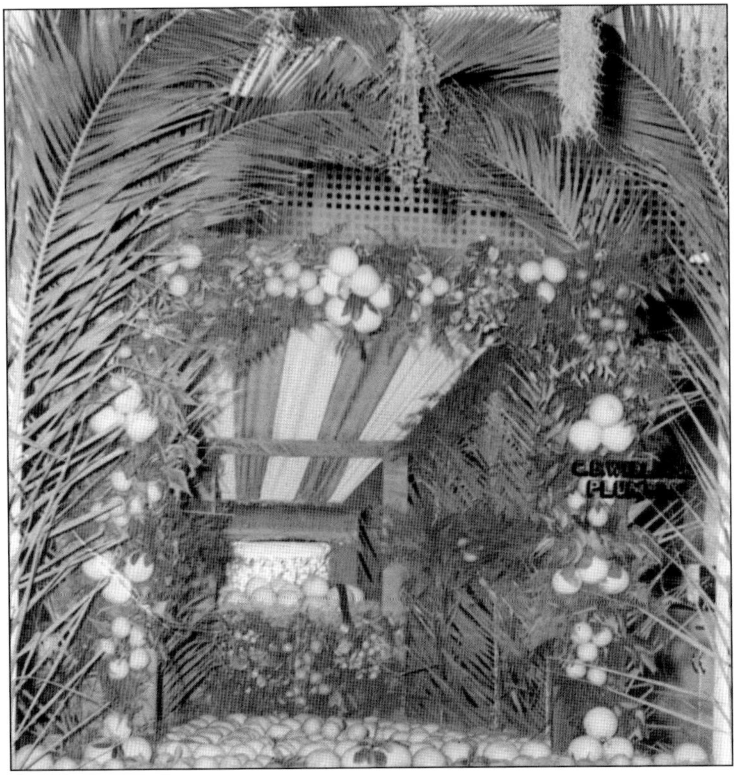

To help promote Mission and the citrus industry, and to stimulate business, decorative shop and store windows were a consistently integral part of the Texas Citrus Fiesta for many years. In 1947, the C.B. Williams Plumbing Company won first place for its elaborate shadowbox design (pictured). Citrus products form the central "picture."

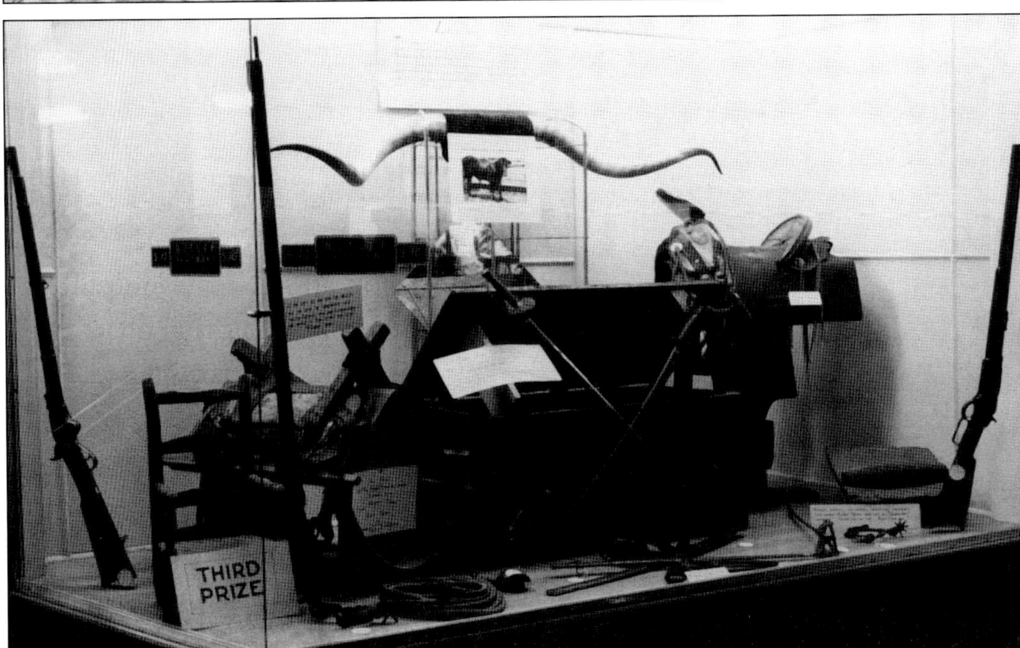

The 1952 third-place winner was the entry from Scott's department store (pictured). The Texas Citrus Fiesta borrowed artifacts representing pioneer life in the Rio Grande Valley from Texas Memorial Museum in Austin. The horns (top) came from a steer named Old Bill, owned by Roy Conway in the 1930s. Old Bill was believed to be the last native longhorn in the Mission area.

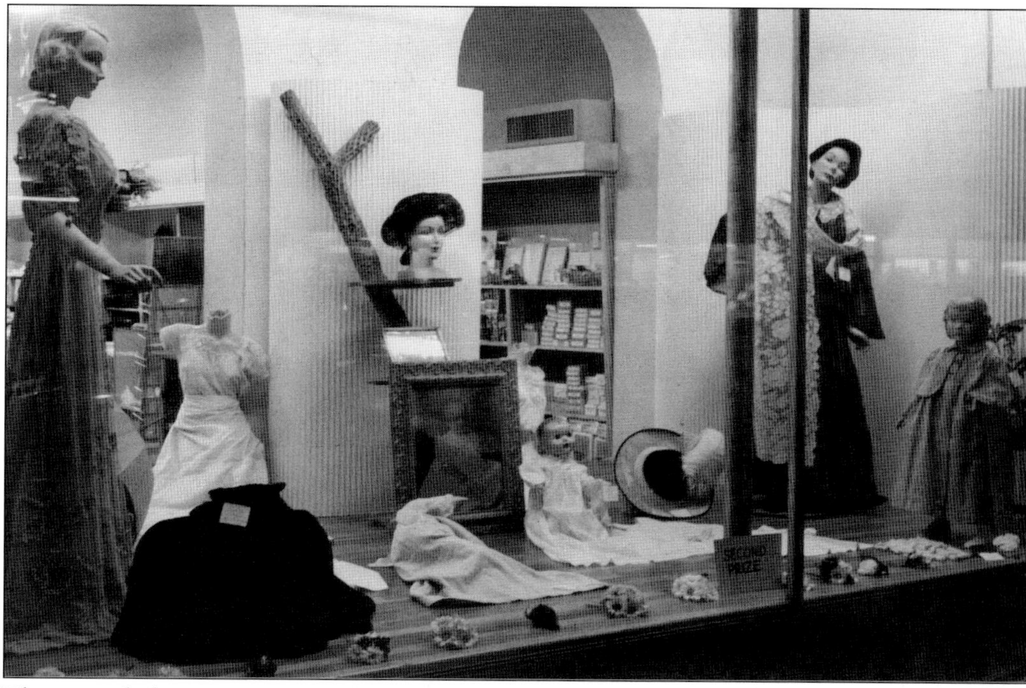

The second-place winner in 1952 was Ben Sam's Shop, located at 913 Conway Avenue. Store decorators reflected the historical theme "Fiesta Under Six Flags" by showing changes in women's clothing styles over a period of 50 years. The decorators borrowed costumes from Mission-area ladies willing to share their collections.

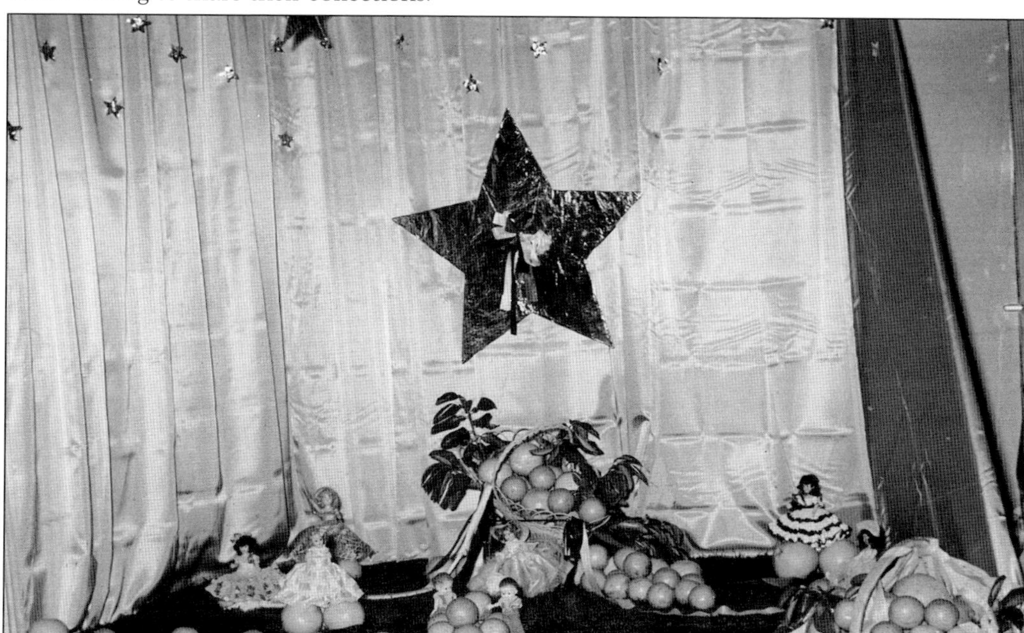

In 1953, C.R. Anthony's Department Store won an honorable mention with its window display, dedicated to the theme "Fiesta Under the Stars." Small, elaborately costumed Nancy Ann Storybook dolls, placed here among the green plants, baskets, and clusters of fruit, were popular with girls.

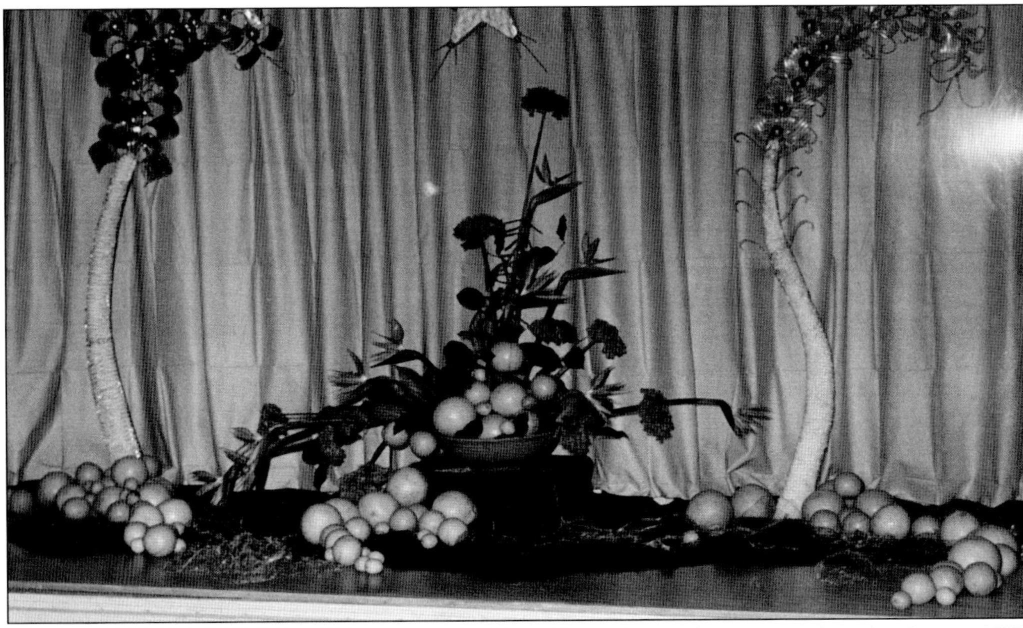

Williams Flower Shop received an honorable mention for its elegant window display in 1953. Sponsored by home demonstration clubs and garden clubs, flower exhibits were a regular part of the Texas Citrus Fiesta. Poinsettias were especially popular, and a group of Mission women created the only all-poinsettia club and flower show in the country. Maurine Duncan's poinsettia arrangements won many honors, and she became a nationally accredited flower show judge.

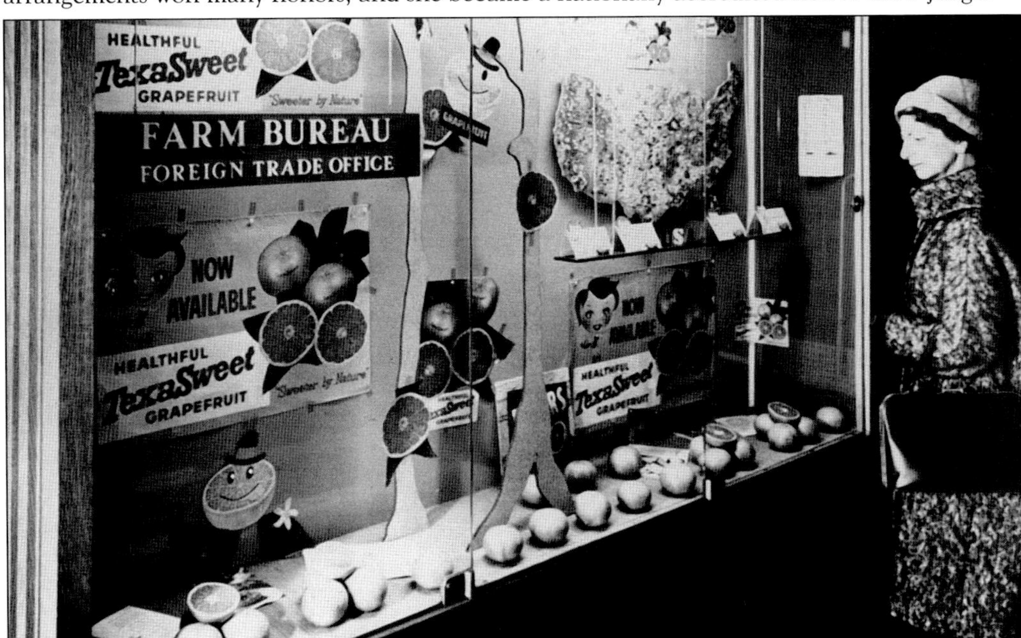

This is not an entry in the fiesta window decoration contest, but an elaborate promotional display of Ruby Red grapefruit at the American Farm Bureau's sales office in Rotterdam, the Netherlands. The office did not take orders of citrus fruit, but it provided European importers with American suppliers' contact information. The woman in this 1960 image is unidentified.

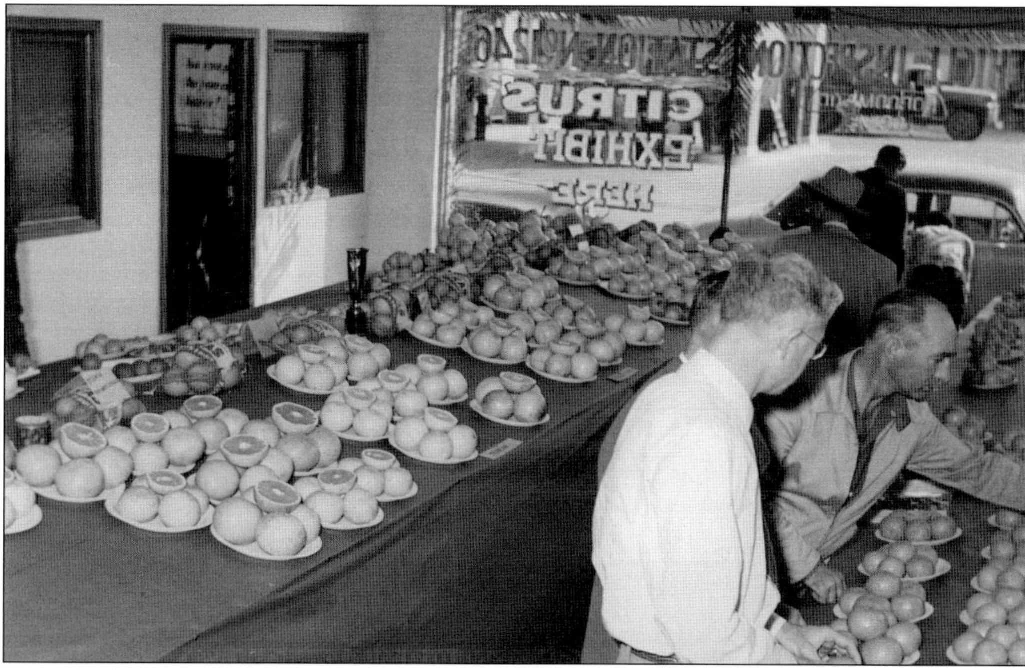

In 1953, Spikes Motor Company hosted the citrus and flower exhibits in its showroom. "Vehicle Inspection Station No. 1246" can be seen in reverse on the window. The two men are unidentified.

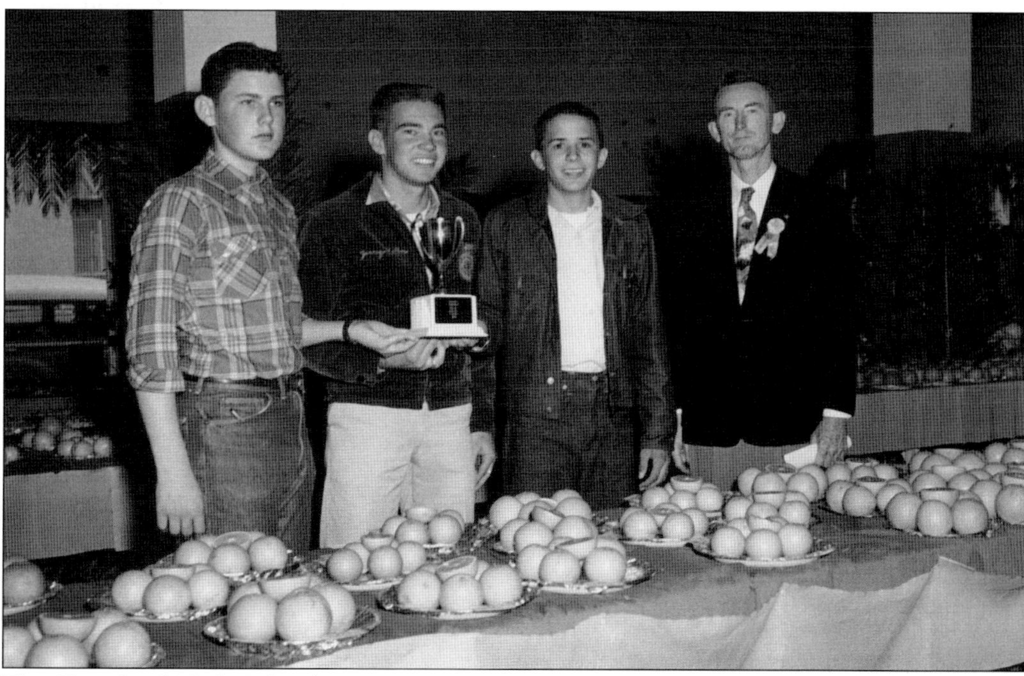

The Sharyland High School Future Farmers of America (FFA) members won the citrus fruit-judging contest four years in a row. In 1956, the fourth year, students scored 2,575 points. The winning students in 1956 are, from left to right, Gary Wright, Jerry Koller, and Larry Chauvin. At far right is R.F. Wilson, sponsor.

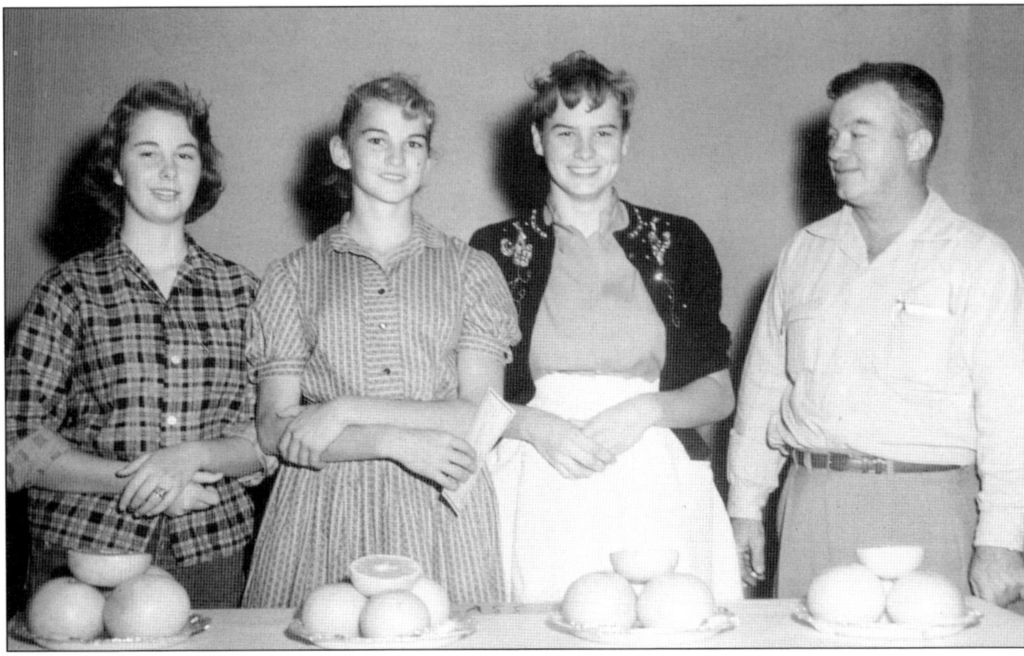

Beginning in 1957, girls from Mission and Sharyland High Schools Future Homemakers of America (FHA) were allowed to enter the fruit-judging contest. Members of the Mission High School FHA, top team, junior division, are seen here at the 1958 contest. They are, from left to right, Linda Lindsey, Nancy Housel, and Janie Weber. Harold Randle (far right) was chairman of the fruit-judging contests. The team earned 2,135 points.

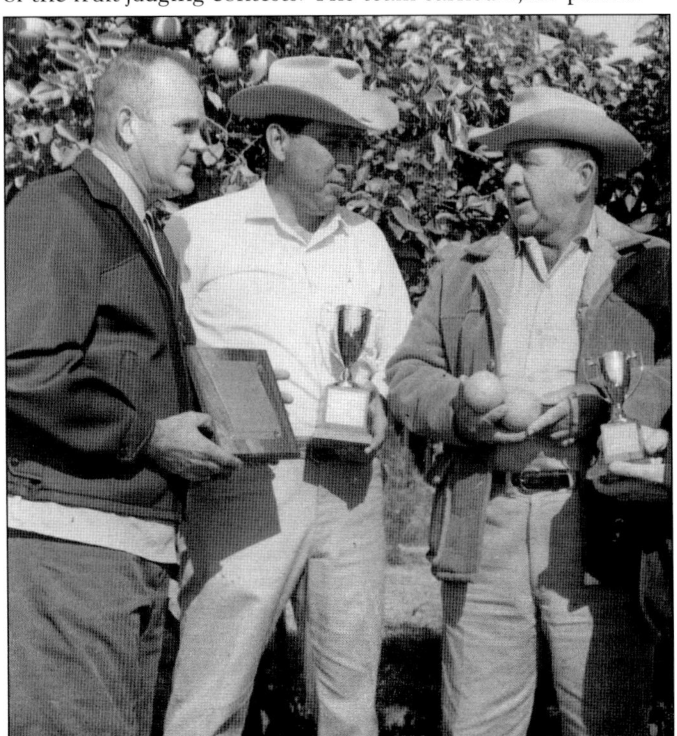

Chairmen for the 1969 citrus exhibit at 1004 Conway Avenue hold the trophies for FHA and FFA contest winners. The men are Dutch Karcher (left), Hidalgo County Extension Agent; Jim Jarrett (center), vocational agriculture teacher, Sharyland High School; and Joe Correa, vocational agriculture teacher, Mission High School. The fourth trophy, just visible at far right, is held by the unidentified chairman of the rock and mineral exhibit.

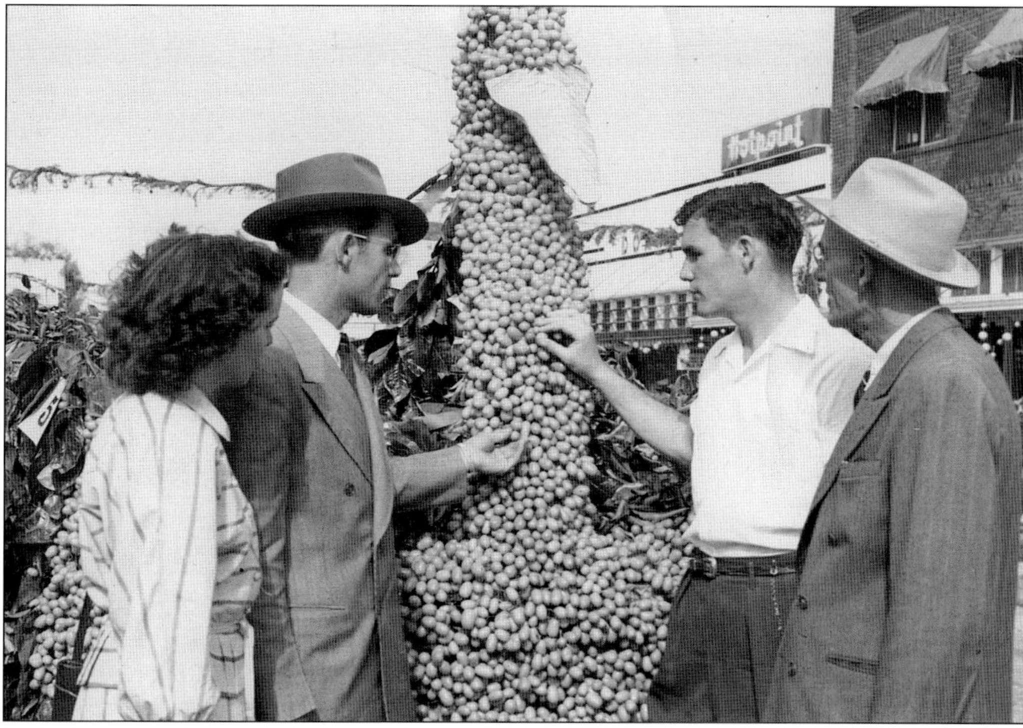

After the Parade of Oranges, floats were parked along a side street so visitors could take a close look at them. Inspecting this swan float in 1948 are, from left to right, Mrs. and Mr. Cecil Rusk, Benny Rusk (in white shirt), and D.L. Rusk, father of the brothers. Cecil was Mission High School band director and a Golden Gloves sponsor. Benny was a professional heavyweight boxer.

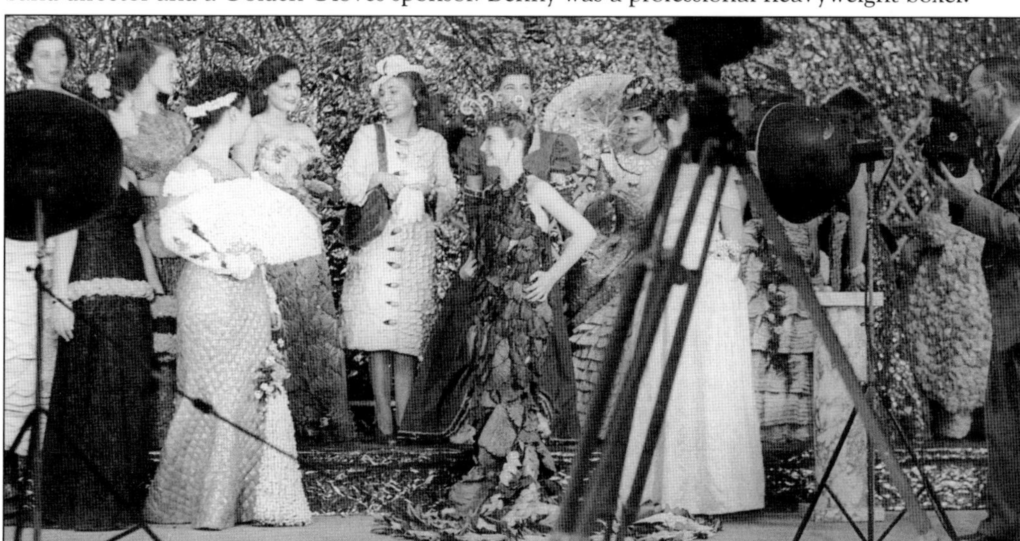

This photograph, taken by Eugene E. Dondlinger, shows several of the 1947 style show contestants in relaxed conversation. They are, from left to right, (first row) Pat Price, Mrs. Donald Bentsen (with fan), Katherine Root, and Betty Jo Knox, Queen Citrianna X (behind the camera tripod); (second row) Mary Jane Seabury, Mrs. J. Forrest Palmer, Jacqueline Meeker, Mrs. Magus Smith, Virginia Ann Henry, Alla Dean Carlile, unidentified, and Eleanor Morelius.

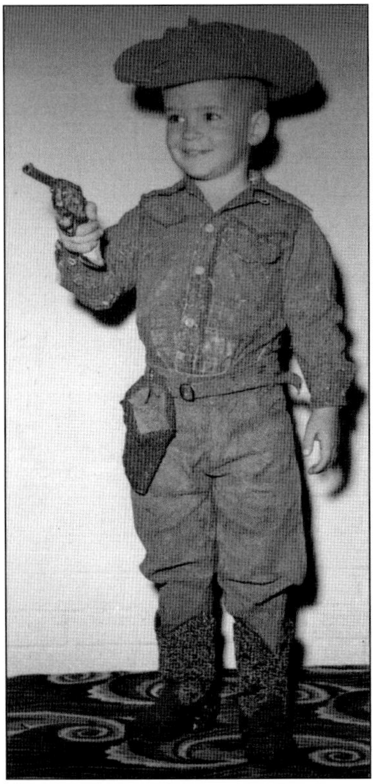

The first Children's Promenade took place at the just-opened Memorial Gymnasium at 10:00 a.m. on Saturday, January 21, 1950. Instead of parading decorated pets, doll buggies, tricycles, or bicycles, the 25 young contestants modeled costumes made of natural products. Seen here is Jimmy Miller, winner of the second division (ages 5–7). His father, Jim Miller, served as mayor of Mission from 1970 to 1973. The small cowboy grew up to be a dentist.

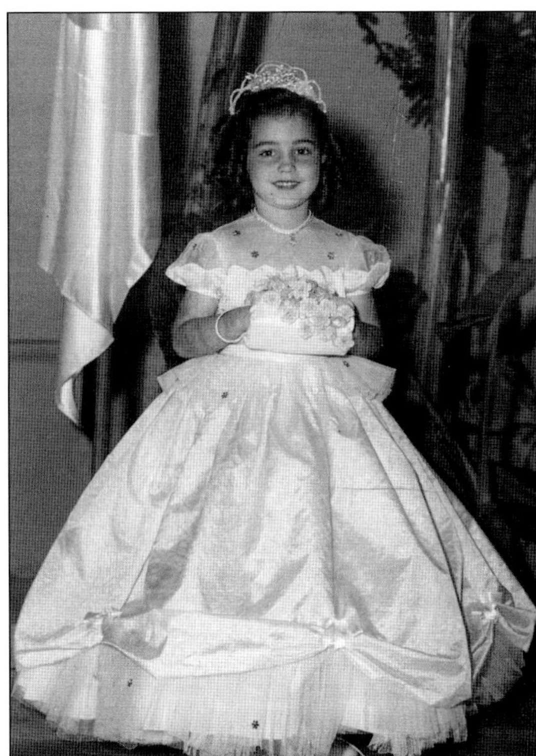

With the opening of Memorial Gymnasium, children's events moved indoors, where they were no longer subject to inclement weather. The Princess Anna contest, begun in 1951, was limited to six-year-old girls. The first Princess Anna, Carol Ellen Faulkner (McAllen), ruled over the Junior Style Show in 1951. Seen here in 1952 is Mary Jo Schroeder of Mission, Princess Anna II.

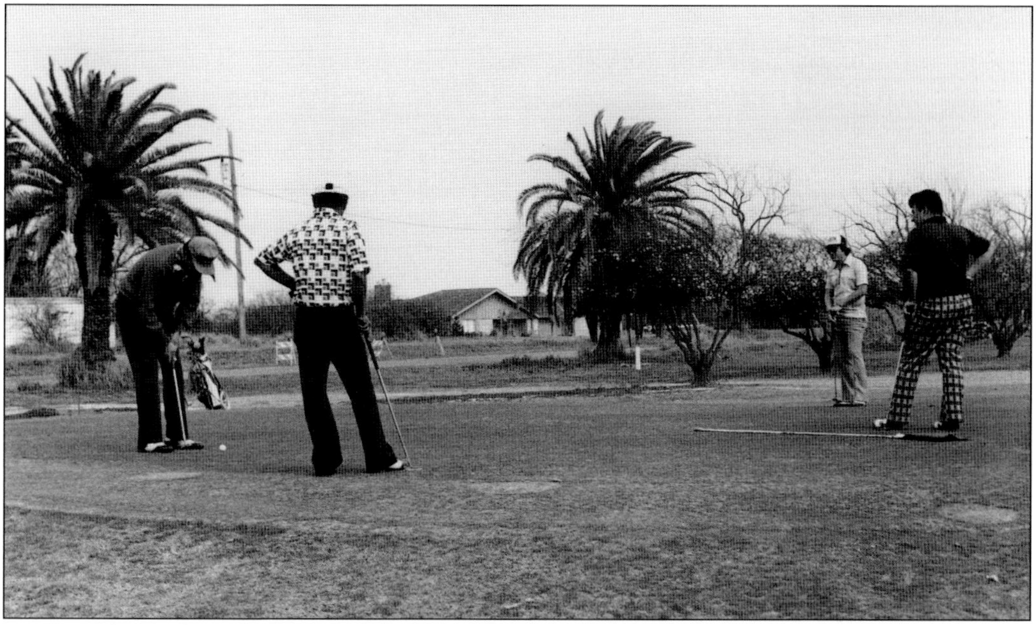

Mission's first golf tournament occurred in 1933, and beginning in 1934, the Golden Grapefruit Golf Tournament took place each year during the Texas Citrus Fiesta. At first, the tournament was held on Sundays, then Saturday and Sunday afternoons, and by the 1950s, it was held over two days, the weekend before the official opening of the fiesta. This undated photograph shows unidentified golfers focused on their game.

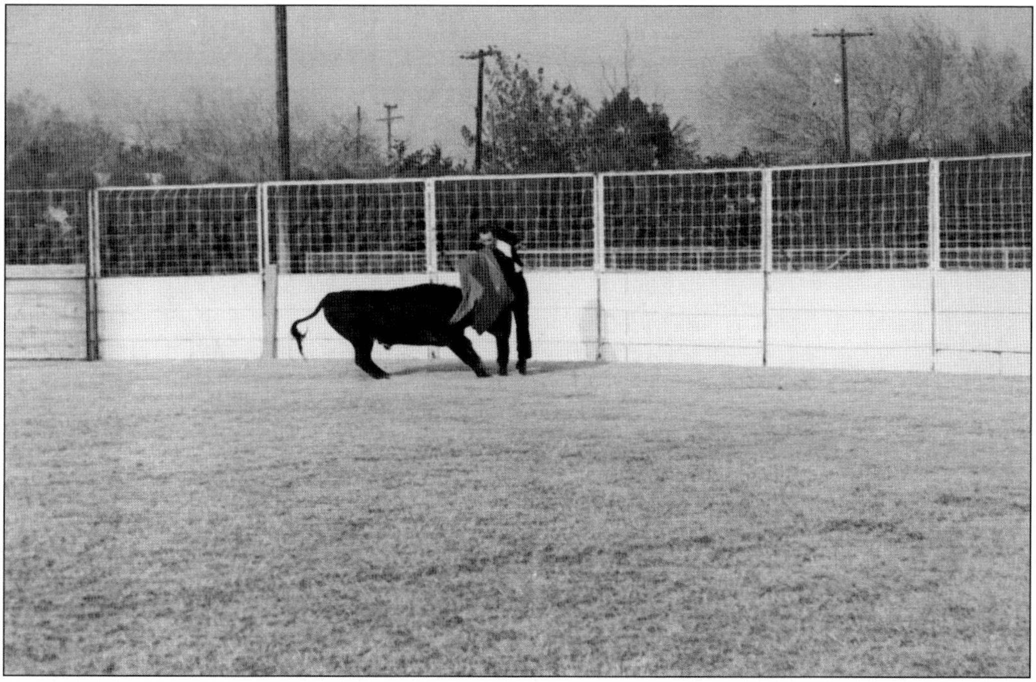

A bloodless bullfight provided entertainment for the 1966 celebration, which had a theme of "Fiesta of Fun and Flowers." The toreros were Dr. Tom Payte, Ramiro Calderón, and Fred Renck (pictured).

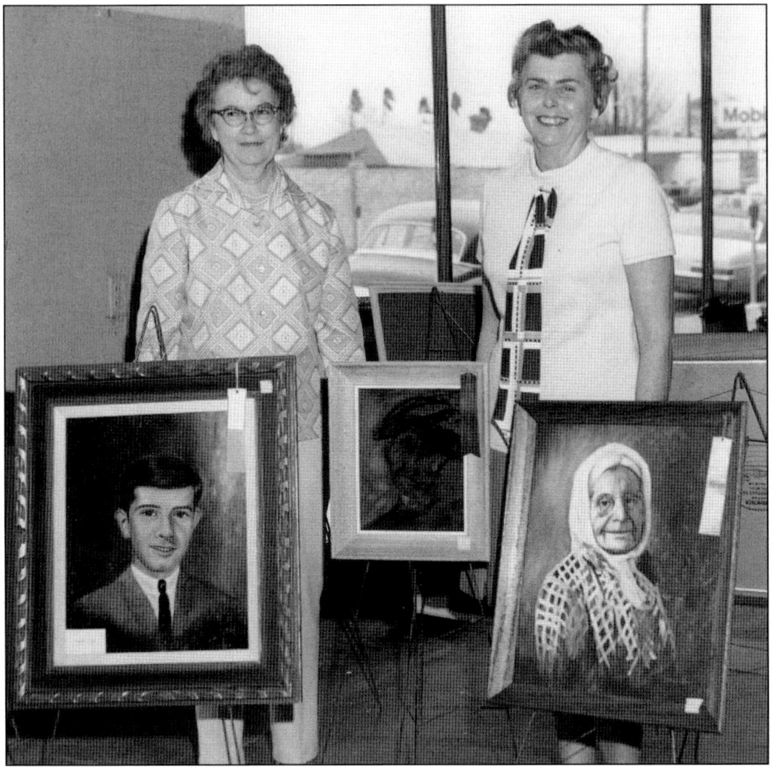

Mrs. Al Nordmeyer (left), art exhibit chairman, and Mrs. Ed Schmidt, cochairman, show the 1970 winning entries in the oil portrait division of the art contest. The sweepstakes winner for that division was Henrietta Treviño of Edinburg.

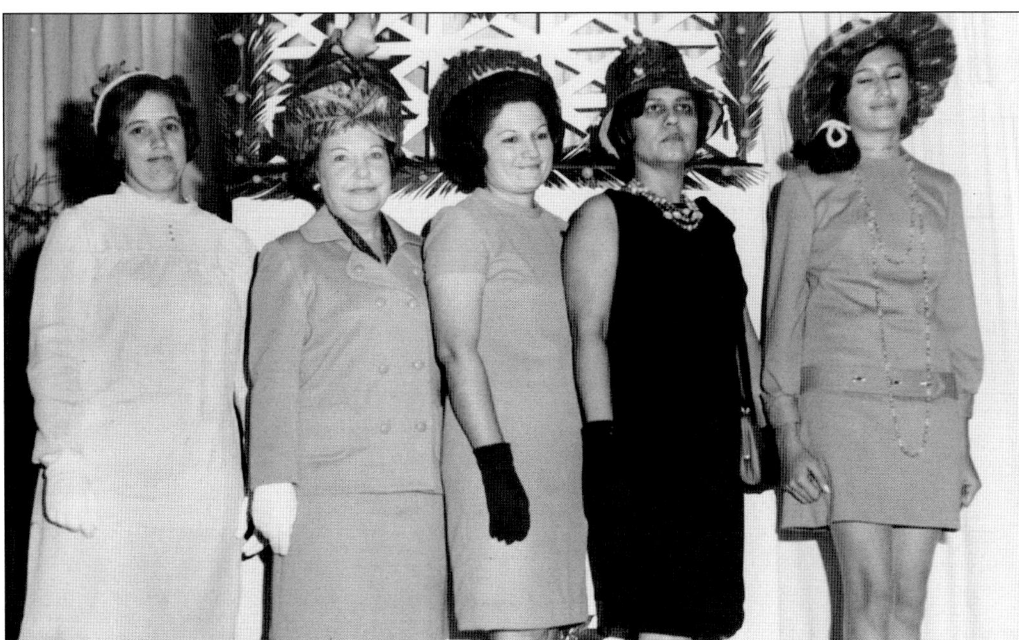

For several years, ladies decorated hats with citrus, flower, and vegetable parts in a popular contest. The winners and their divisions in 1970 are, from left to right, Mrs. Jim Moran, nonperishable; Mrs. Dorothy Stiller, entry from the greatest distance (Marion, Kansas); Mrs. Robert Chapa, most colorful; Mrs. Don Hilbery, flower; and Mrs. Ester Peña, fruit.

Four

Fiesta Royalty

The 1932 Texas Citrus Fiesta ended with the coronation of W.D. Toland as King Grapefruit I and Marguerite Daniel as Queen Citrianna I. The coronation took place at Lions Park with a backdrop of citrus-bearing trees. The Pageant of Citrus, directed by teacher Arthur Hayes, featured about 100 people in several vocal and dance numbers. The Mission High School Band provided the music. High school girls performed the jarabe tapatío (of the three or four "couples," half the girls wore china poblana costumes and half wore charro outfits). During the jarabe tapatío, rain caused the lights to go out, and the girls, perched on unsteady benches, danced to the beams of automobile headlights.

Seven duchesses from throughout the Rio Grande Valley, along with attendants and a duke (escort), represented their home cities. Each duchess was named a princess of a citrus variety. The first royal court also included two heralds, a maid of honor, four ladies-in-waiting, two train bearers, a crown bearer, a jester, and a master of ceremonies. The Queen's Ball followed the coronation, and the next Queen Citrianna was announced during the ball.

By 1982, the coronation event had made adjustments to changing times. For example, the Ex-Kings Association, begun in 1948 by former King Citrus honorees, selected its new King Citrus each year from the Mission citrus industry. His identity remained unknown until his appearance at the beginning of the coronation. Crowned by the previous year's King Citrus, the new king in turn crowned Princess Anna and Queen Citrianna. The C.B. Curtis Award went to someone who had provided invaluable service to the Texas Citrus Fiesta.

Another new feature was the presentation of Princess Anna, who ruled over the Tangerine Court of young princesses and pages.

Most of the early coronation traditions continue today.

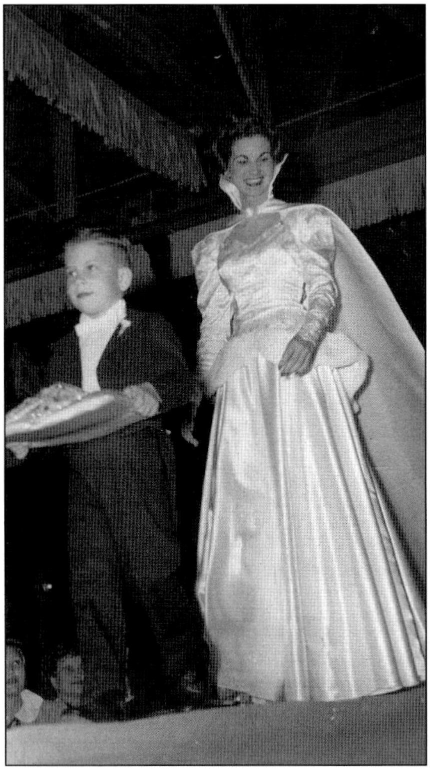

Doris Ann Pierce of Harlingen was crowned Queen Citrianna XI in 1948. Here, she walks along the ramp inside the recreation hall at Moore Field, north of Mission. Seating was designed to be no more than 20 feet from the ramp, which was placed in the center of the rows of seats. Johnny Montgomery, age five, is her crown bearer. Maurine Duncan designed Queen Citrianna's train.

The theme for the 1948 Texas Citrus Fiesta was "A Carnival of the Rainbow," and the coronation featured a background of blue sky and white clouds with a large rainbow overhead. Here, George Tillson, King Citrus XI, crowns Doris Ann Pierce, Queen Citrianna XI. At left is Lillie Marie Garcia (Rio Grande City), First Princess. On the right are Johnny Montgomery (Mission), Crown Bearer, and Patsy Carson (Mission), Second Princess.

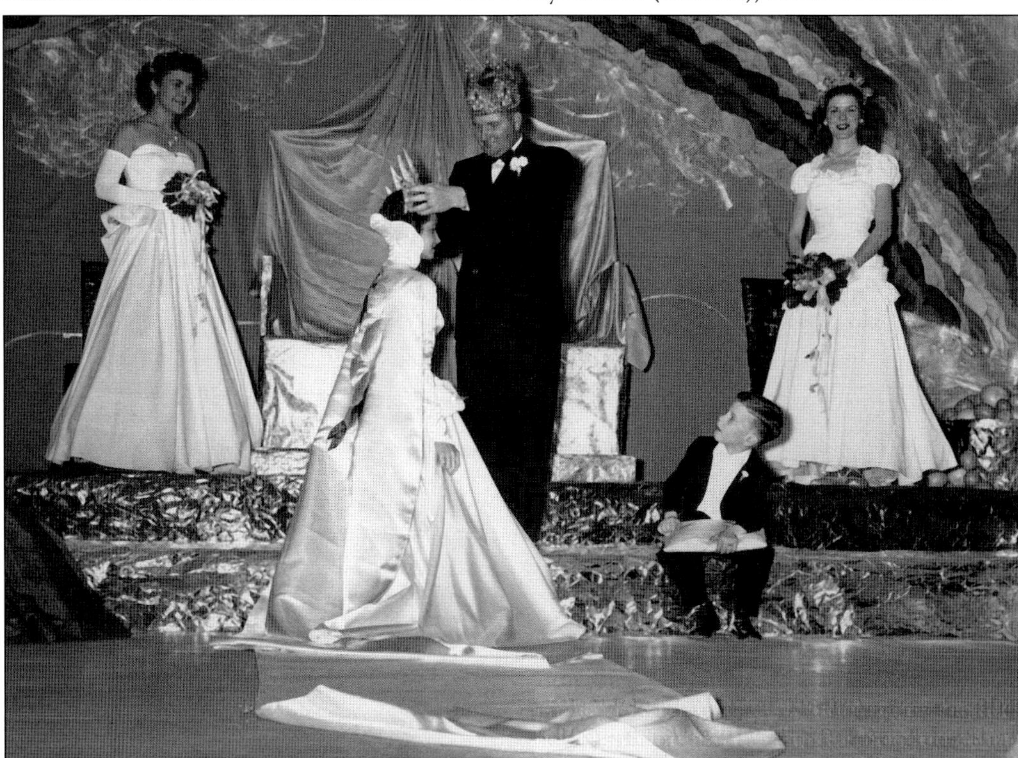

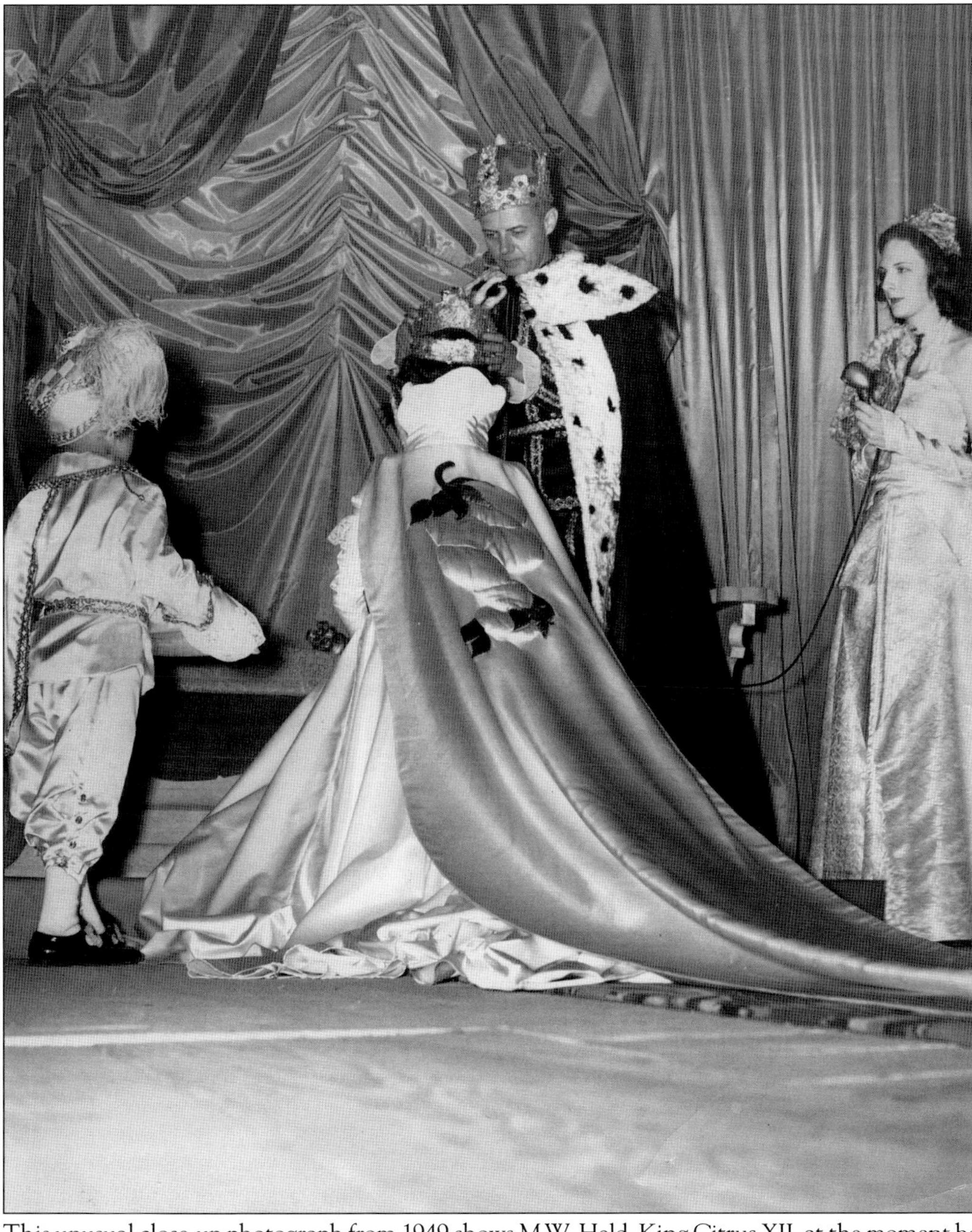

This unusual close-up photograph from 1949 shows M.W. Held, King Citrus XII, at the moment he crowns Bonnie Sue Morgan, Queen Citrianna XII. Jack Edwin Wilson (left), Crown Bearer, holds the satin pillow upon which he brought the crown. On the right, Ann Harrison (Sharyland), First Princess, waits with the microphone. The coronation took place at the National Guard Armory/ Fiesta Building. The official title for Queen Citrianna XII was Empress of the Carnival of the Sun. Morgan, 17, was a senior at Mission High School. Harrison, 16, was a senior at Sharyland High School. Held was engaged in the citrus industry, and his wife served on the Texas Citrus Fiesta's executive committee for several years. In 1950, Mrs. Held became the first woman to be named chairman of the fiesta's board of directors.

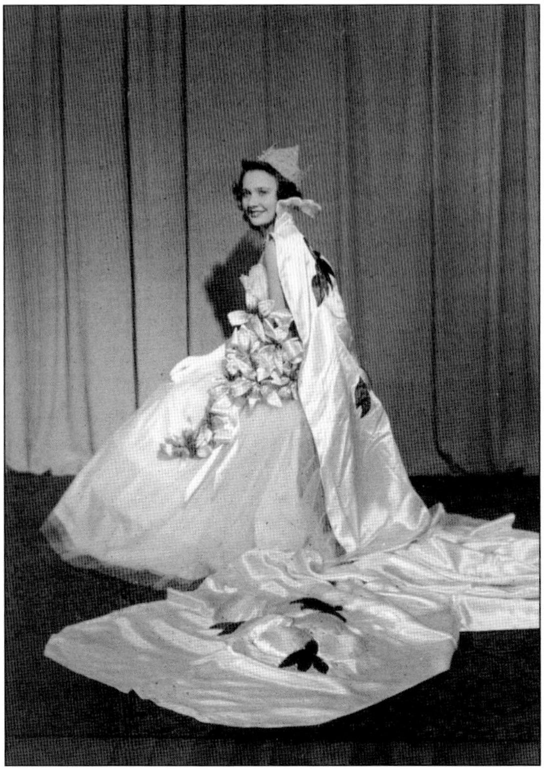

Wilma Cutler served as Queen Citrianna XIII in 1950. The third Queen Citrianna from Raymondville, she wears a gown of white satin and carries an orchid corsage made from grapefruit peel. The theme that year was "Fiesta del Rancho Grande." King Citrus XIII, twenty duchesses, two junior princesses, two senior princesses (chosen from the 1949 court), a lady-in-waiting, a crown bearer, and two pages made up the court.

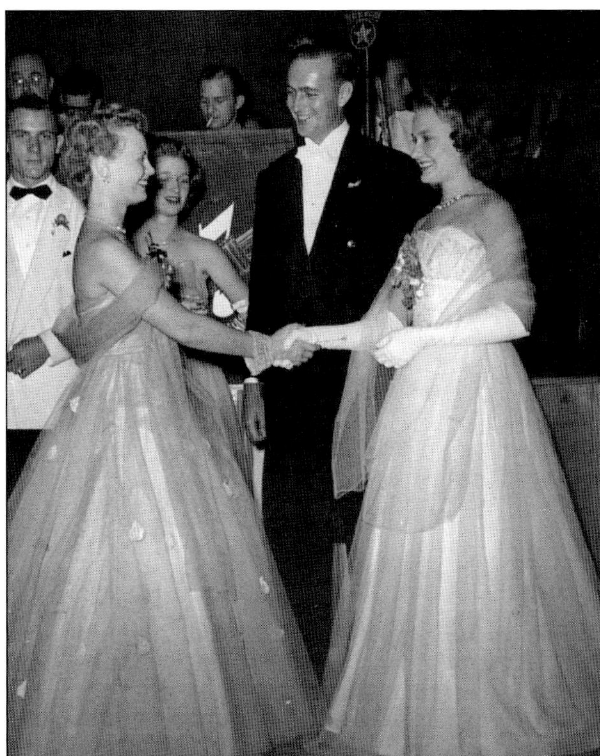

At the conclusion of the 1950 Queen's Ball, Fosteene Spikes of Mission (left) receives congratulations from Wilma Cutler, Queen Citrianna XIII (right) after the announcement that Spikes had been chosen Queen Citrianna XIV to reign over the 1951 Texas Citrus Fiesta. James M. Blankenbaker, King Citrus XIII, stands at center.

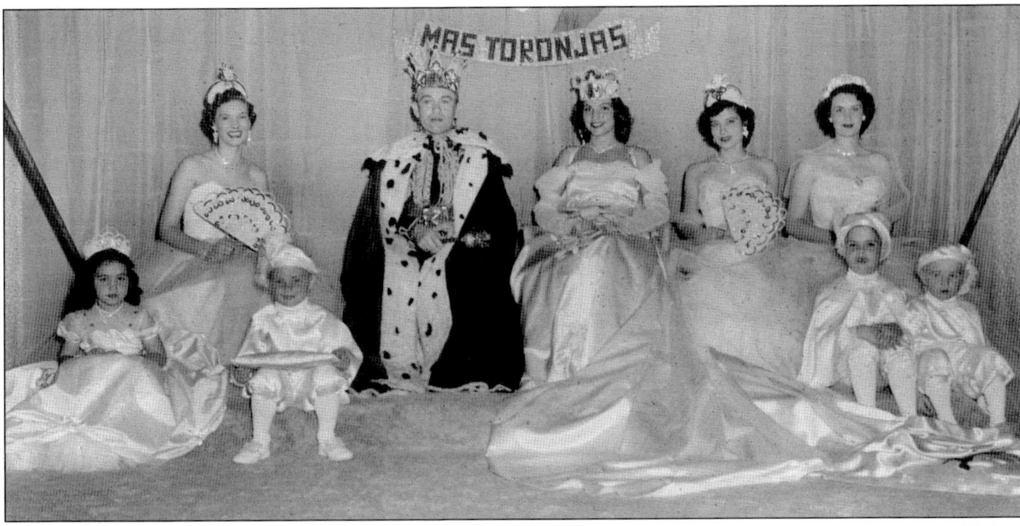

The 1952 royal court is seated just below a royal crest with the motto "Más Toronjas" ("More Grapefruit"). Posing here are, from left to right, (first row) Mary Jo Schroeder, Princess Anna II; Gary Ray Robinson, Crown Bearer; Hollis Rankin Jr. and Andrew Lee Rone, Train Bearers; (second row) Gerry Chandler, First Princess; Marshall Walden, King Citrus XV; Dorothy Hortness, Queen Citrianna XV; Amelia Reyna, Second Princess; and Betty McDougle, Lady-in-Waiting.

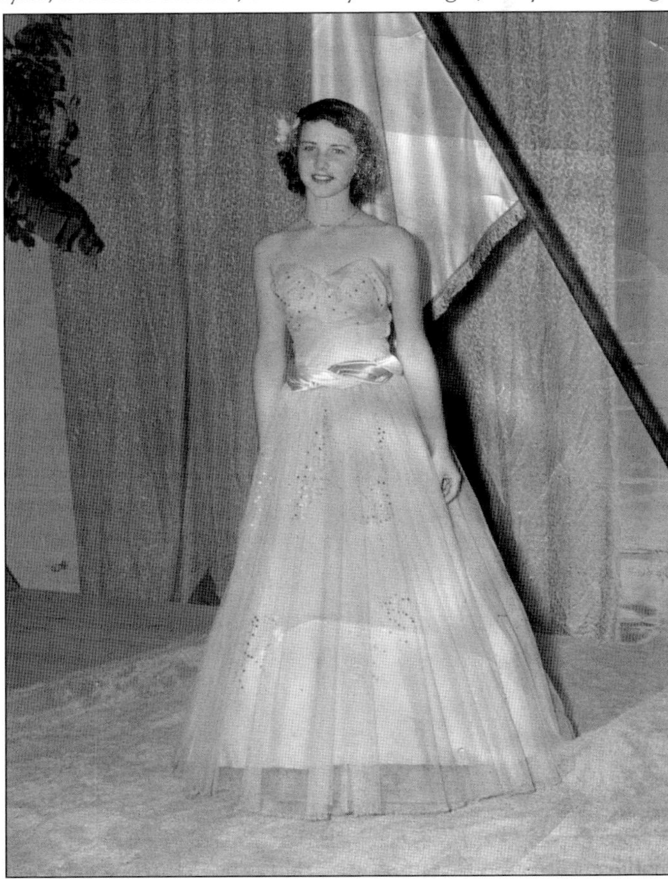

Patia Link of Weslaco, seen here as the 1952 Duchess of Lemon, was named First Princess for the 1953 Texas Citrus Fiesta. Gerry Chandler, Princess of Grapefruit Blossom, was selected for 1953 Queen Citrianna, but she was disqualified when she got married. Link became Queen Citrianna XVI in 1953. The theme that year was "Fiesta Under the Stars."

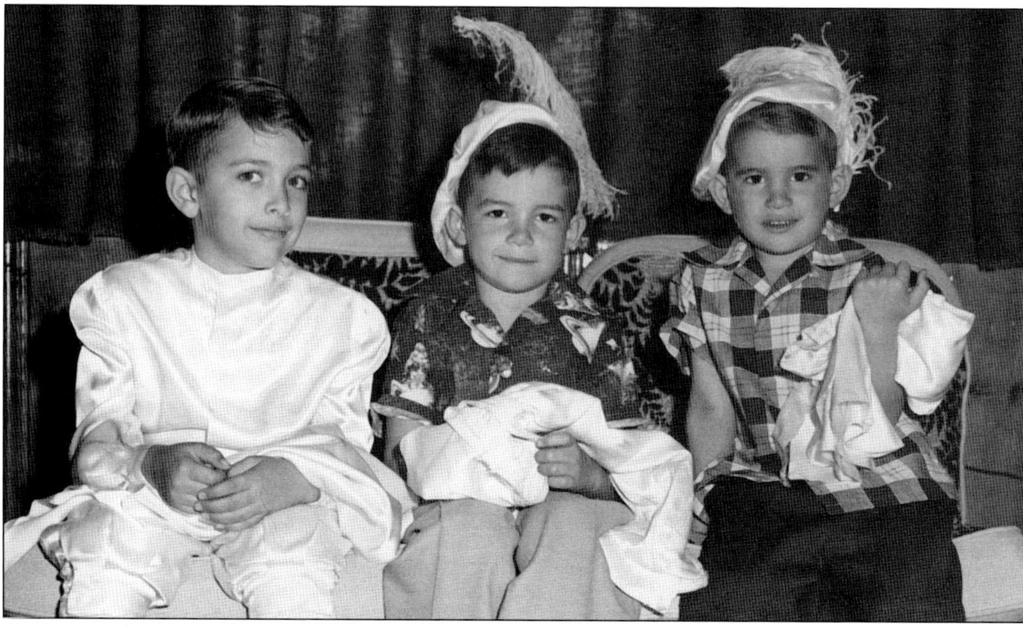

Receiving their new costumes made of white satin in 1953 are pages Gary Hoekstra (left), Train Bearer; Jimmy Hall (center), Train Bearer; and David Hall, Crown Bearer. All three were from Mission, and Jimmy and David were brothers. According to the January 30, 1953, *Mission Times*, the background was a "sky garden of twinkling stars, floating clouds, and a skyline of citrus trees."

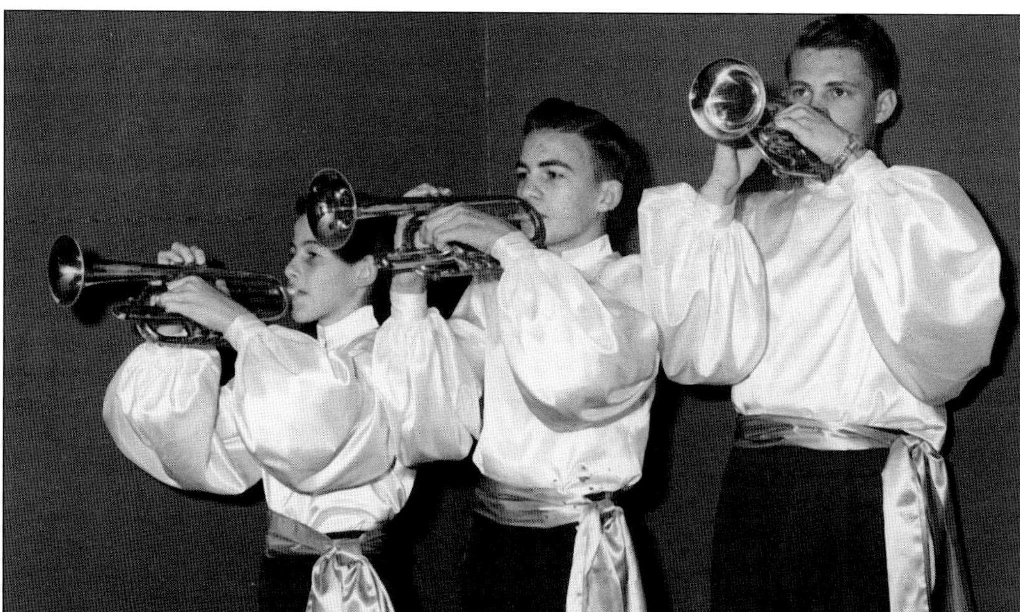

Heralds announced the arrival of King Citrus XVI and members of the Court of Citrus. A trumpet fanfare introduced each coronation event. Mission High School band members seen here in 1953 are Bob Bourgeois (left), Jim Van Cleave (center), and Warren Shropshire. King Citrus XVI, Eugene M. Goodwin II of Mission, was a citrus nurseryman and third-generation member of the pioneer Goodwin family in Mission's citrus industry.

In 1953, "Fiesta Under the Stars" featured an elaborate throne room at the Memorial Gymnasium. Patia Link, Queen Citrianna XVI, wears a dress replicating the one worn by England's Queen Elizabeth II during her June coronation. Shown here are, from left to right, Link; Eugene M. Goodwin II, King Citrus XVI; Lana Cheryl Bentsen, Princess Anna III; and David Hall, Crown Bearer.

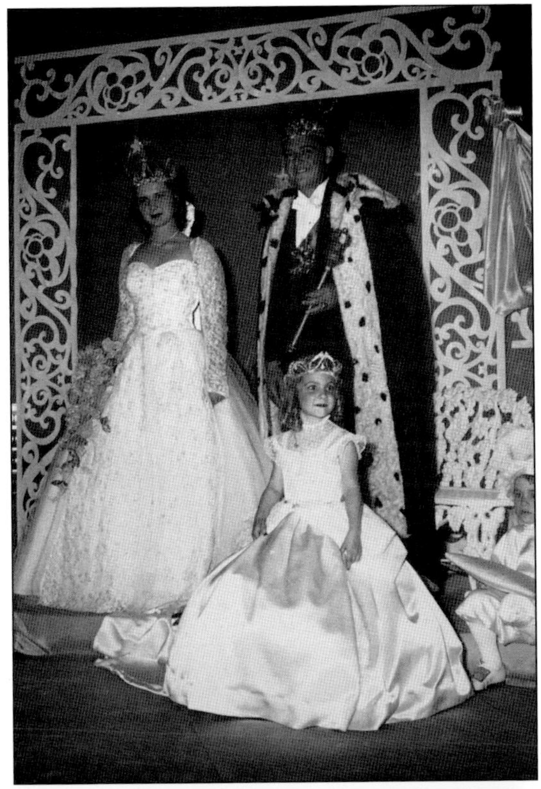

Sometimes, lighter moments occurred during the otherwise serious coronation. Seen here in the 1955 event are, from left to right, (first row) Pages Roger Bell, Betito Reyna, and Johnny Miller; (second row) Betty Lee Smith, Queen Citrianna XVIII; Chester W. Showers, King Citrus XVIII; and Paula Rogers, Second Princess. To emphasize the theme "Citrus for the World," tropical shrubs and fruit decorate a large medallion of the North American hemisphere.

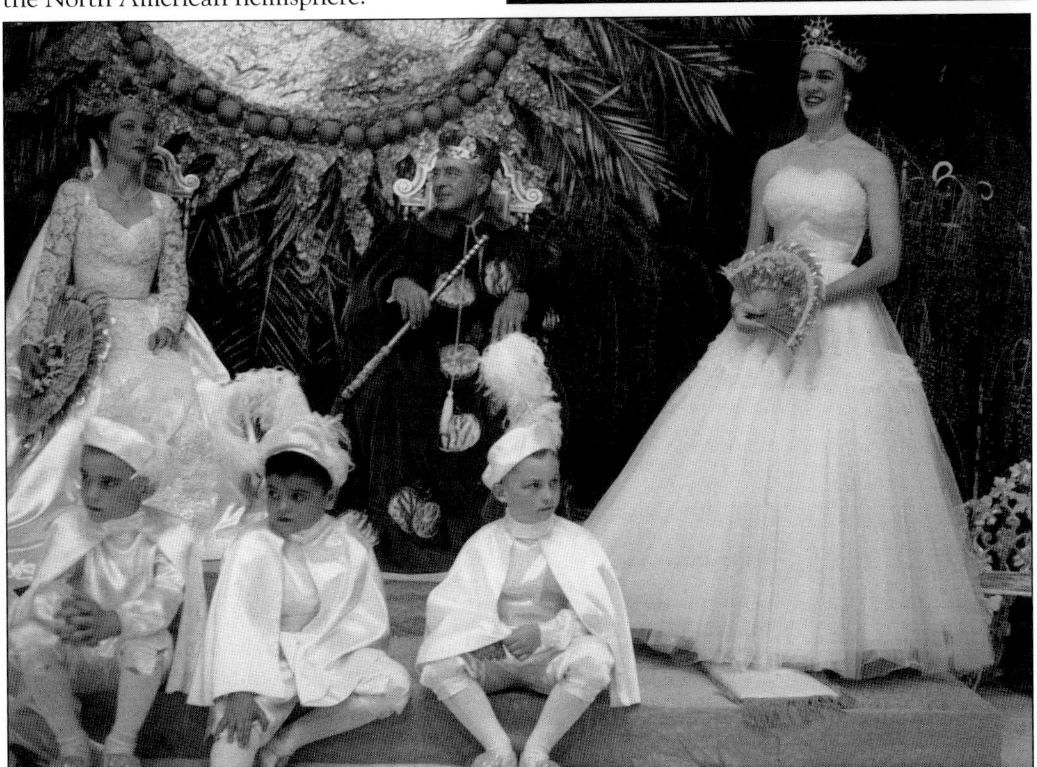

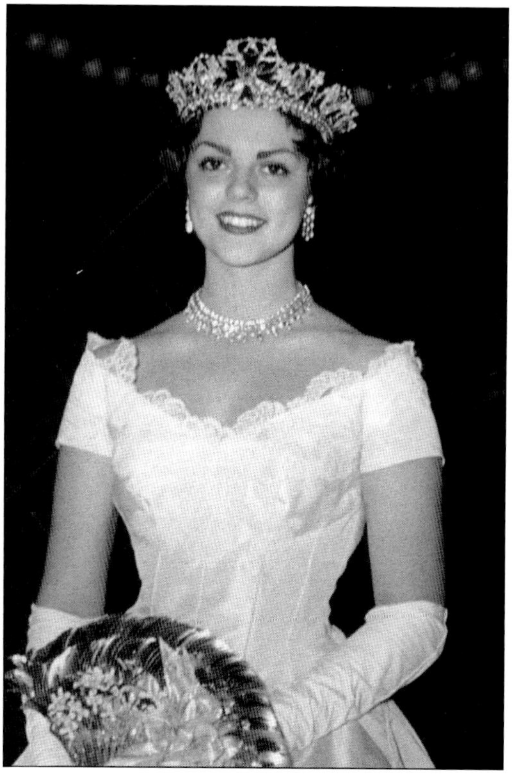

Jeanette Waters, Queen Citrianna XIX, ruled over the 1956 Court of Citrus. The daughter of R. Newell Waters, a prominent Weslaco architect, and Mrs. Waters, Jeanette had previously competed for Farm Bureau Queen (1954) and served as Duchess of Lemon (1955). A cheerleader, band twirler, and class officer at Weslaco High School, she was a freshman at the University of Texas in 1956. King Citrus XIX was Joe L. Crump.

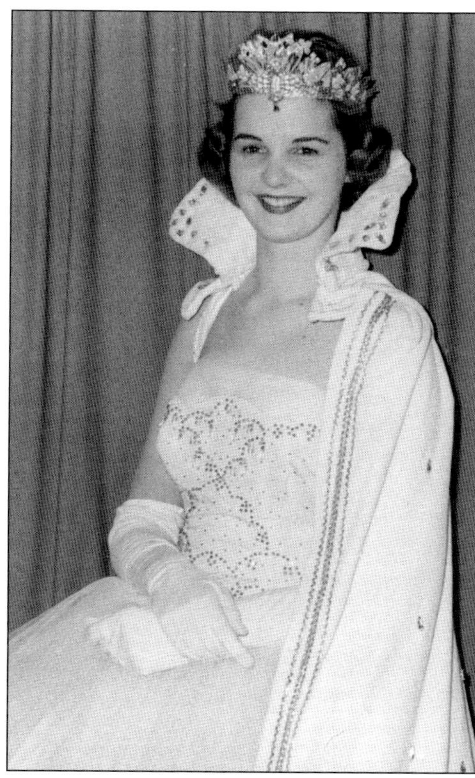

Tall, red-haired Sandra Ruth Kimbriel reigned as Queen Citrianna XXI in 1958. She modeled product costumes in the 1955 and 1956 style shows. In 1956, she was Duchess of Calamondin, representing San Juan. The City of San Juan sponsored her float, a basket full of oranges, which won third place. She was named First Princess for the 1957 court. A drawing of her by Billie Bruns graces the 1958 program cover.

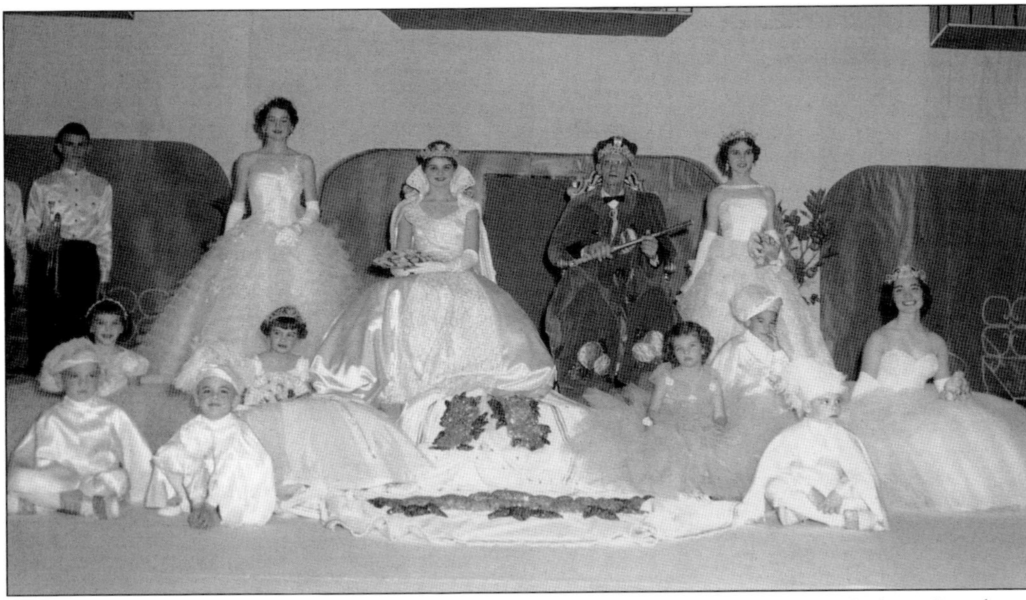

Members of the 1958 royal court are, from left to right (first row) Train Bearers Robert Goodwin, Mike Trolinger, and Charles Osteen; (second row) Georgeanna Amyx, Lady-in-Waiting; Ellen Blankenbaker, Princess Anna VIII; Glenda Rowe, Lady-in-Waiting; Gregg Holbrook, Crown Bearer; and Mildred Ruth Lawler, First Princess; (third row) Jimmy Bourgeois, Herald; Sally Lei Walker, Lady-in-Waiting; Sandra Ruth Kimbriel, Queen Citrianna XXI; Herbert P. Truhe, King Citrus XXI; and Judy Seitz, Second Princess.

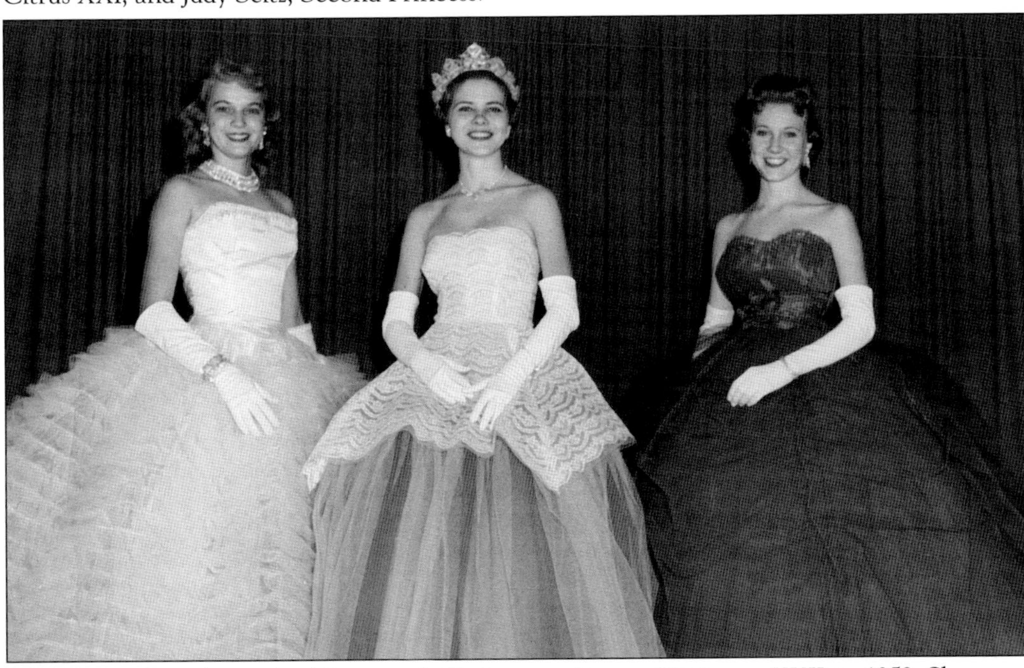

Lucy Ann Moon (center) of Raymondville became Queen Citrianna XXII in 1959. She was a student at Raymondville High School. Posing with Moon for a portrait are Ann Irene Norman (left), of Weslaco, First Princess, and Shirley Baggett of Mission, Second Princess. J. Harold Randle ruled the court as King Citrus XXII.

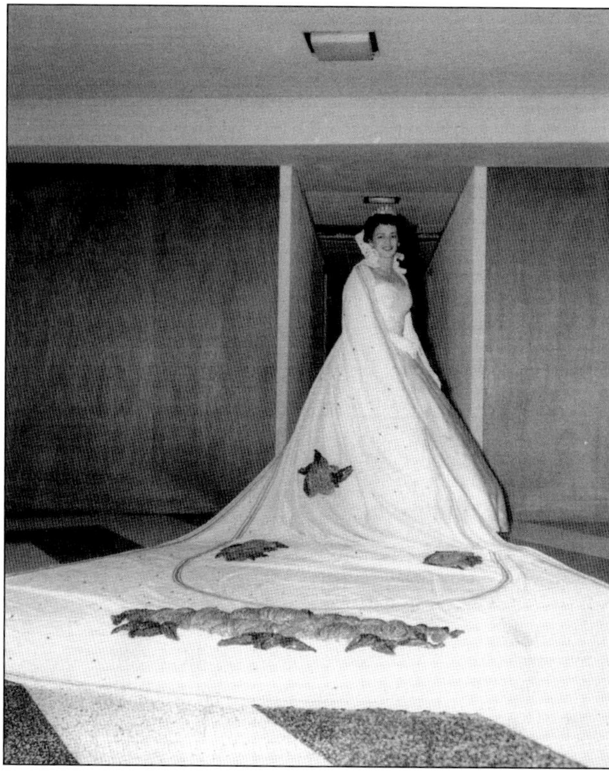

In 1961, Mary Lovey Wood, Queen Citrianna XXIV, was an 18-year-old freshman at Southwestern University. The fifth Queen Citrianna from Mission, she had previously served as Lady-in-Waiting to Queen Citrianna XXII, Lucy Ann Moon, in 1959 and as Duchess of Ruby Red Grapefruit in 1960. King Citrus XXIV was Harry Thompson.

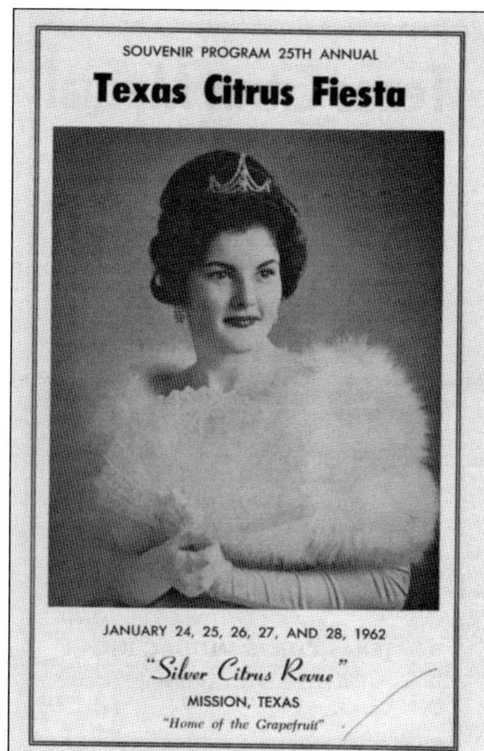

In 1959, the executive board authorized the printing of a souvenir program to be sold during the Texas Citrus Fiesta. In 1962, a photograph, rather than a drawing, of Sharyn Ruth Shropshire, Queen Citrianna XXV, marked another turning point in the event's programs. Subsequent program covers feature a portrait of Queen Citrianna. The 1962 theme, "Silver Citrus Revue," celebrated the 25th anniversary of the fiesta. David C. Blevins was King Citrus XXV.

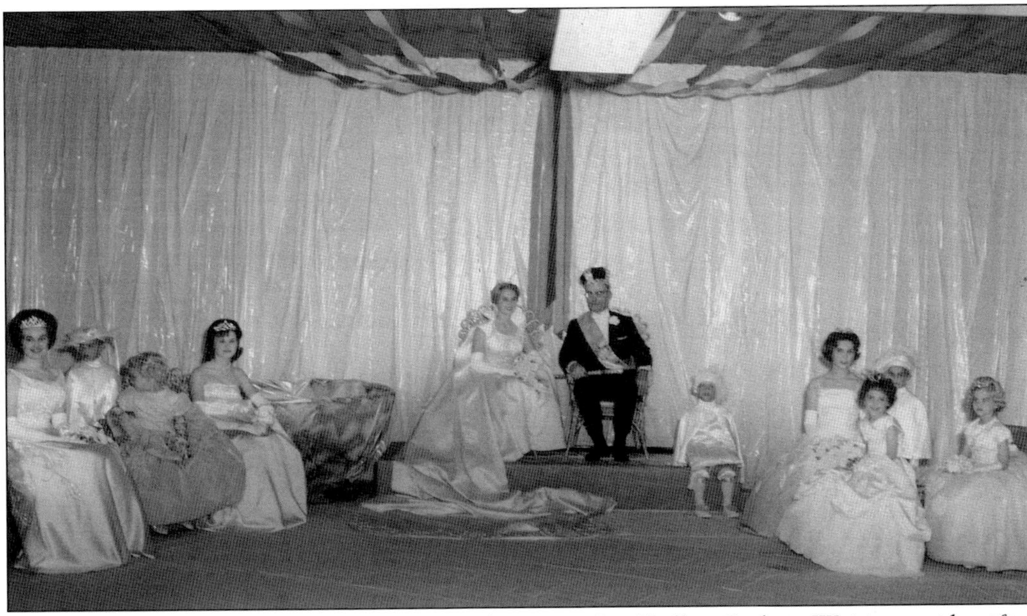

Members of the 1963 court are, from left to right, Laurie Sue Phillips, Lady-in-Waiting; unidentified Train Bearer; Candace Leah Hild, First Princess; Mary Jo Lynch, Princess of Orange Blossom; Patricia Marie Lenoir, Queen Citrianna XXVI; C.B. Curtis, King Citrus XXVI; Keith Wright, Crown Bearer; Barbara Nordmeyer, Princess of Grapefruit Blossom; unidentified train bearer; Jill Faye Saxon, Princess Anna XIII; and Jill Annette Powers, Second Princess.

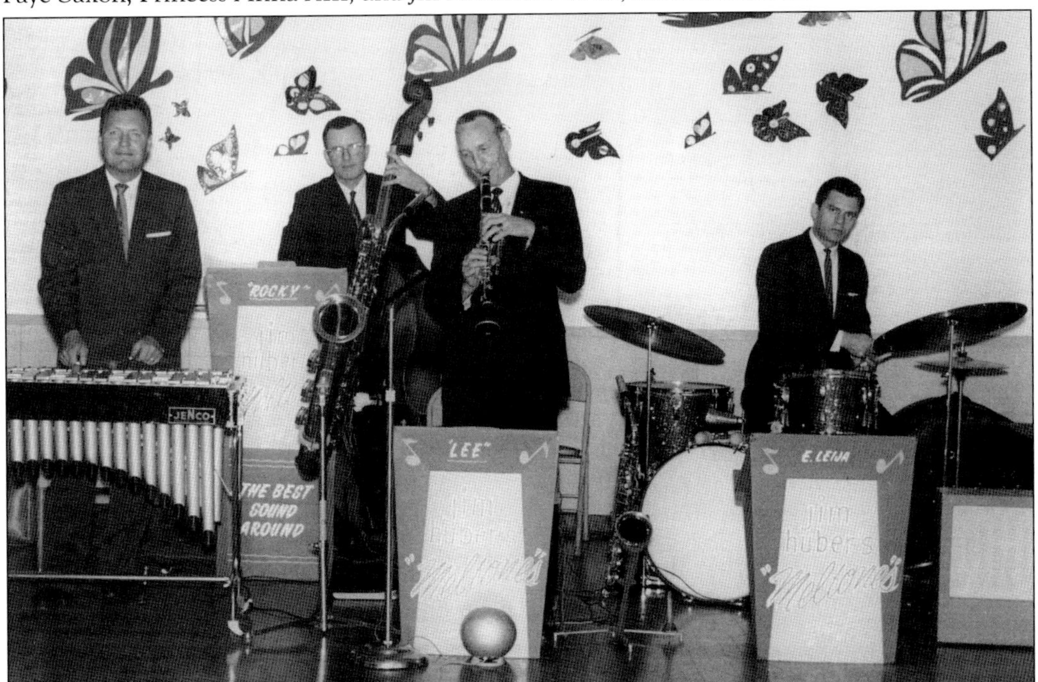

In 1963 and 1964, Mel Huber and His Meltones provided dance music for the Queen's Ball, held at the Mission Community Center. Tickets for the dance cost $5 per couple. The band provided a fanfare at midnight to signal the announcement of the next Queen Citrianna.

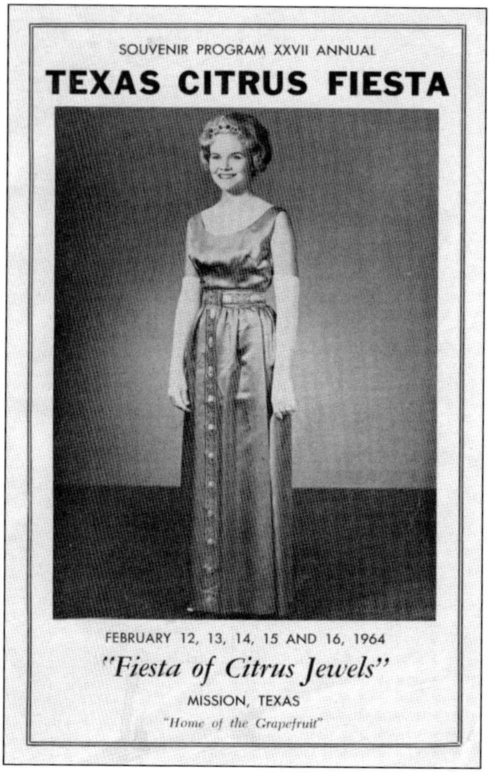

The 1964 Texas Citrus Fiesta took place in February, with the theme "Fiesta of Citrus Jewels." Seen here on the souvenir program cover is Marylyn Kay Mitchell of Sharyland, Queen Citrianna XXVII. Age 17, she was president of the Sharyland High School senior class and lived on a citrus farm. She studied citrus grading and packing for her role as Queen Citrianna. Blaine H. Holcomb was King Citrus XXVII.

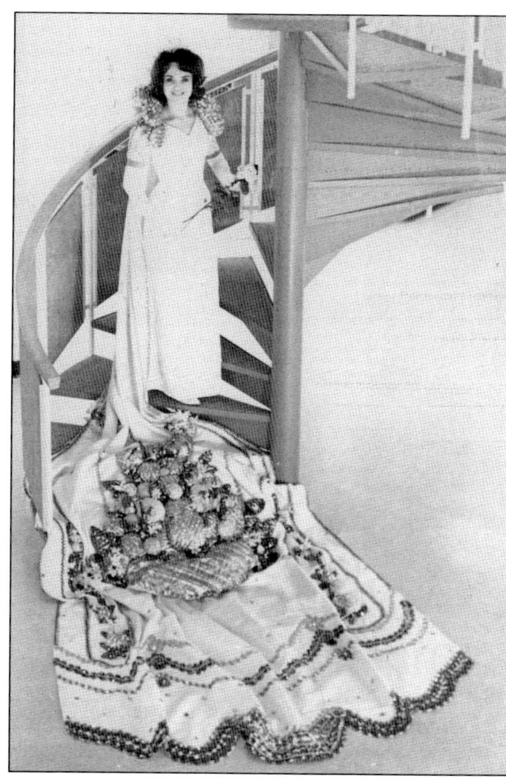

Alys Virginia Taylor, Princess Anna V in 1955, became Queen Citrianna XXIX in 1966. She represented Mission as Duchess of Marsh Seedless Grapefruit. Taylor attended Mission High School, where she was FFA Sweetheart, cheerleader, and a National Honor Society member. Here, she is depicted on the staircase at the new Mission High School library. King Citrus XXIX was Claborne B. Brazeal.

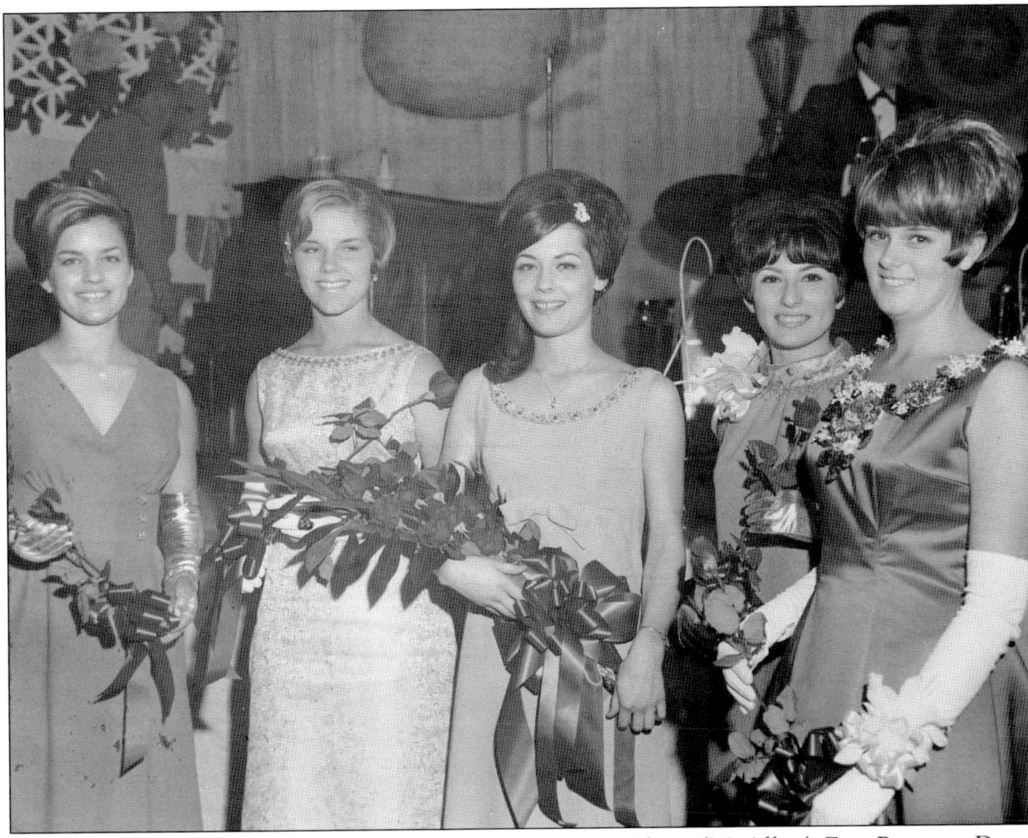

Members of the 1969 court are, from left to right, Virginia Chase (McAllen), First Princess; Dawn Conway (Pharr), Second Princess; Cheryl Ann Garrett (Harlingen), Queen Citrianna XXXII; Laura Beard (San Benito), First Alternate; and Ellen Blankenbaker (Mission), Second Alternate. King Citrus XXXII was Lloyd M. Bentsen Sr.

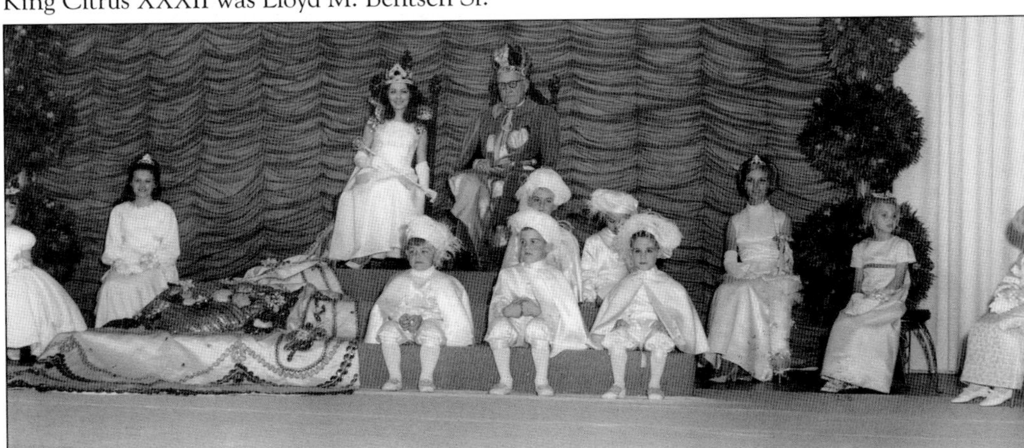

The 1969 court includes, from left to right, (first row) Troy Esquivel, Ralph Young, and Michael Medkiff; (second row) David John Ridling and Blake Brandt; (third row) Keli Jo Cobb, Princess Anna XIX; Paula Reynolds; Cheryl Ann Garrett, Queen Citrianna XXXII; Lloyd M. Bentsen Sr., King Citrus XXXII; Dawn Conway; Merry Kathryn Moskal; and Sheryl Ann Underwood. A shirred blue net curtain and antique chairs from the Enrique Flores family provide ambiance.

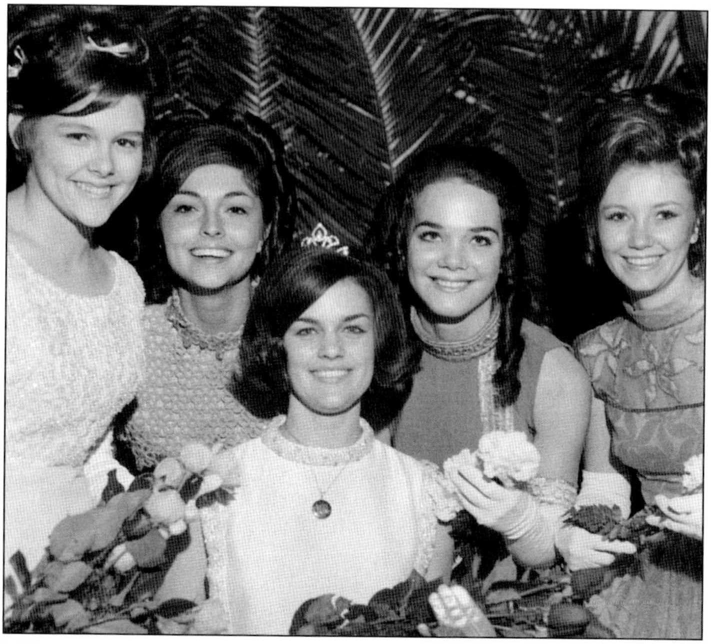

Seen here in 1969, members of the 1970 court are, from left to right, Debra Jo Ludwig (Mission), First Princess; Gilma Longoria (Pharr), Second Princess; Virginia Ann Chase (McAllen), Queen Citrianna XXXIII; Gloria Gene Moore (Edinburg), First Alternate; and Connie Sue Garfield (San Juan), Second Alternate. Chase abdicated because of her college schedule, and Debra Jo Ludwig became Queen Citrianna XXXIII. King Citrus XXXIII was C.H. "Hubert" Thompson.

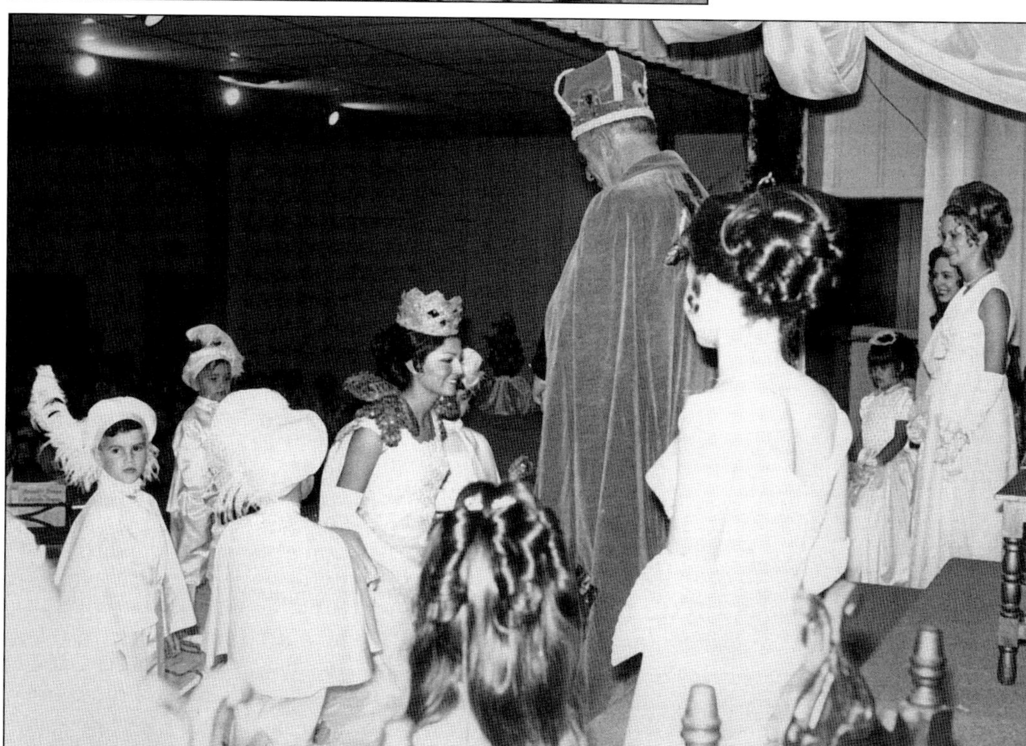

James P. Walsh (McAllen), King Citrus XXXIV, crowned Gilma Longoria (Pharr), Queen Citrianna XXXIV, in February 1971. As Princess of Grapefruit Blossom, she competed against 21 other contestants in 1970. Members of her court were Catherine Brumley (Edinburg), First Princess; Vicki Lynn Strobel (Donna), Second Princess; Nancy White (Mission), First Alternate; and Martha Dizdar (McAllen), Second Alternate.

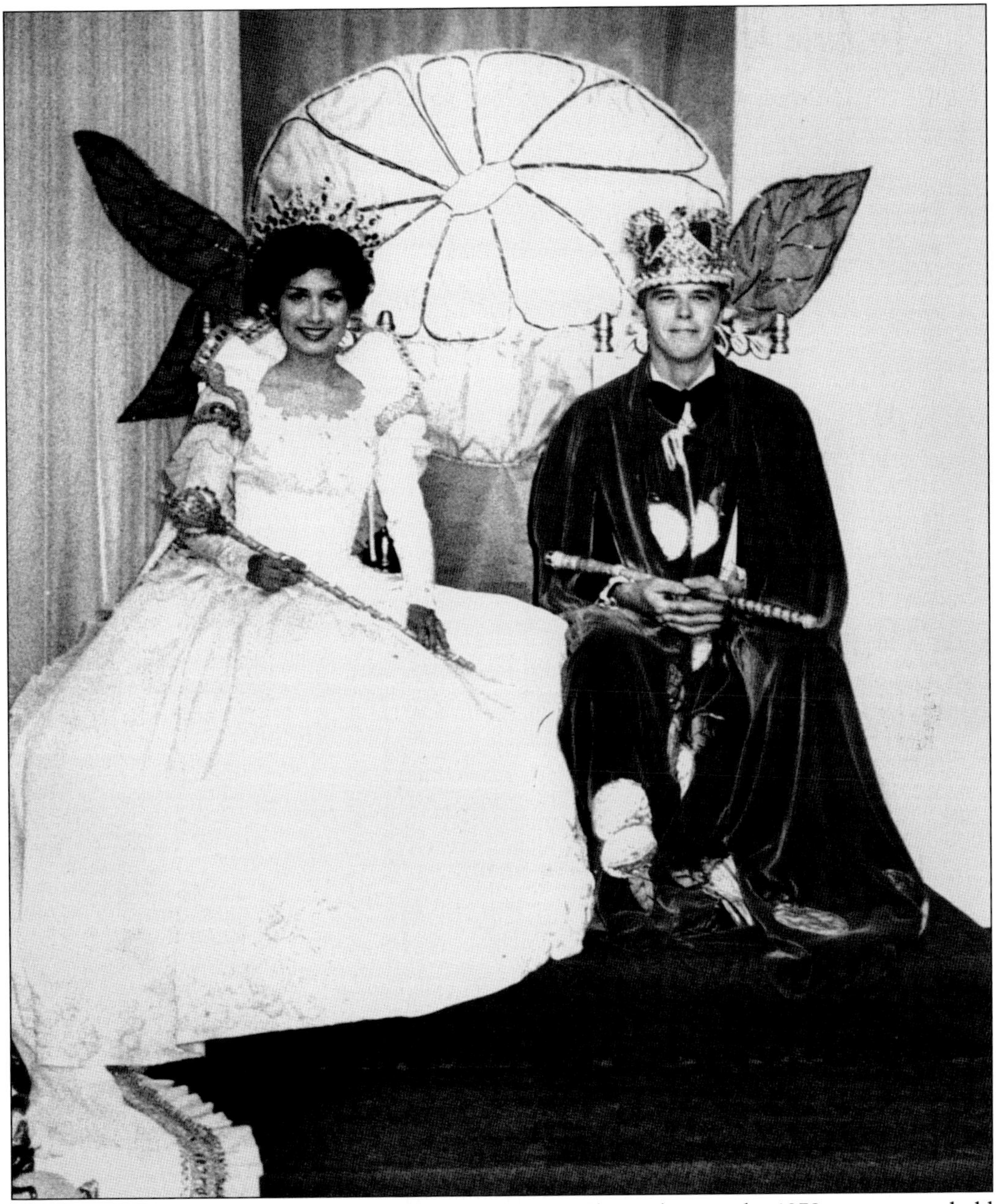

Denise Hernández (Edinburg), Queen Citrianna XLI, is shown here at the 1978 coronation, held on February 1 at the Mission Community Center. The scholarly queen earned a bachelor's degree from Pan American University a year and a half after her May 1976 graduation from Edinburg High School, both times with honors. At age 20 in 1978, she was in the process of earning a master's degree in counseling and guidance from Pan American University Graduate School. Hernández received the titles of Miss Edinburg (1975) and Miss Bicentennial (Edinburg, 1976). She represented Edinburg in the 1976 Texas Citrus Fiesta and, as Princess of Orange Blossom, joined the royal court in 1977. Bill Thompson (right) is King Citrus XLI, and Leticia Yvette Parras was Princess Anna XXVIII. The theme of the celebration was "Disney Kaleidoscope—Mirrored in Citrus."

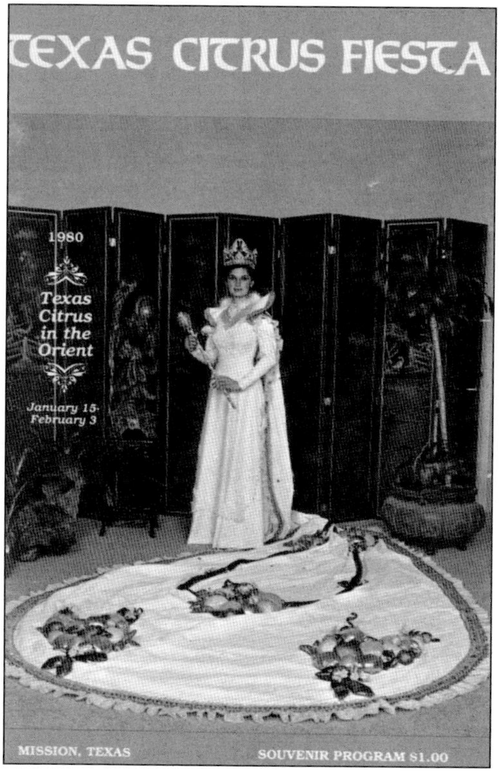

In 1980, Kathryn Lucille Swayze, Queen Citrianna XLIII, was a senior at Raymondville High School. She took part in numerous high school activities and worked at the Raymondville Bank of Texas. King Citrus XLIII was Ken Martin, and Princess Anna XXX was Melissa Ann Pérez of Edinburg. The program cover, seen here, has evolved from black-and-white to full color.

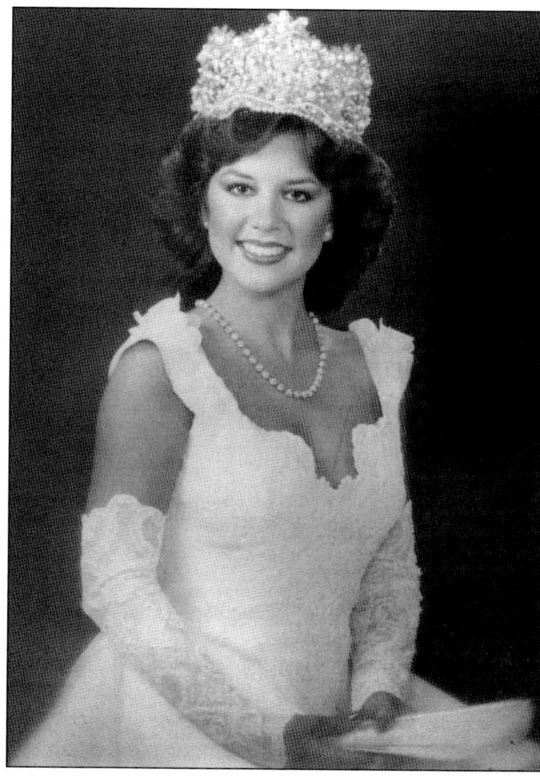

Annette Thompson (Weslaco), Queen Citrianna LXV, joined Andrew Hill Jr., King Citrus LXV, to reign over the 1982 court. Tiffany Ann Mann, Princess Anna XXXII, likewise ruled over the Tangerine Court, composed of more than 20 girls. The fiesta theme that year was "Citrus—Deep in the Heart of Texas."

Five

A Focus on Children

Children have been integral to the Texas Citrus Fiesta since the first celebration, serving as crown and train bearers. During the "Coronation and Pageant of Citrus," youngsters of different ages performed dances and the "March of the Harvest," and Mission High School band members provided the music. Arthur Hayes organized most of the entertainment for the first pageant.

Research does not indicate whether children participated in their own parade in 1932, but they did two years later. In 1936, as a "novelty feature" of the fiesta, a children's parade was organized into two divisions, one for children wearing costumes and one for children with their pets. According to the *Mission Times* of December 11, 1936, spectators lined Conway Avenue to watch "the tiny, costumed youngsters parade their pets, which included dogs, cats, and monkeys."

The children's parade, renamed the Junior Parade in 1940, remained a special part of the fiesta, and the children's unpredictable behavior added to the enjoyment of the adults. After World War II, Mission citizens returned to the traditional events of the fiesta with great energy. There were indications that the Junior Parade was not going to be "revived" in 1947, according to the *Mission Times*, but popular sentiment demanded its return.

To avoid inclement weather, the children's event moved indoors to Memorial Gymnasium in 1950, and emphasis shifted to a citrus and vegetable style show, like that of the adults. The Princess Anna contest began in 1951, and the winner was chosen from photographs. Today, there are as many as 200 entrants, each identified by number only until the winners are announced. Princess Anna is accompanied by youngsters in the Tangerine Court, and they participate as princesses, pages, train bearers, crown bearers, and style show models.

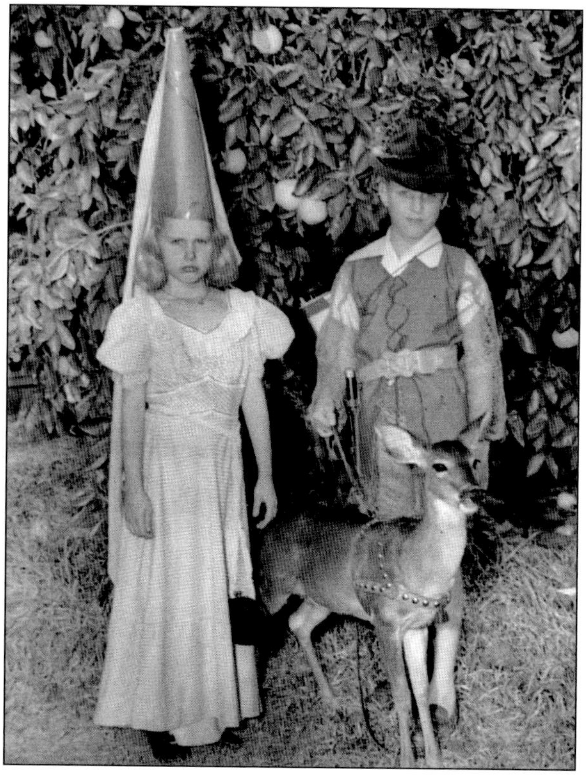

Siblings Kathleen and Wallace Bohannon, representing storybook characters, are dressed as Maid Marian and Robin Hood, respectively. Seen here in 1947, they won first place in the pet division of the Junior Parade with their four-month-old fawn.

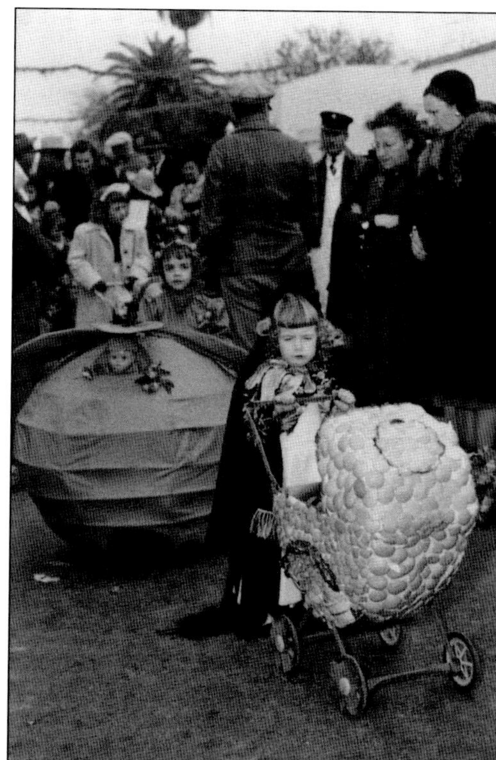

The doll buggy parade was limited to children ages seven and under. The 1948 winner was Linda Looney (left of center), whose doll can be seen peeking out of the "orange." The young lady in front, pushing the doll buggy covered with citrus halves, is unidentified.

The 1948 Junior Parade, tricycle division, began at 10:30 a.m. on Saturday, January 17. The youngsters walked or rode from Mission City Hall, down Conway Avenue to Ninth Street, and returned to city hall. The two children at left are unidentified. At right are Brad Findley and his sister Jennifer. Citrus bundles dangled from store canopies, and palm fronds concealed the bases of streetlights.

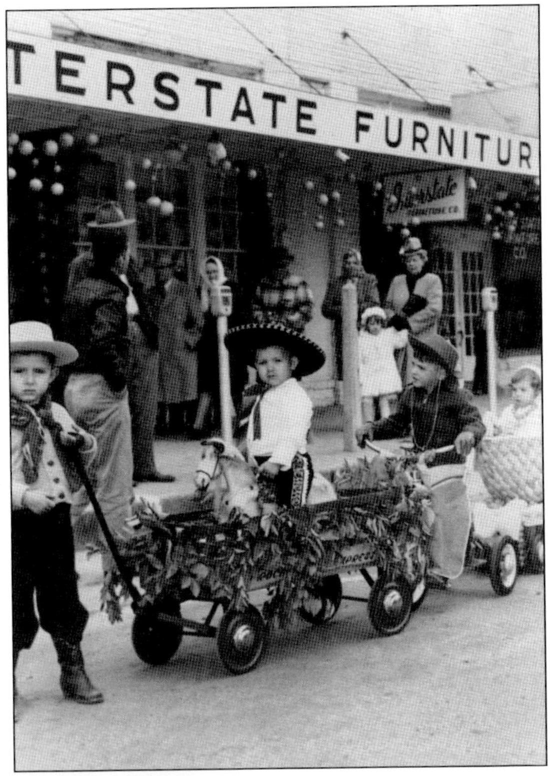

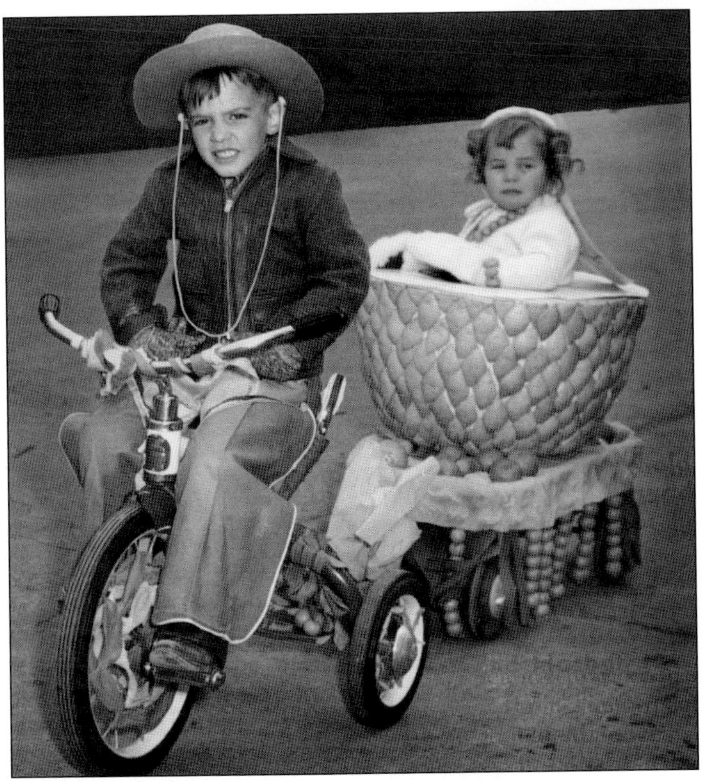

Brad Findley, four, pulls a wagon loaded with a replica of half a grapefruit containing his sister Jennifer Lynn, two, in the 1948 Junior Parade. They won first place in the tricycle division. Brad served as a page in the 1950 coronation.

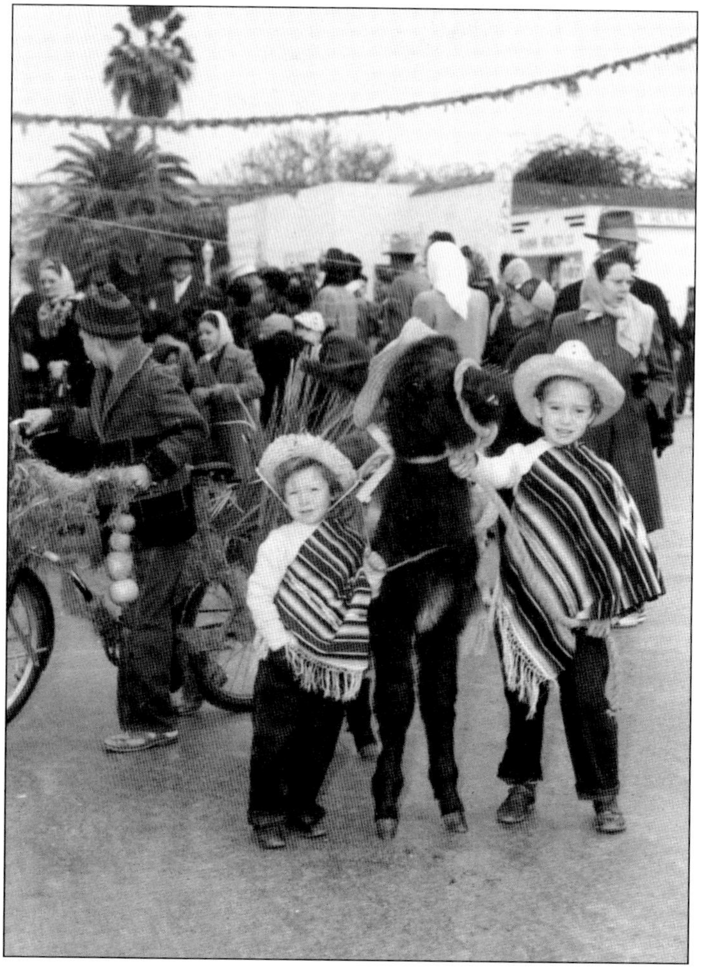

In 1948, sisters Jean Dawson, four, and Rosalie Dawson, eight, representing Mexican caballeros, led their burro George in the pet division of the Junior Parade. According to the *Mission Times*, George required encouragement from the crowd to step across the finish line. Perhaps George felt more confident after learning that he and the sisters had won first prize.

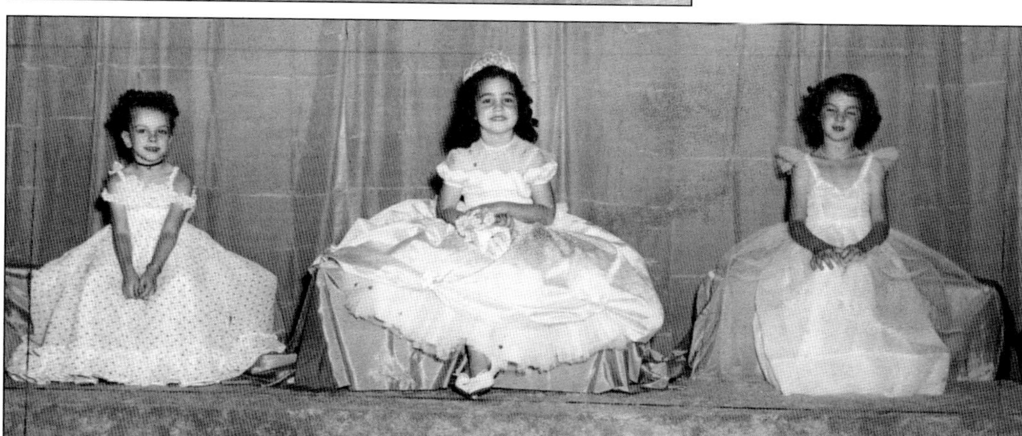

Beginning in 1951, Princess Anna and her court were chosen each year. She reigned over the Junior Style Show, held on Saturday mornings at Memorial Gymnasium, and she and her court participated in the Coronation, Parade of Oranges, and other events. Seen here in 1952 are, from left to right, Cheri Cox (McAllen); Mary Jo Schroeder (Edinburg), Princess Anna II; and Deanne Dair Jones (Mission).

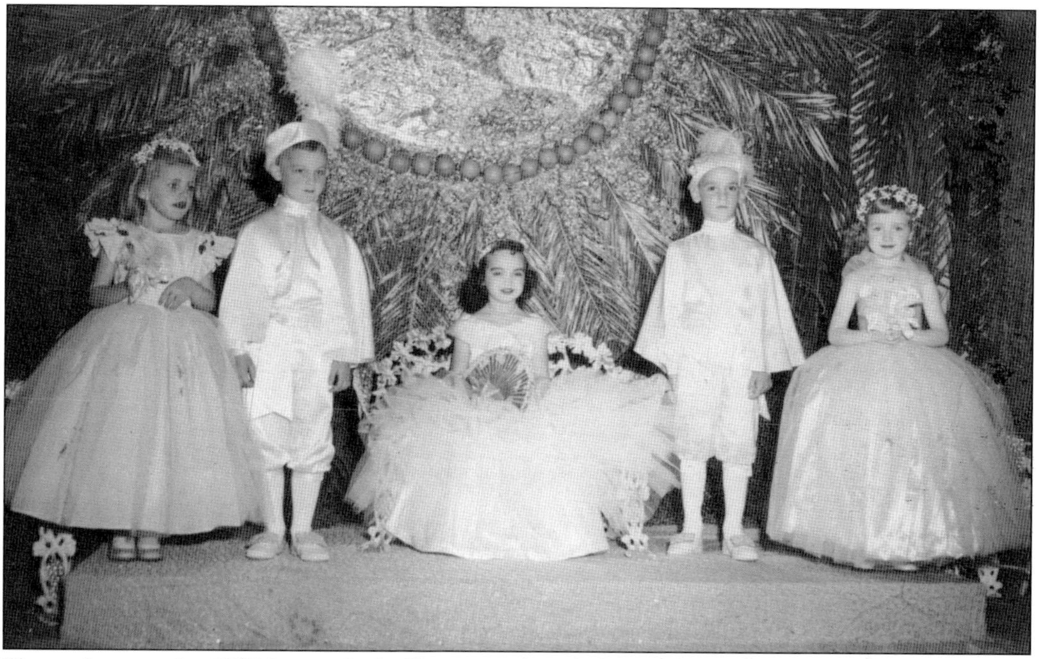

Shown here at the 1955 Junior Style Show are, from left to right, Deborah Darlene Leibengood (McAllen), Princess Alternate; Roger Bell (Mission), Page; Alys Taylor (Mission), Princess Anna V; Johnny Miller (Mission), Page; and Jacque Ellington (Lyford), Princess Alternate. Taylor became Queen Citrianna XXIX in 1966.

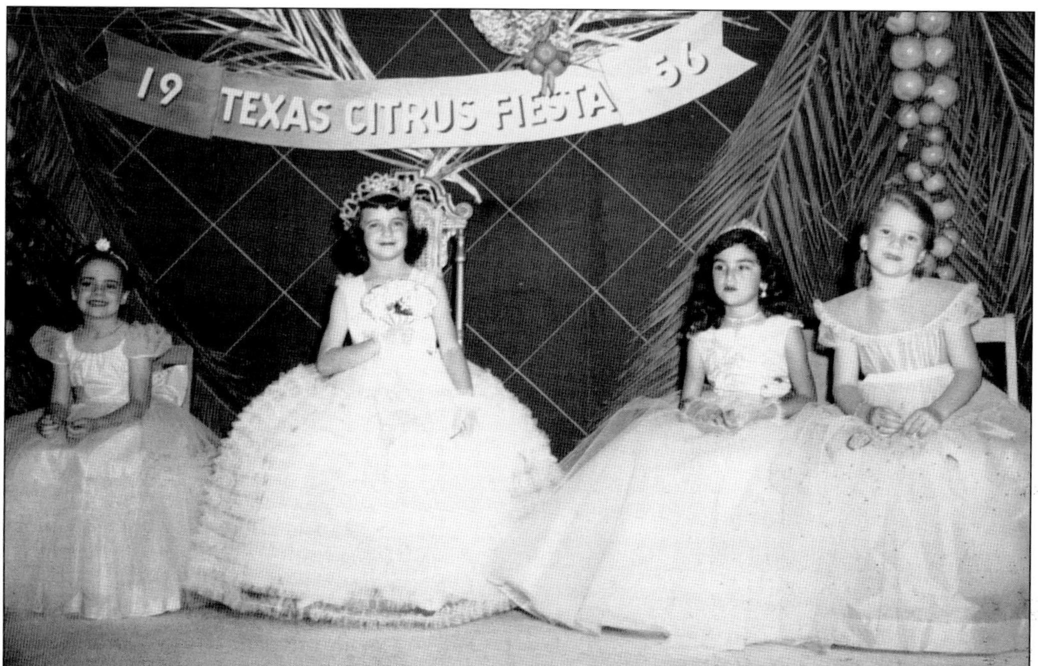

A portion of Princess Anna's court in 1956 appears here. They are, from left to right, Debby Rankin (Mission), First Princess; Janis Evelyn Billue (San Juan), Princess Anna VI; Monica Saenz (Mercedes), Junior Princess; and Carol Jane Smith (San Juan), Junior Princess.

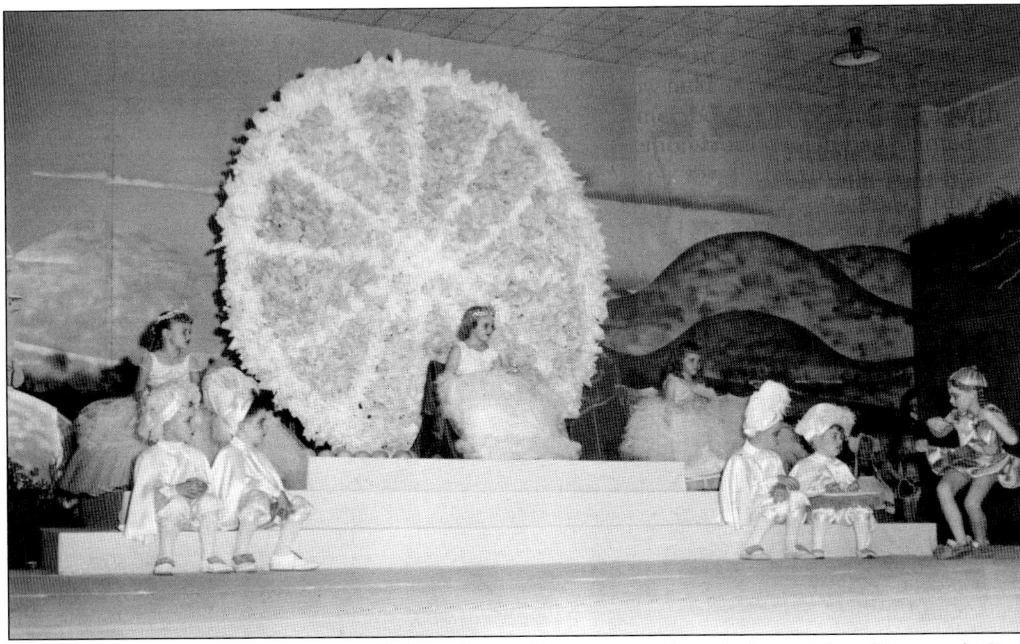

Watching the small dancer (far right) at the 1957 court are, from left to right, (first row) Gary Bentsen, Michael Myers, and Michael Perryman, Train Bearers; and Henry Fankhauser, Crown Bearer; (second row) Jan Ellen Thornton, Second Alternate Princess; Janet Claire Fletcher (Mercedes), Princess Anna VII; and Jane Mulholland, First Alternate Princess. The dancer is unidentified.

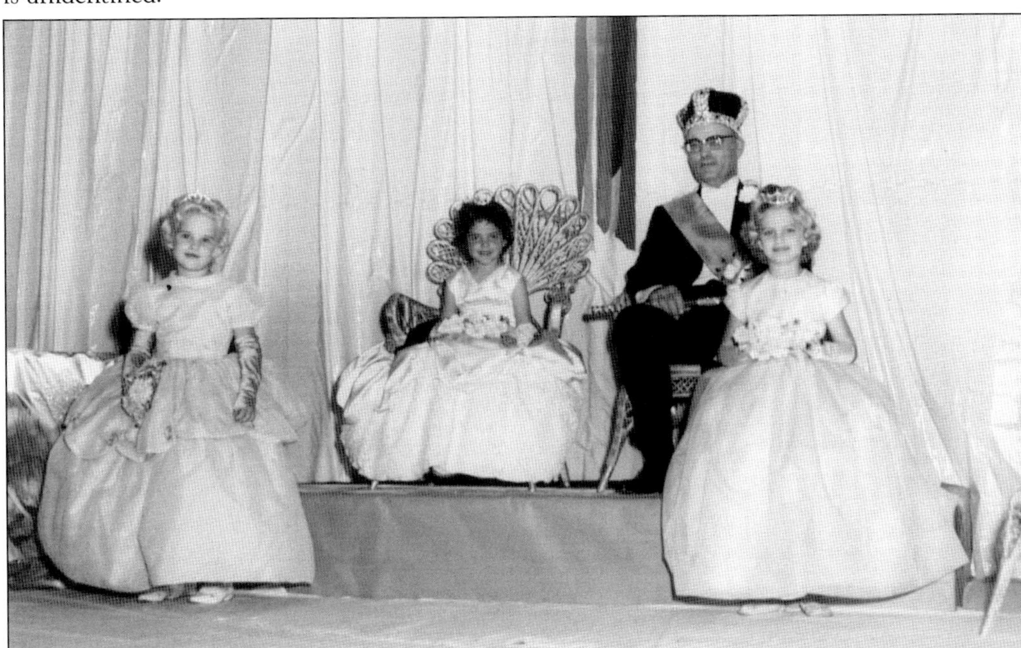

Court members for 1963 are, from left to right, Candace Leah Hild (Mercedes), First Princess; Jill Faye Saxon (San Perlita), Princess Anna XIII; C.B. Curtis (Mission), King Citrus XXVI; and Jill Annette Powers (Mercedes), Lady-in-Waiting.

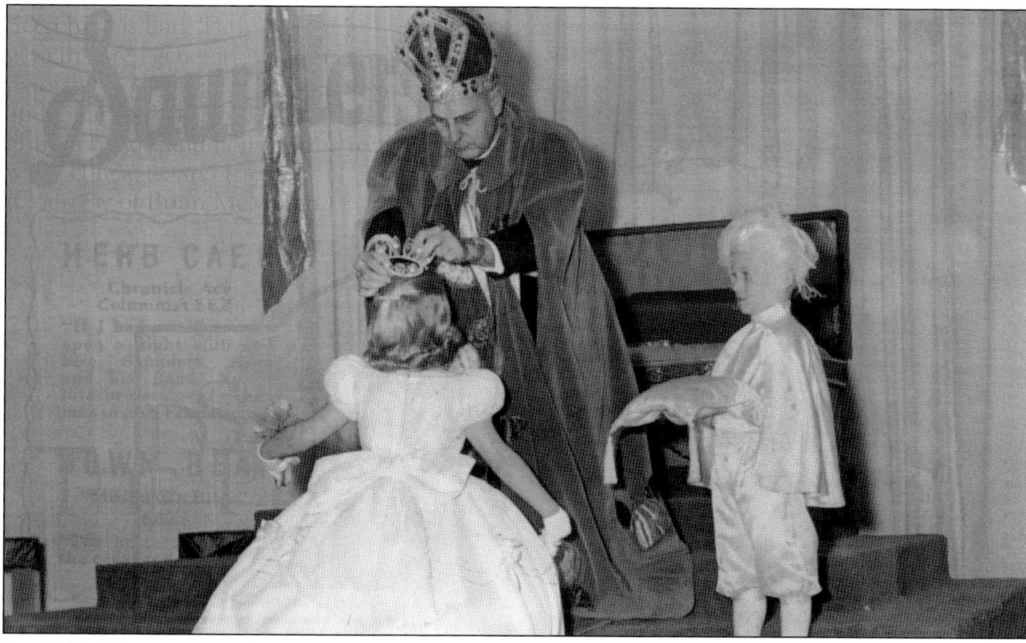

In 1964, Blaine H. Holcomb, King Citrus XXVII, crowns Rebecca King, Princess Anna XIV. The Crown Bearer is Jody Calloway White. A certified public accountant, Holcomb had been manager of the Shary estate and Allan Shivers interests since 1947. He served as president of the Texas Citrus Fiesta, the Mission Chamber of Commerce, and the Mission Lions Club, and he participated in the Texas Citrus Mutual. He and Mrs. Holcomb had four children.

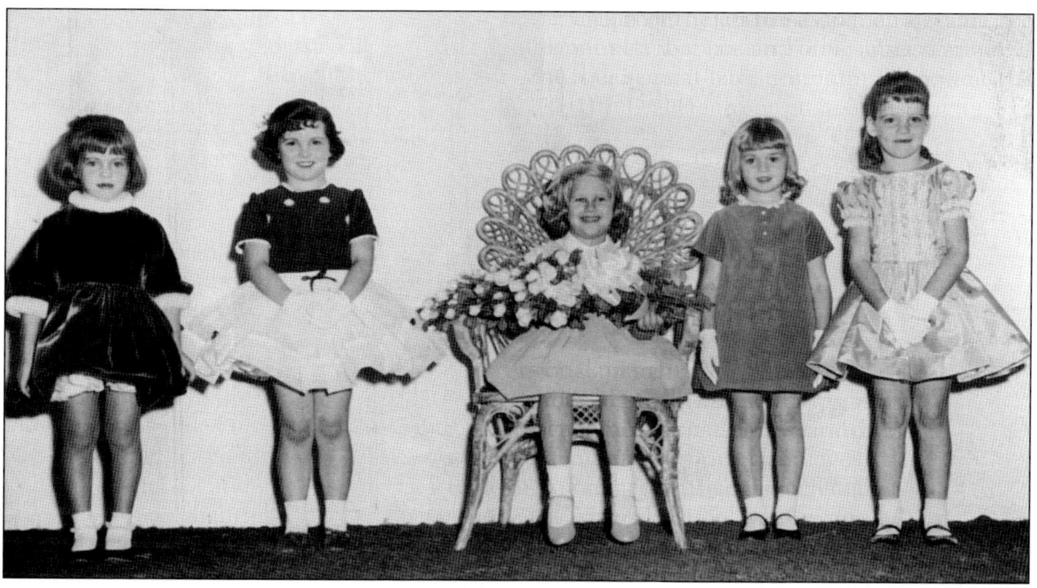

Seen here are Princess Anna XIV and her court in 1964. Pictured are, from left to right, Leslie Taylor (McAllen), Second Alternate; Teresa Moseley (McAllen), Third Alternate; Rebecca King (Mission), Princess Anna XIV; Sherri Lea Barnick (Mission), Second Princess; and Liz Later (Mission), First Alternate.

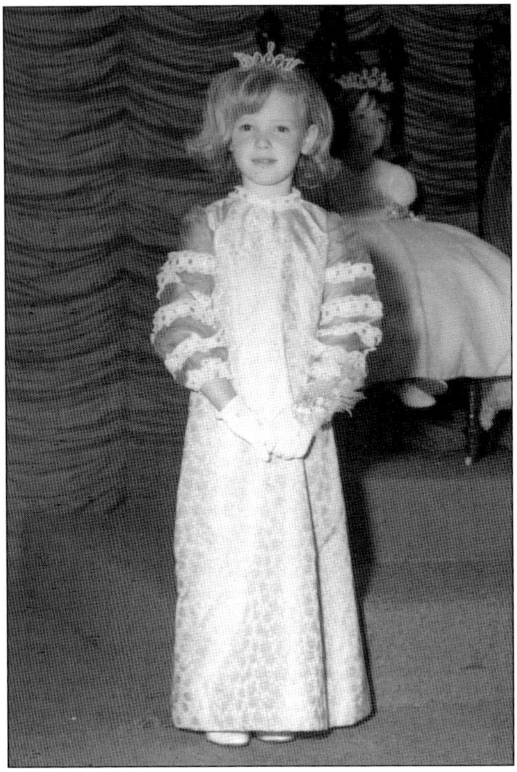

Sheryl Ann Underwood, six, was Second Princess at the 1969 royal court. Her dress of pale blue brocade complemented the dresses of Keli Jo Cobb, Princess Anna XIX, made of white velvet, and Merry Kathryn Moskal, Third Princess, of pink peau de soie.

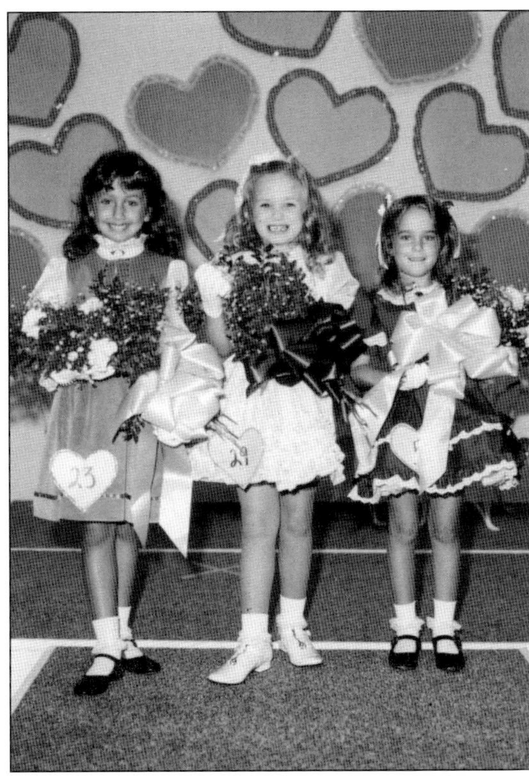

Junior royalty for 1982 are, from left to right, Alma Rosa Revesz (McAllen), Princess of Lime Blossom; Tiffany Ann Mann (McAllen), Princess Anna XXXII; and, Shelly Rae West (Mission), Princess of Lemon Blossom. Mann was the winner out of 29 members of the Tangerine Court.

In 1950, with the opening of the Memorial Gymnasium, the traditional Junior Parade moved indoors. The Children's Promenade took place on Saturday morning, and the youngsters modeled costumes made from citrus and other agricultural products, like those of the adults. Seen here in 1950 are Jimmy Miller (left) and twins Peggy and Tommy Spring.

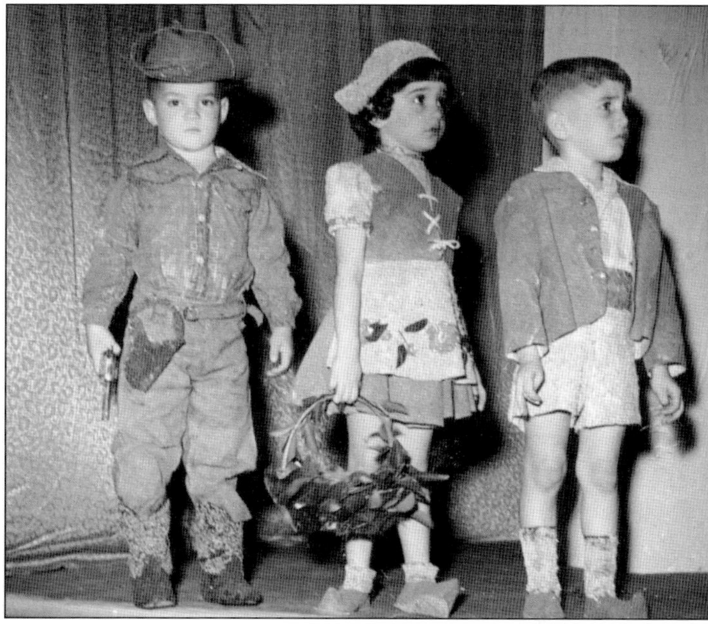

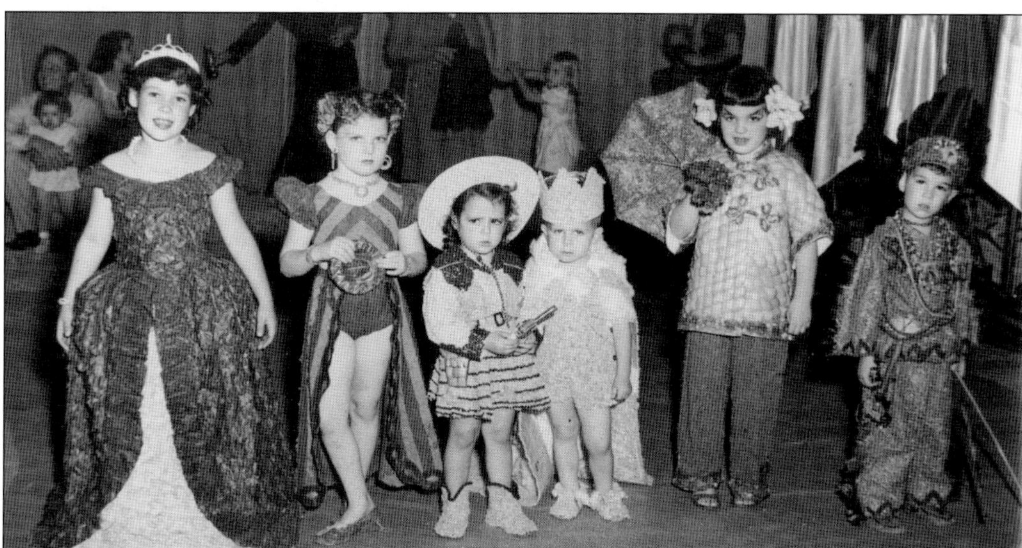

These Junior Style Show prizewinners in 1952 are, from left to right, Peggy Sue Shalla ("Empress Carlota of Mexico"), Janis Lee Keller ("Cuban Dancer"), Lexi Genenwein ("Texas Cowgirl"), David Larry Levermann ("King Cotton"), Lucy Beth Brazeal ("Chinese Girl"), and Bobby Randle ("Indian Chief").

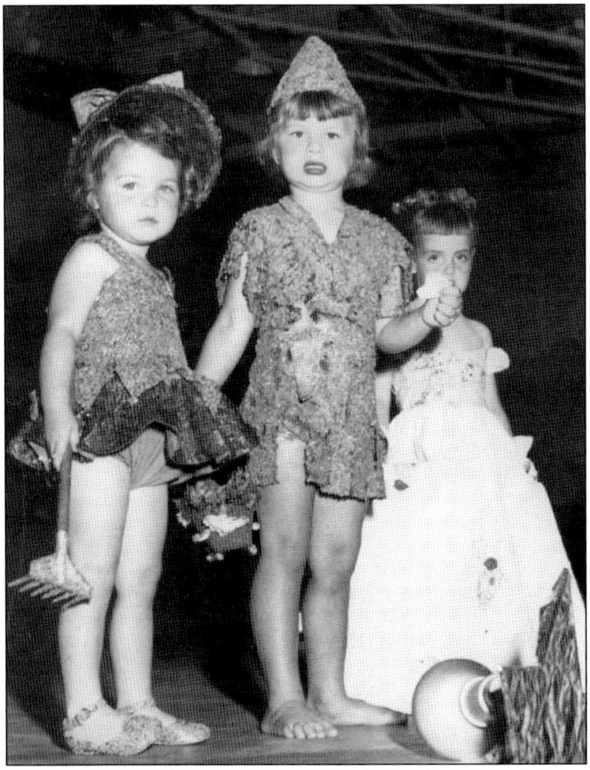

Junior Style Show winners in the two-to-three-year-old division in 1953 are, from left to right, Gail Brady ("Mistress Mary Quite Contrary"), Donna Marie Johnson ("Peter Pan"), and Luann Summers ("Cinderella"). The costumes are made of bougainvillea (Brady), dehydrated grapefruit leaves (Johnson), and grapefruit (Summers).

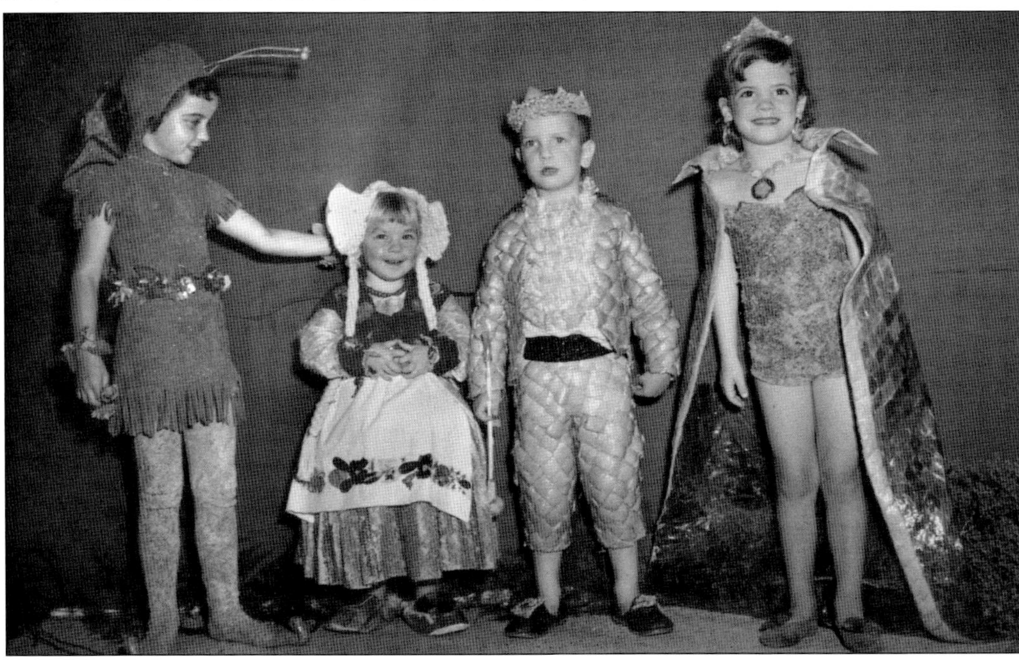

Winners in 1957 are, from left to right, Gail Brady ("Winsome Fairy," third place, four-to-six-year-olds), Denise Gail Reynolds ("Dutch Girl," third place, two-to-four-year-olds), David Martin ("Old King Cole," first place, four-to-six-year-olds), and Marsha Mae Ellison ("A Princess," second place, four-to-six-year-olds).

Maurine Duncan's daughter Diane first appeared in the Junior Style Show in 1958. Dressed as a cowgirl, she placed second in the two-to-three-year-old division. This was the first of many style shows in which Diane modeled, and her costumes were designed and made by her mother.

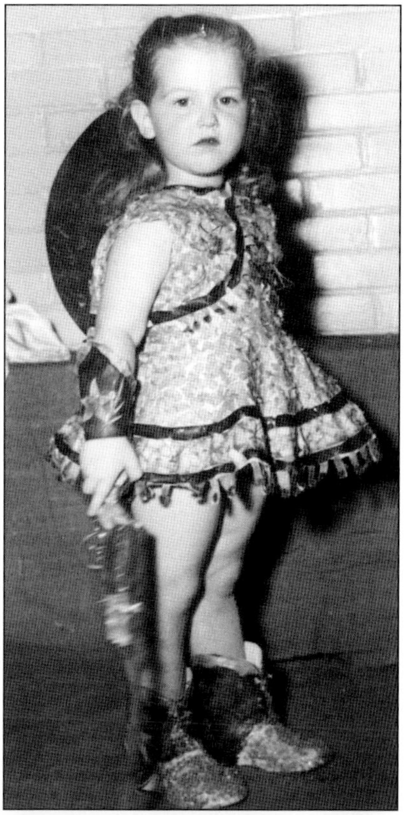

Among the Junior Style Show winners in 1959 are, from left to right, Liz Davey ("1909 Belle of Mission"), Gail Brady ("Golden Goddess of Citrus"), and Suzy Walk ("Mission's 1909 Bathing Beauty"). The costumes reflect the history of Mission during the city's 50th-anniversary celebration in 1959.

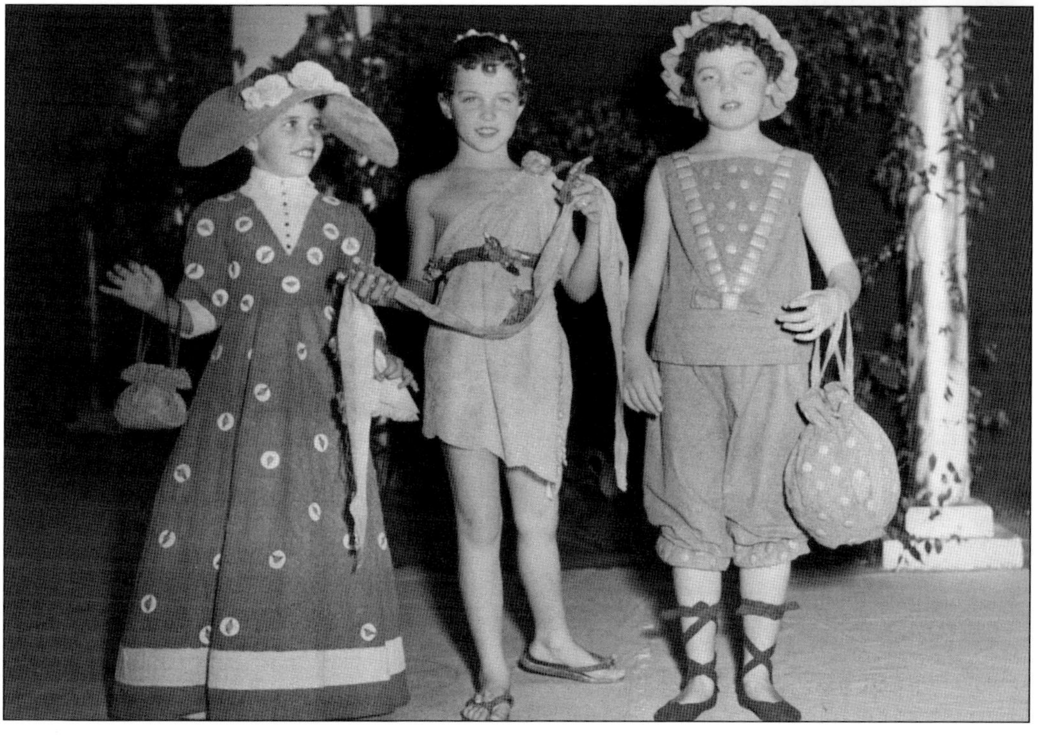

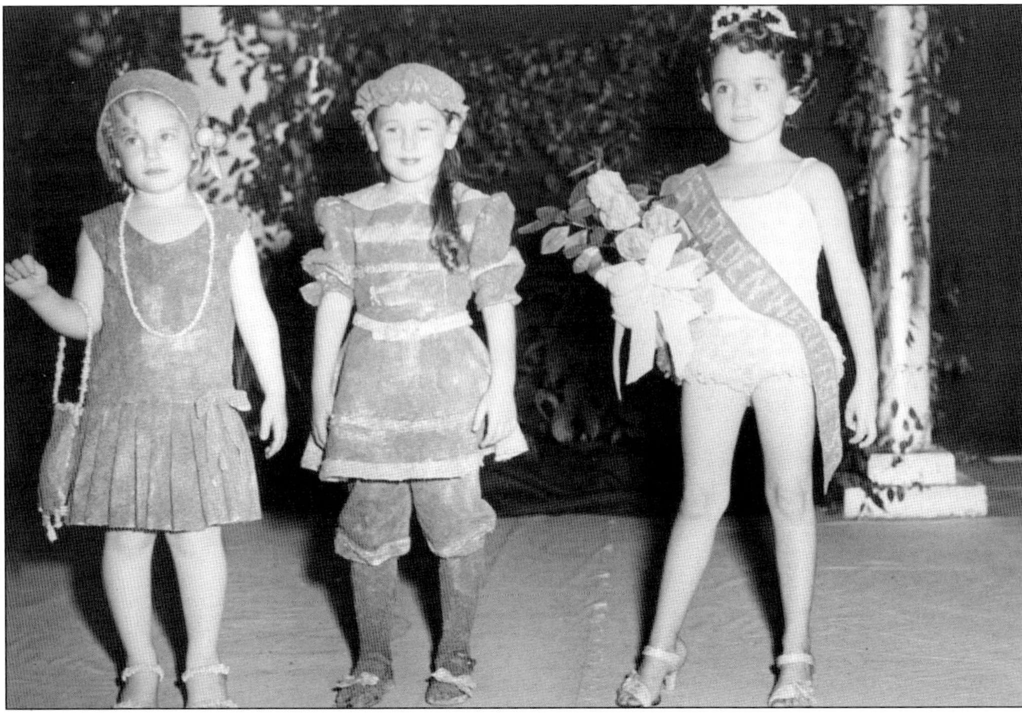

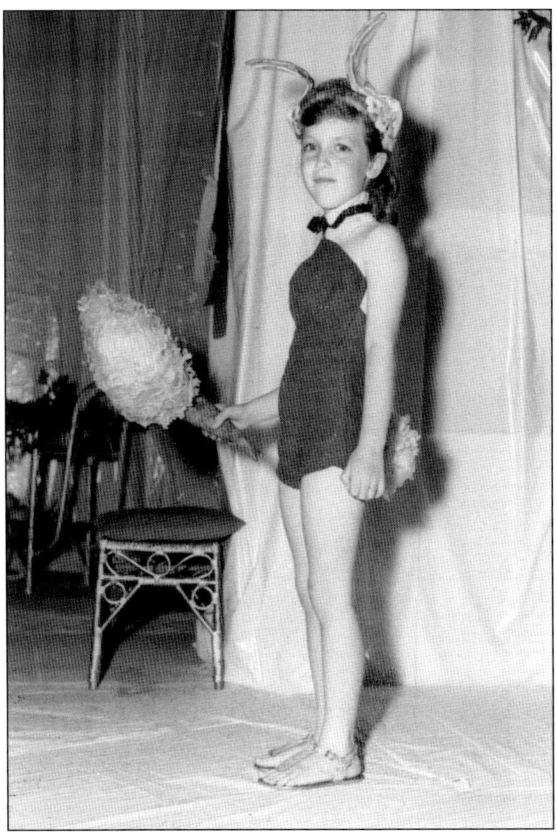

Additional Junior Style Show winners in 1959 are, from left to right, Denese Cannon ("Miss Roaring 20s"), Debbie Lee Cannon ("Miss Gay 90s"), and Pam McNallen ("Miss Golden Heritage of 1959").

In 1963, Diane Duncan, who had won first place in the four-to-six-year-old division in 1962, returned to compete in the seven-to-eight-year-old division as "A Playmate Bunny." Both years, she was sponsored by the Order of Rainbow Girls. In 1963, she won third place.

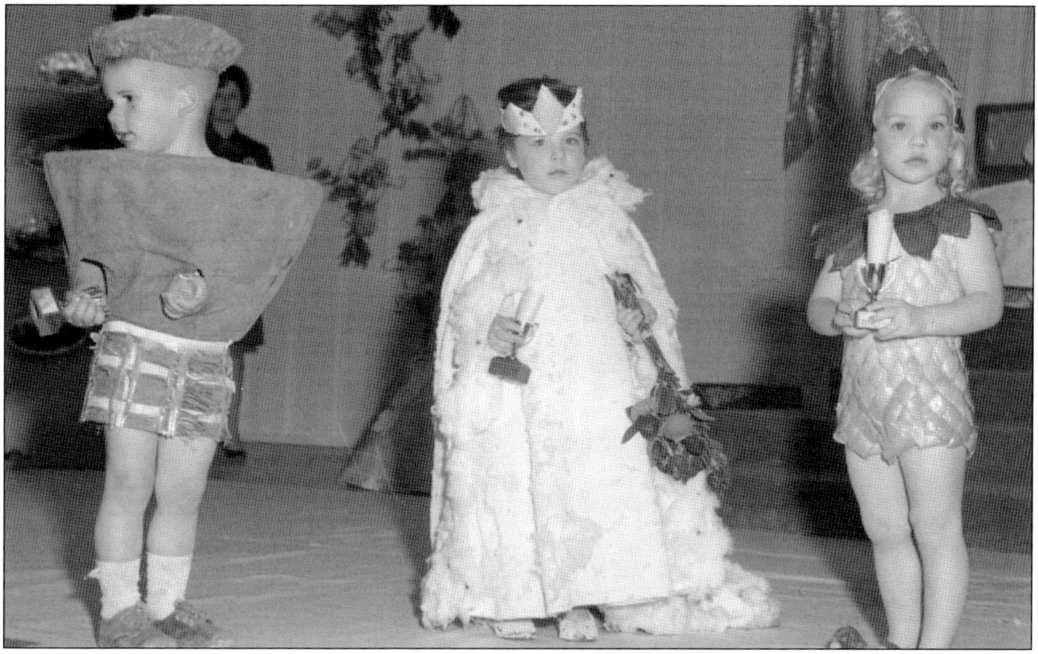

Winners in the 1964 Junior Style Show in the two-to-three-year-old division are, from left to right, Barton Wade Daniel ("Scotsman"), Gay Showers ("Little Miss America"), and Bunny Fryer ("A Pixie"). Costume materials are citrus products (Daniel), ground white corn with cotton "ermine" trim (Showers), and fresh citrus peel and leaves (Fryer).

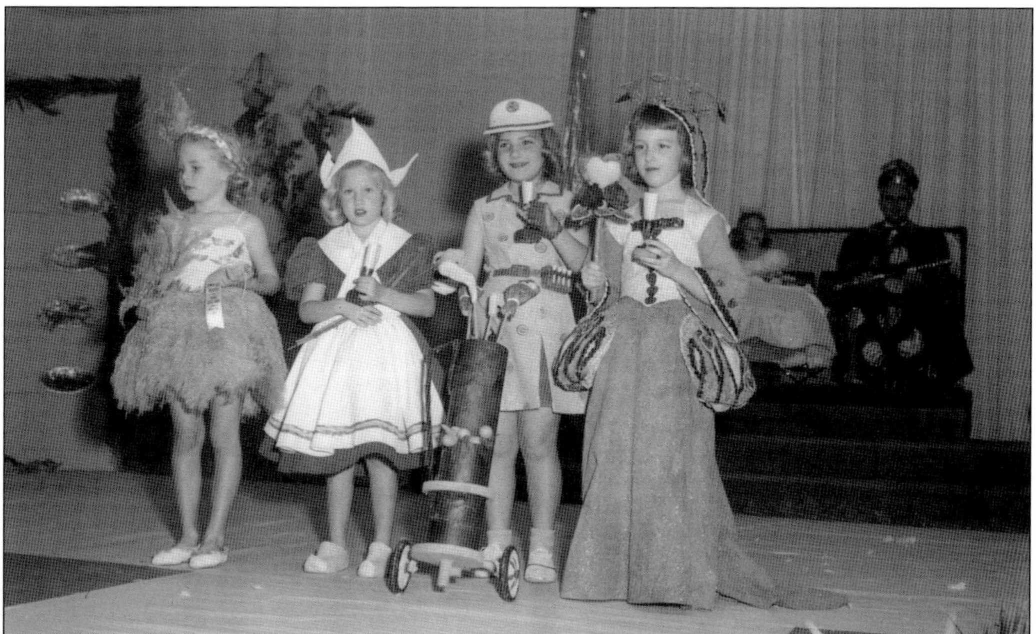

Winners in the six-to-eight-year-old division in 1964 are, from left to right, unidentified, Patricia Ann Mettle, Becky Fryer, and Diane Duncan. The Dutch costume (Mettle) is made of dried curly parsley and citrus pulp.

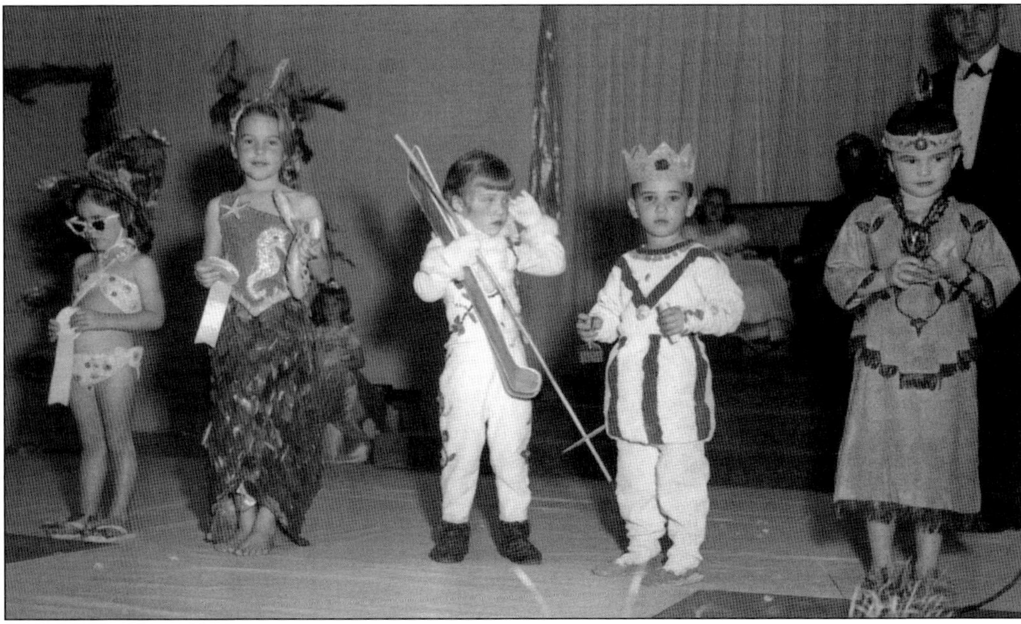

Additional product costume winners in 1964 are, from left to right, Beverly Birdwell, Sheri Willeford, Beverly Fryer, James Brewer, and Lisa Sue Barnick. Corn covers the ski suit (Fryer), which is trimmed with cotton "fur." The costume worn by "Prince Charming" (Brewer) is made of popcorn.

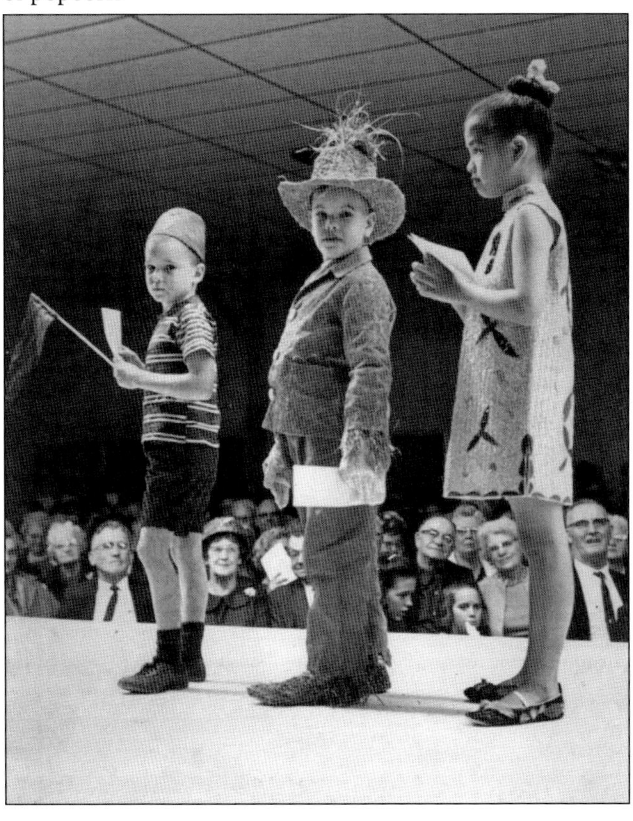

Costume winners in the six-to-eight-year-old division in 1966 are, from left to right, Johnny Jones ("Circus Spectator"), Clay King ("Scarecrow"), and Jo-Jo Shiba ("China Doll"). Shiba's dress features a mandarin collar, slits on each side of the skirt, and a dragon on the back. Cantaloupe seeds cover the dress in horizontal and vertical rows. The style show took place at the Mission Community Center.

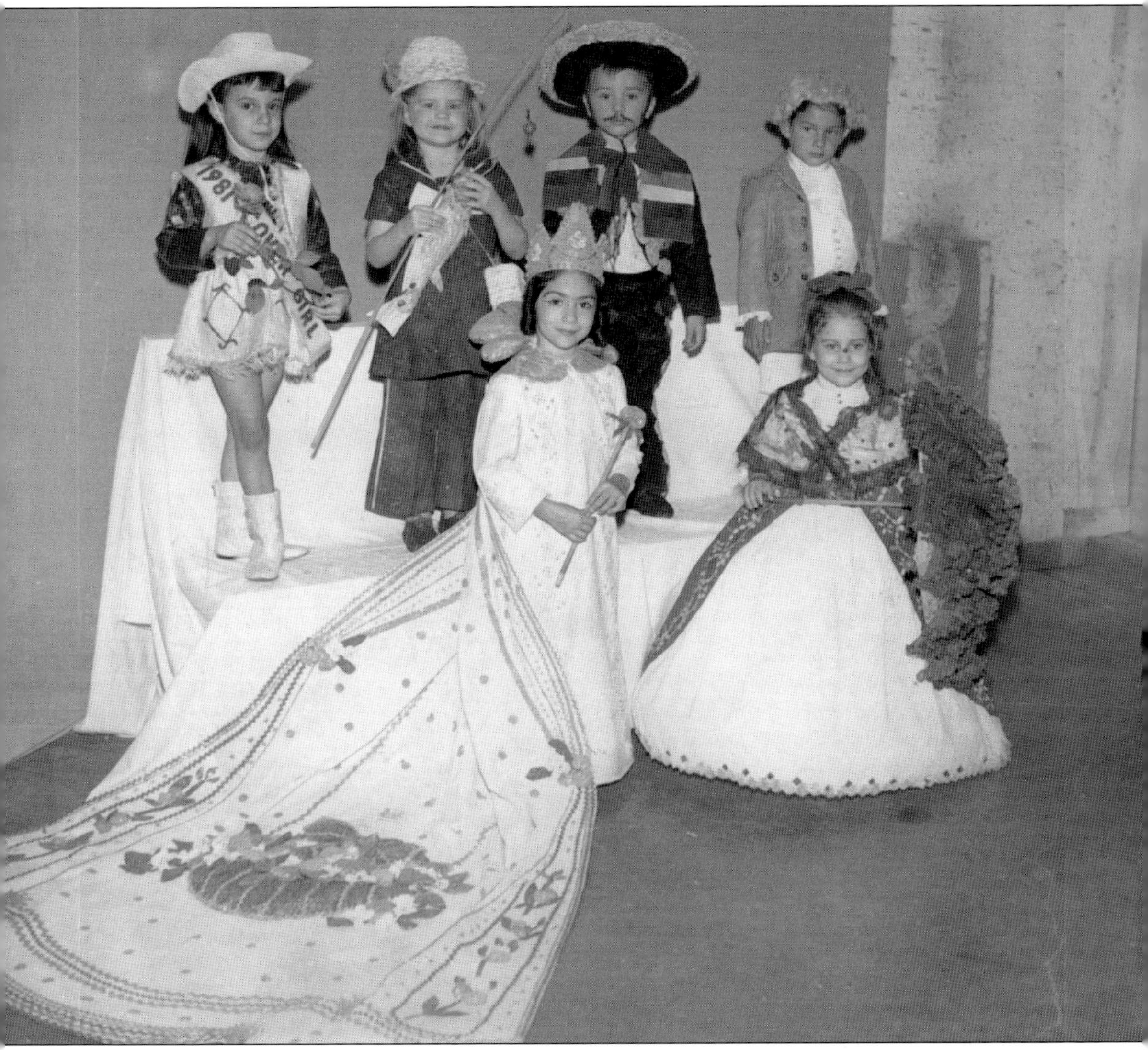

By 1970, costume models were subdivided by age and theme. Here, four- and five-year-old models illustrate "Celebrations Along the Rio Grande Border," a subtheme of "Fiesta Magic—Valley Style." Shown here are, from left to right, (first row) Valerie Valverde and Melissa Lea Willems; (second row) Clara Hinojosa, Ginger Lee Bennett, Javier Ortiz, and Marc Barrera. Valerie, "Miniature Queen Citrianna from the Texas Citrus Fiesta," won the Princess Anna trophy based upon her high score. Melissa, as "Martha Washington," represents the George Washington Days celebration at Eagle Pass. Clara wears a Western outfit to signify the Cover Girl Contest presented by the Rio Grande Valley Livestock Show at Mercedes. Ginger symbolizes the Port Mansfield Fishing Tournament. Javier is a miniature charro from Brownsville's Charro Days. Marc, as "George Washington," signifies Laredo's George Washington Days festival. The costumes and accessories were required to have 100 percent coverage by Rio Grande Valley products.

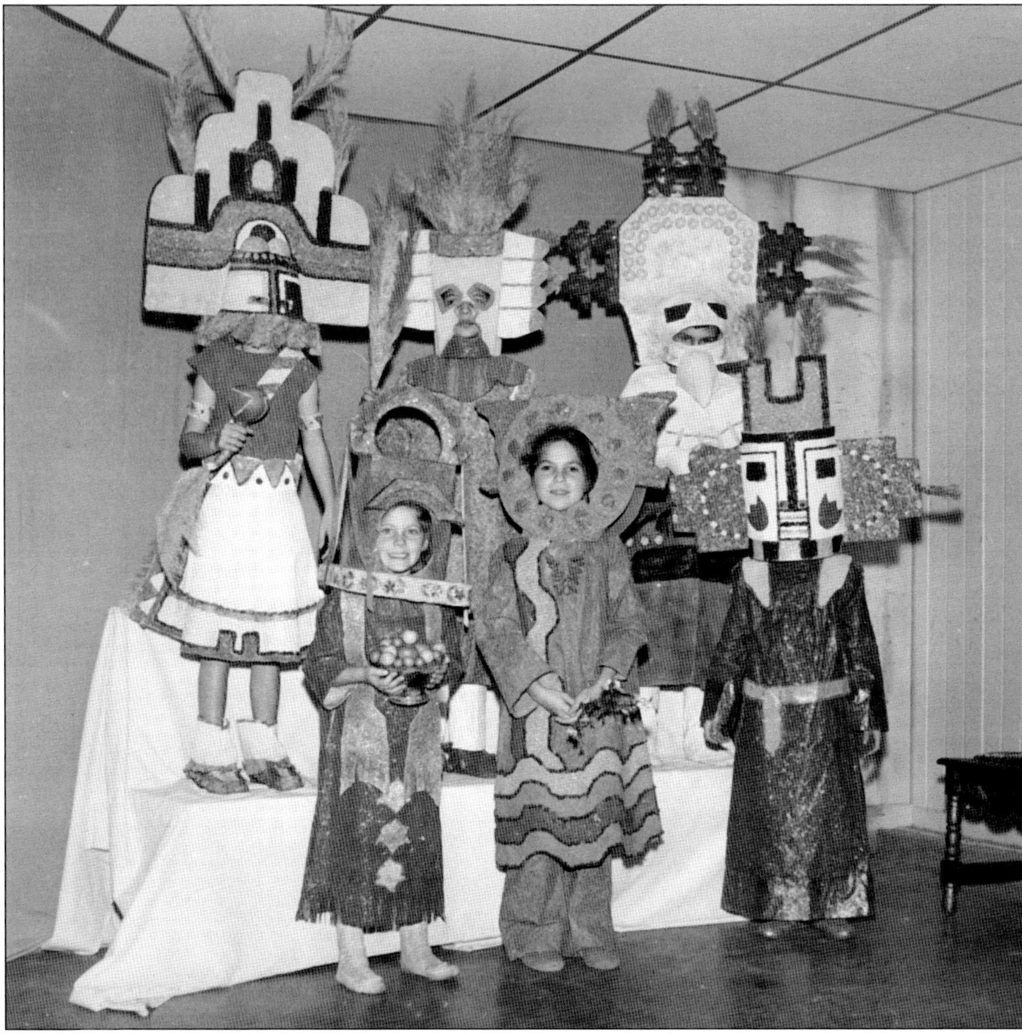

In 1970, children of grade-school age wear costumes designed to represent kachina dolls from the Southwest. Wearing elaborately constructed costumes are, from left to right, (first row) Lorraine Helle ("Rainbow"), Norma Dovalina ("Little Flower of the Peach Tree"), and Cynthia Gearhart ("Good News of the Citrus Fiesta"); (second row) Kathy Nattrass ("Spirit of Sky and Rain"), Dolores Guerrero ("Planting Time"), and Robert Austin ("Corn Grinding"). Norma Dovalina received the Princess of Citrus Blossom trophy for her high score. Among the unusual natural products used were seeds from the dishrag gourd, citrus meal (cattle food), roses, blooms of the Hawaiian golden showers tree, peach blossoms and seeds, avocado seeds, bluebonnets and plumbago flowers, nandina berries, sunflowers, and toasted ground citrus peel. More standard products were corncobs and other corn products, bougainvillea, poinsettia petals, pampas grass, grapefruit and oranges (leaves, peel, and seeds), bell pepper seeds, onion seeds, Mexican morning glory seeds, and banana leaves.

Six

The Parade of Oranges

In the first Parade of Oranges, 27 floats proceeded through downtown Mission, where citrus trees lined the route. (A float for Queen Citrianna I and her court appears on page 15.) Prizes adding up to $200 were awarded for the best floats.

In 1936, E.E. Marburger served as chairman of the parade committee, and prizes were raised to $275. Floats were separated into two divisions, commercial and noncommercial, and the grand-prize winner received $100. First-place winners were awarded $50 each, and second-place winners received $25 each. The parade formed at Sixteenth Street and passed down Conway Avenue to Sixth Street, and a reviewing stand for officials and judges was located at Tenth Street and Conway Avenue. During these years of the Great Depression, monetary awards were indeed welcome.

Judges, who were not from Mission, used various criteria to choose the winners in the float competition. Besides excellence in design and execution, each float had to reflect the theme of that year's fiesta and use citrus fruit in its design. The amount of fruit required for eligibility in the competition varied with the availability of the citrus crop. After hurricanes, freezes, or severe drought, the float competition committee and judges accepted a lower percentage of citrus than in years when production was normal.

Selection of the next year's Queen Citrianna and her court was partly based on each young lady's appearance and manner on the floats during the parade.

Between 1951 and 1956, Texas Citrus Fiesta officials, the royal court, and members of the Mission Chamber of Commerce formed a caravan on the Saturday before the fiesta opening. They traveled to cities throughout the Rio Grande Valley, inviting residents to attend the celebration.

Decorated automobiles, marching bands, clowns, members of fraternal organizations, horsemen, military officers, dignitaries, and fiesta officials made up additional parts of the parade. Celebrities such as Mission's own Cleo Dawson and actress Sissy Spacek (in 1977) thrilled the thousands of spectators who anticipated the colorful parade each year.

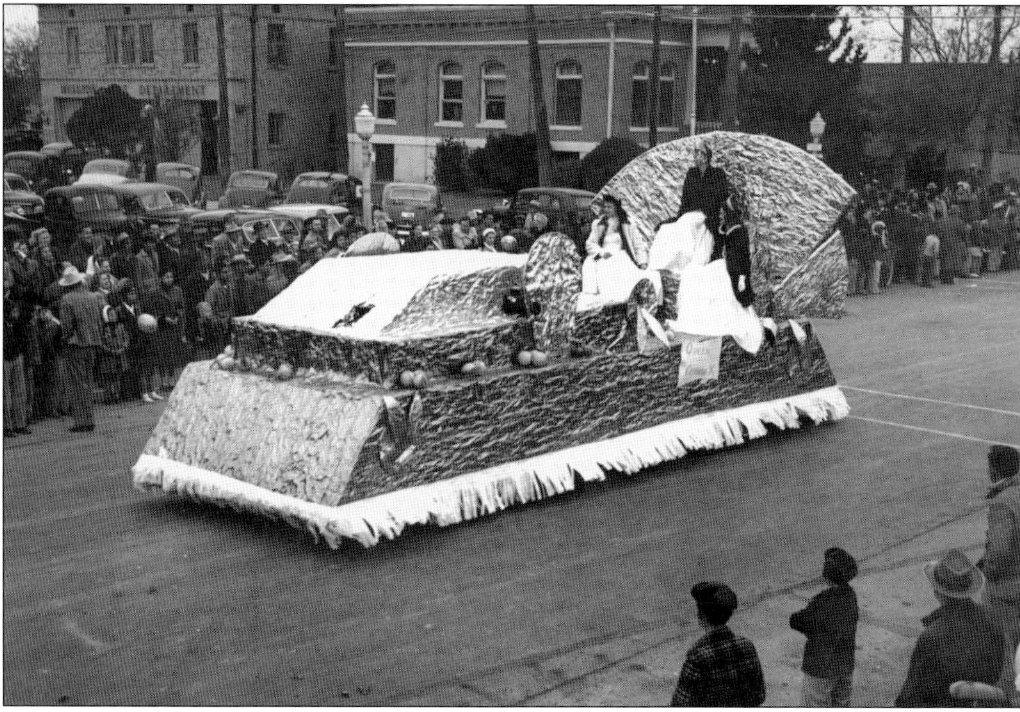

The 1947 Parade of Oranges brought a return to happier times. The royal float, seen here, carries Betty Jo Knox, Queen Citrianna X, and John D. Hulsey, King Citrus X. Ladies-in-Waiting Gerda Lee Klunkert and Doris Ann Pierce joined them. Some 25,000 spectators watched the parade of 26 units, including floats, highway patrolmen, US Marines, and Boy Scouts and Girl Scouts. This scene was captured by Mission photographer Eugene E. Dondlinger.

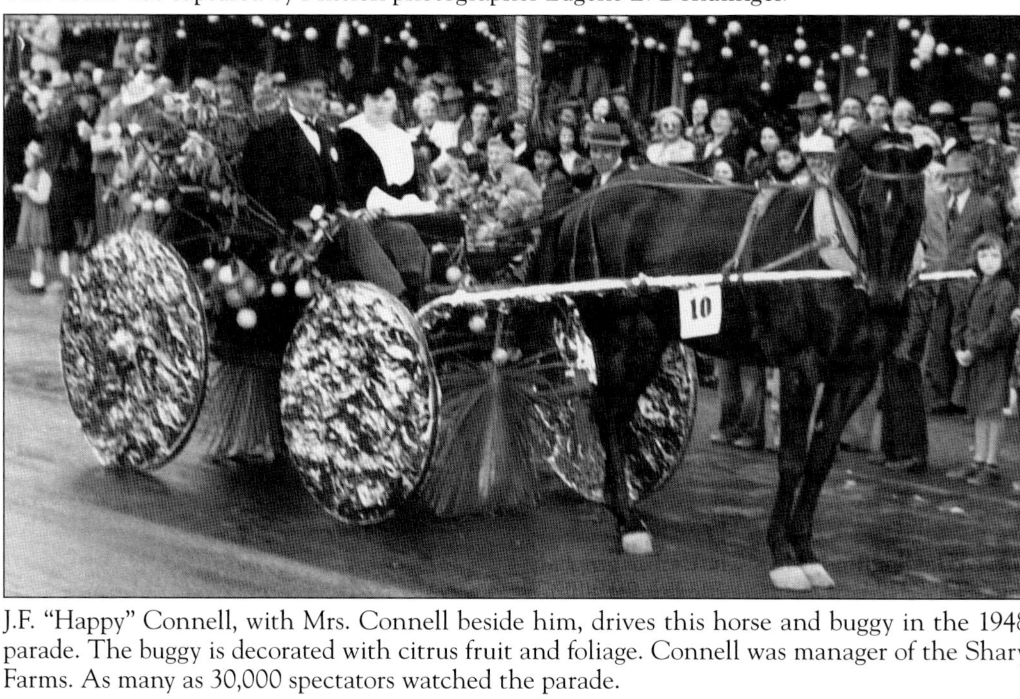

J.F. "Happy" Connell, with Mrs. Connell beside him, drives this horse and buggy in the 1948 parade. The buggy is decorated with citrus fruit and foliage. Connell was manager of the Shary Farms. As many as 30,000 spectators watched the parade.

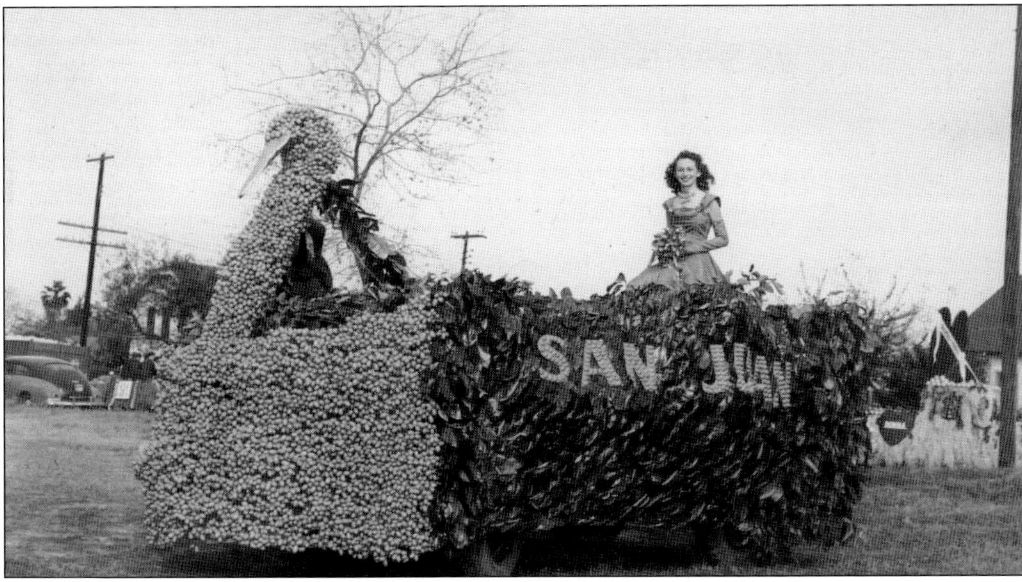

In 1948, this float, sponsored by the San Juan Lions Club, won the first prize of $125 in the float competition. The golden foreground figure, made of kumquats, represents a swan. Jane Ellen Mellenbruch, Duchess of Kumquat, rides atop the stately float, which required thousands of kumquats and citrus leaves. (A close-up view of the swan can be seen on page 41.)

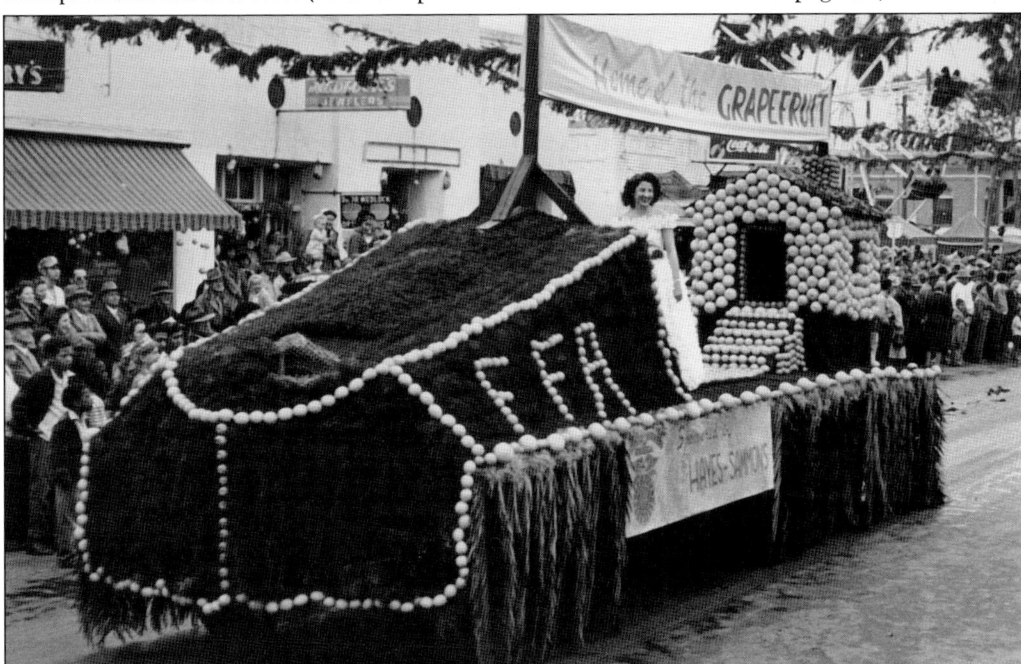

The float seen here, entitled "Home of the Grapefruit" and sponsored by Hayes-Sammons Hardware Company, was decorated by students in the Mission High School Future Farmers of America program. Riding on the float is June Custer, FFA Sweetheart. The float won first place in the commercial division in 1948. The house is made of grapefruit and the roof of citrus leaves, while a pathway of lemons leads to the steps.

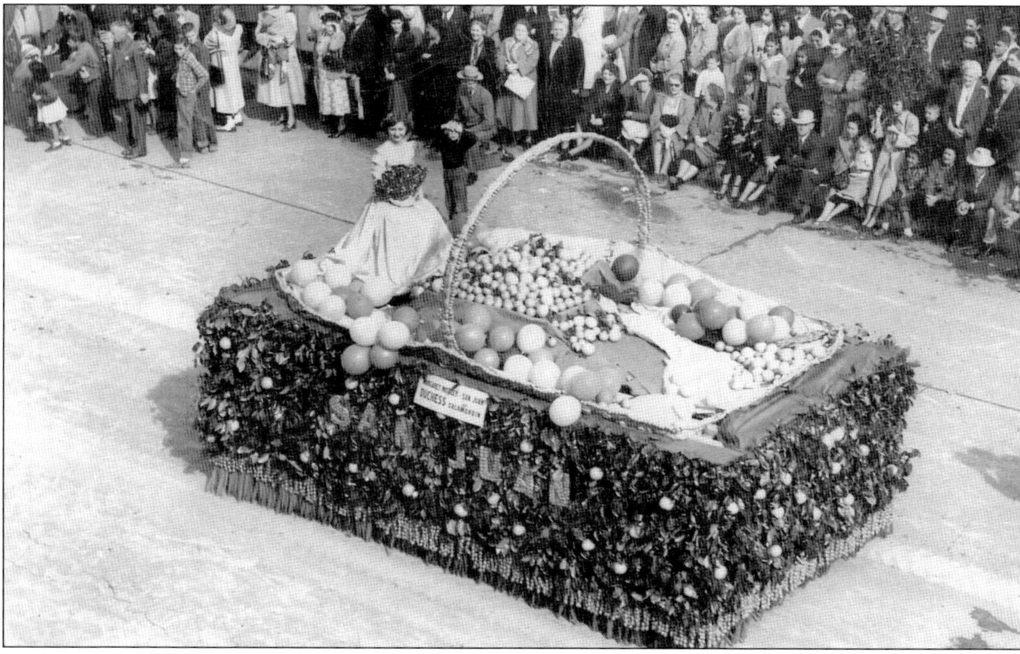

Margaret Motley (San Juan), Duchess of Calamondin, represents the San Juan Lions Club, which sponsored this float in 1949. Filled with real citrus fruit and large balloons in citrus colors, this "basket of fruit" expressed the idea of fruit on its way to market. The float won third place and $75 for the club.

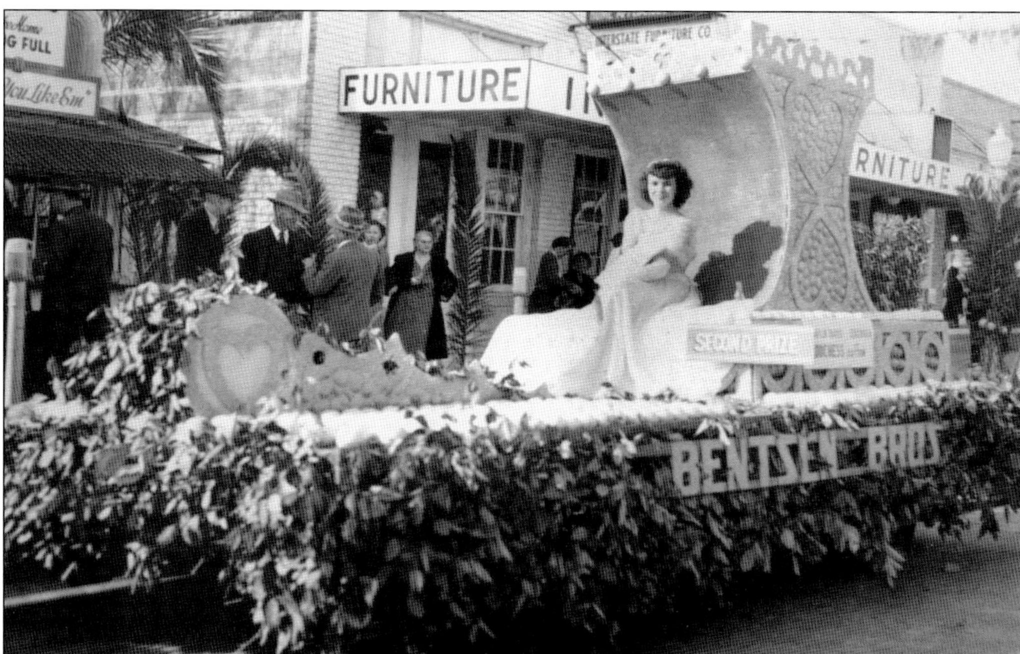

Bentsen Brothers sponsored this second-place winner in the commercial division of the float contest for 1949. Marilyn Davis (Edcouch), Duchess of Cotton, rides on the "chariot" decorated with citrus fruit, citrus peel, and leaves. The sponsors received an award of $100.

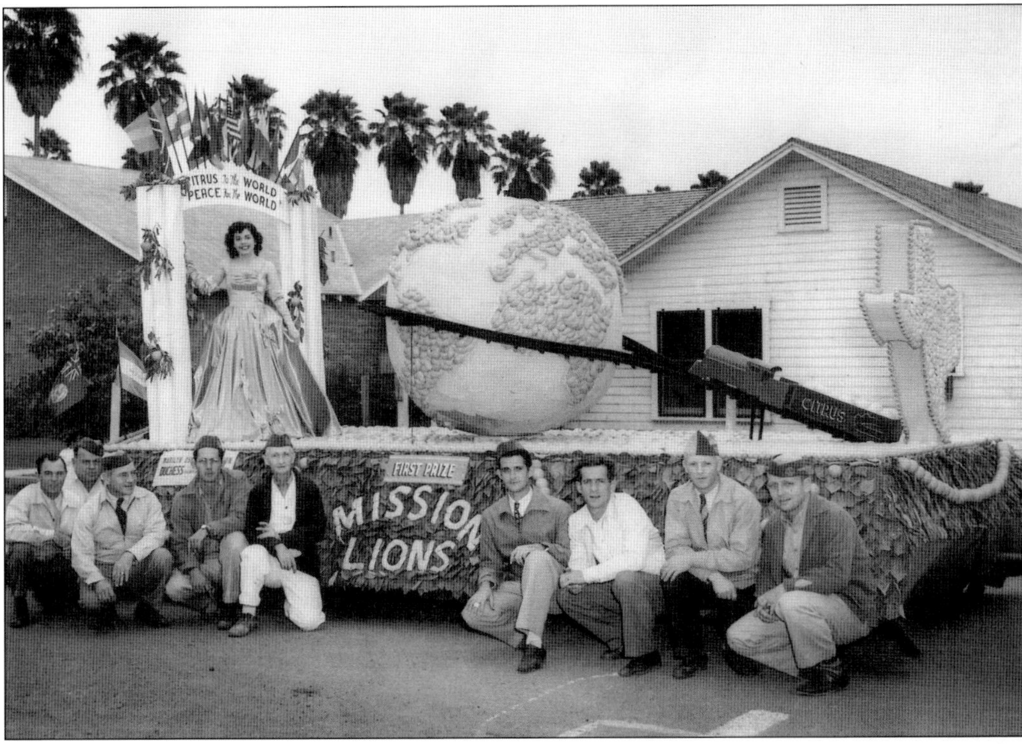

The 1949 first-place winner, out of 33 entries, was sponsored by the Mission Lions Club. Marilyn Osburn (Mission), Duchess of Pink Grapefruit, stands beneath an archway topped by the flags of 13 nations. At the front of the float, a map of Texas is decorated with citrus fruit. A train carries citrus fruit to all the world's continents, made of citrus fruit on the globe.

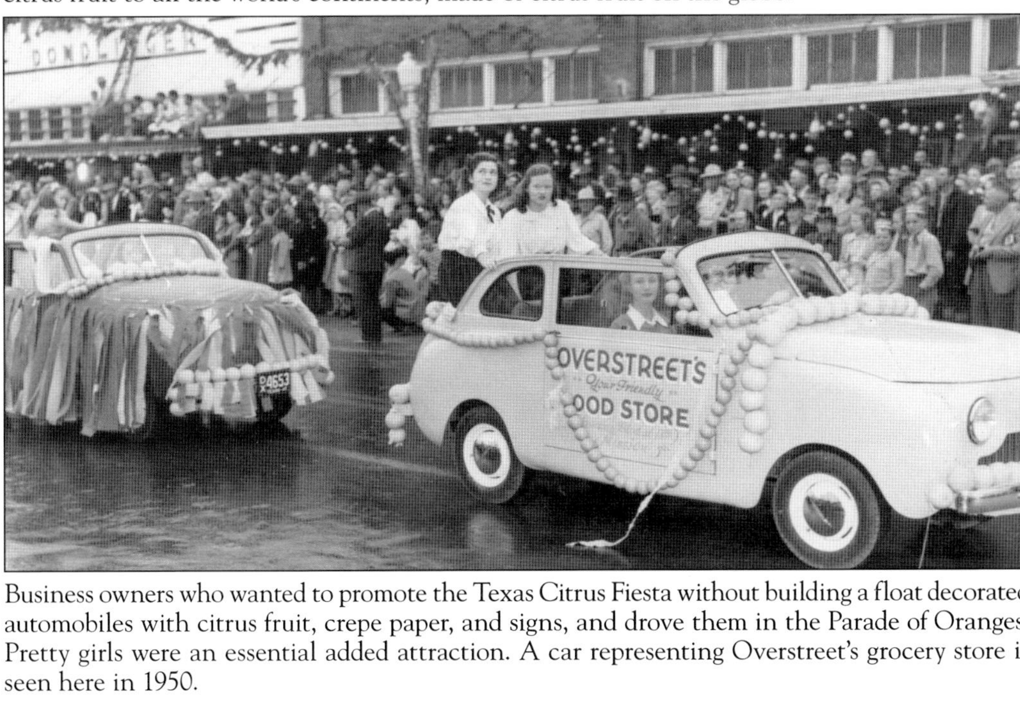

Business owners who wanted to promote the Texas Citrus Fiesta without building a float decorated automobiles with citrus fruit, crepe paper, and signs, and drove them in the Parade of Oranges. Pretty girls were an essential added attraction. A car representing Overstreet's grocery store is seen here in 1950.

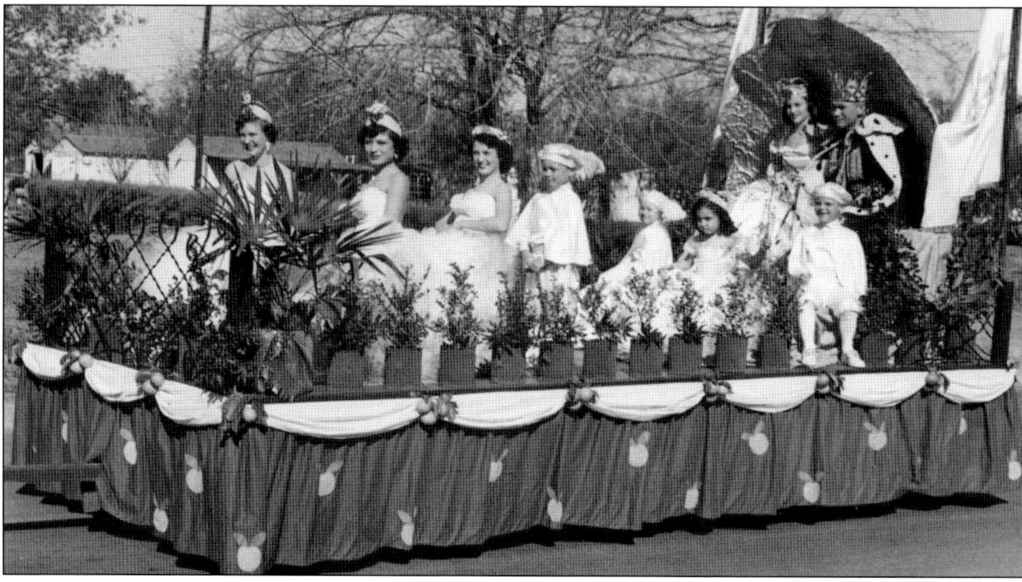

The Mission Chamber of Commerce sponsored the 1952 royal float. Dorothy Hortness, Queen Citrianna XV, and Marshall M. Walden, King Citrus XV, are seated at the far right. Starting at the front of the float are, from left to right, Gerry Chandler, First Princess; Amelia Reyna, Second Princess; Betty McDougle, Lady-in-Waiting; Gary Ray Robinson, Crown Bearer; Andrew Lee Rone, Train Bearer; Mary Jo Schroeder, Princess Anna II; and Hollis Rankin III, Train Bearer.

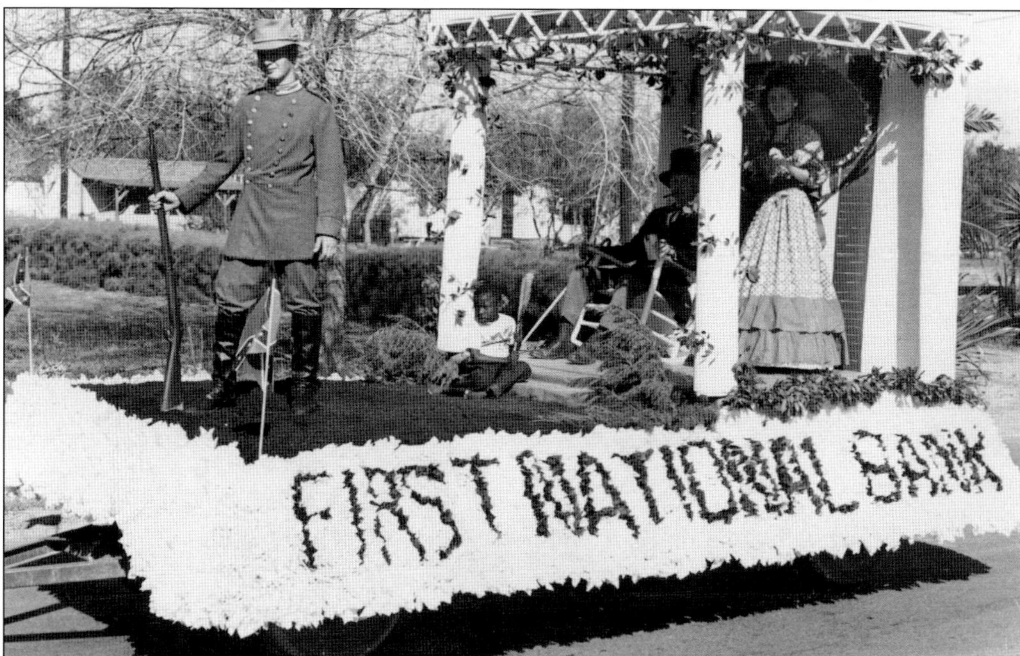

Adhering to the "Fiesta Under Six Flags" theme in 1952, this float represents Texas in the Confederacy and won first place. Calvin Cox, wearing a Confederate soldier's uniform, stands in front of the Southern-style veranda. Al Graham, a Southern "colonel," sits in a rocking chair, while Southern "belle" Mary Louise Robertson stands beside him. Philip Akin, on the veranda steps, waves a fan.

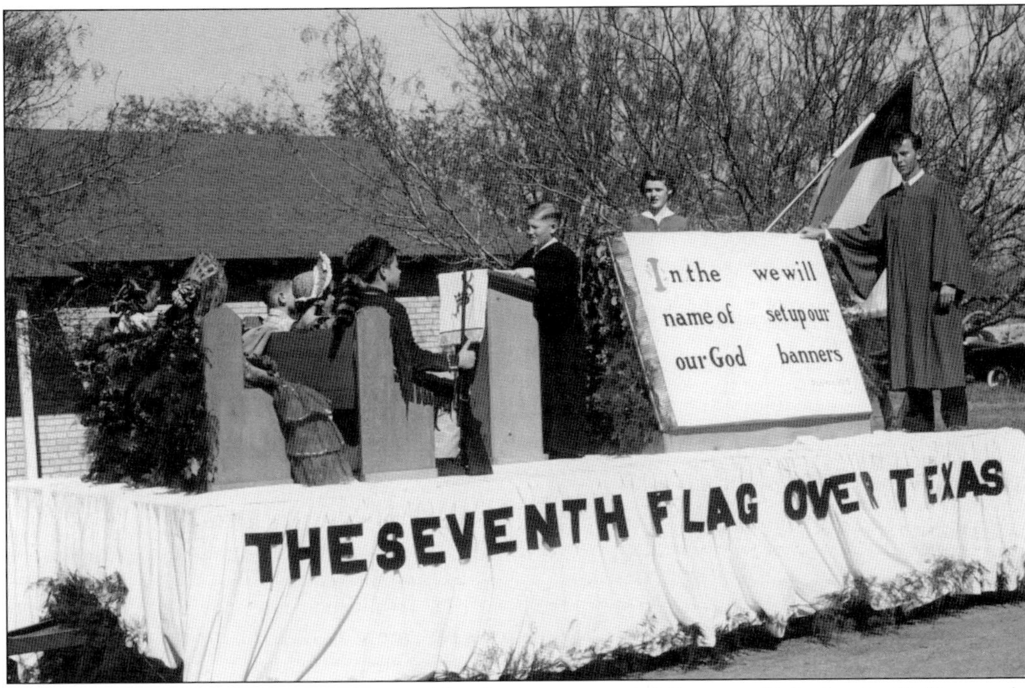

The Seventh Flag over Texas, presented by the Ministerial Alliance of Mission in 1952, was the Christian flag. Standing within a replica of a church interior, Michael Hugh portrays a minister, while Allen Bourgeois and Nina Harper serve as flag bearers. The congregation represents the six periods of Texas history: Pearl Austin (Spain), Phillip Bridgewater (France), Carmen Laura de la Garza (Mexico), Jimmy Showers (Texas), Mary Virginia Richards (Confederacy), and Darrell Buck (USA).

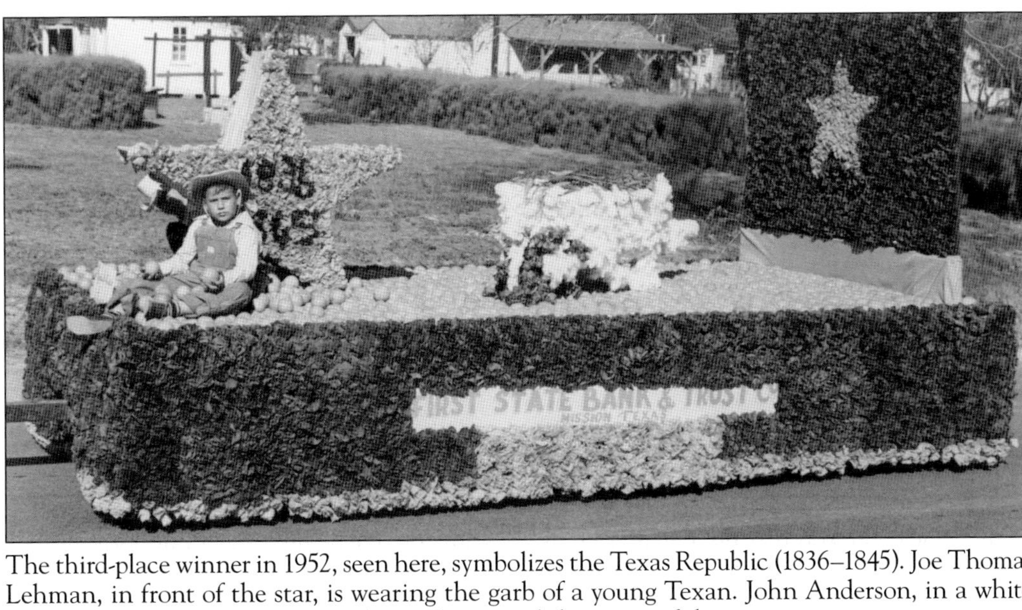

The third-place winner in 1952, seen here, symbolizes the Texas Republic (1836–1845). Joe Thomas Lehman, in front of the star, is wearing the garb of a young Texan. John Anderson, in a white hat and seated on the opposite side, peeks around the point of the star.

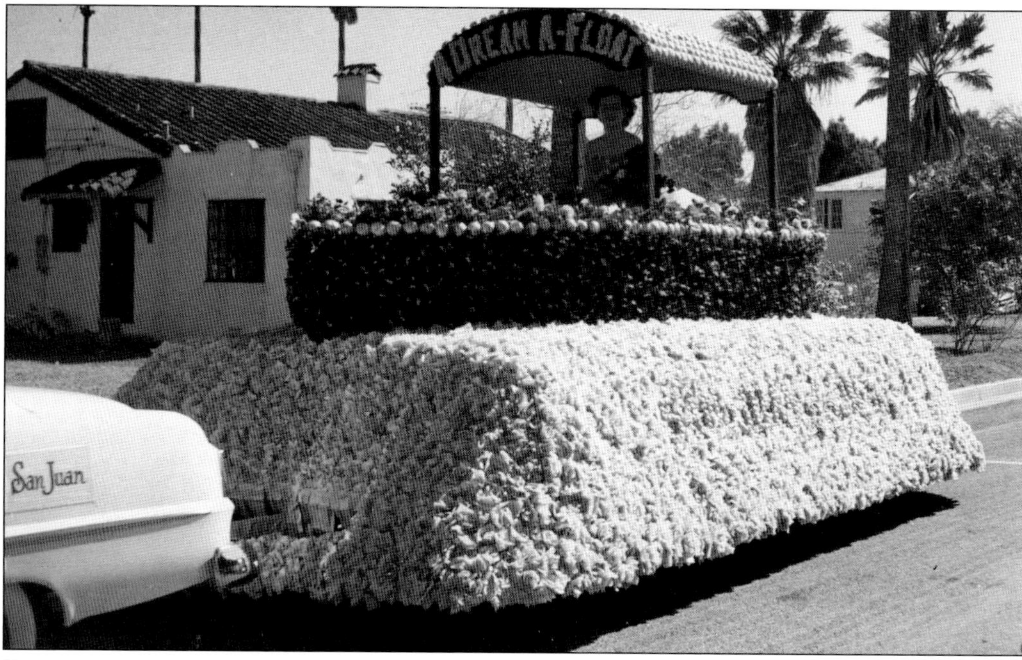

First-prize winner in 1953 was this float, designed as a gondola similar to those of Mexico's Floating Gardens. Sponsored by the San Juan Lions Club, the gondola, covered with flowers and fruit, appears to be floating on waves made of crepe paper. Earline Hinkle, representing San Juan as Duchess of Calamondin, rides beneath the canopy of the gondola.

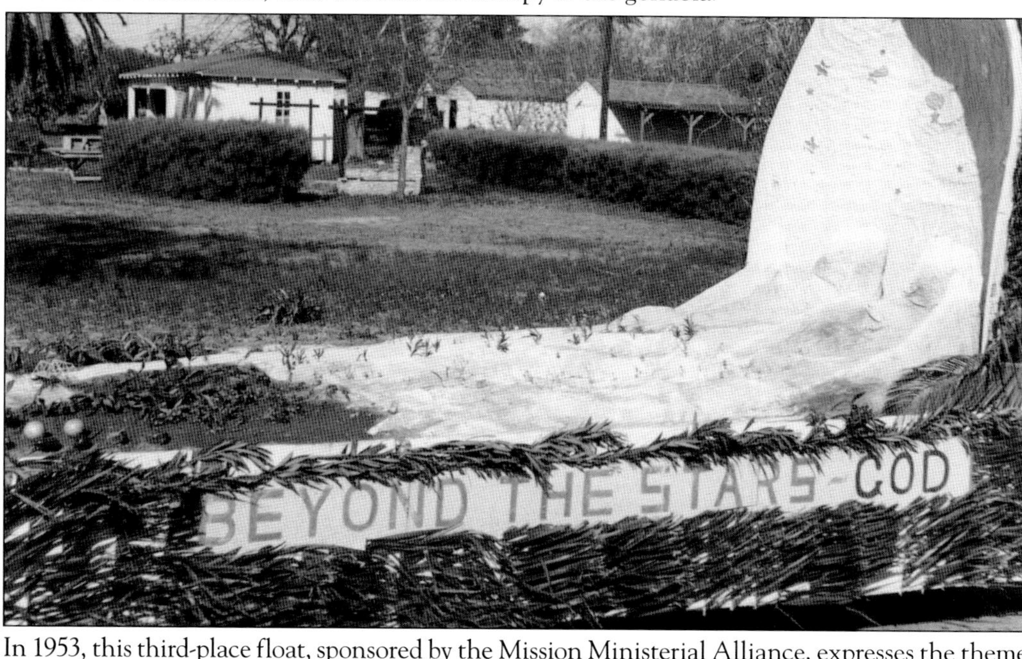

In 1953, this third-place float, sponsored by the Mission Ministerial Alliance, expresses the theme of "Fiesta Under the Stars" by adding the phrase, "Beyond the Stars—God." Mission ministers chose the same theme for their Sunday sermons during the week of fiesta. The float shows the course of the Rio Grande from the Rio Grande Valley to its source in the Rocky Mountains, and beyond, to the clouds, the stars, and God.

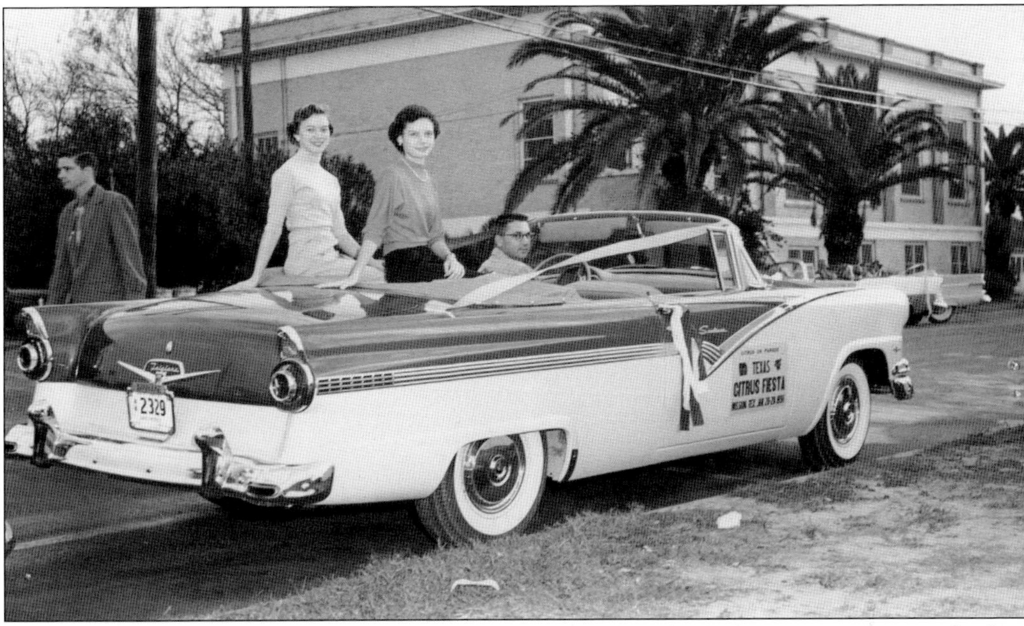

For several years during the 1950s, Texas Citrus Fiesta officials, duchesses, sponsors, and others formed a large caravan to travel to Rio Grande Valley cities on the Saturday before the opening of the fiesta to invite people to the celebration. Seen here on January 21, 1956, are Janis Stutz (left), Shirley Smith (right), both of Mission, and an unidentified driver. At least 20 convertibles formed part of this caravan.

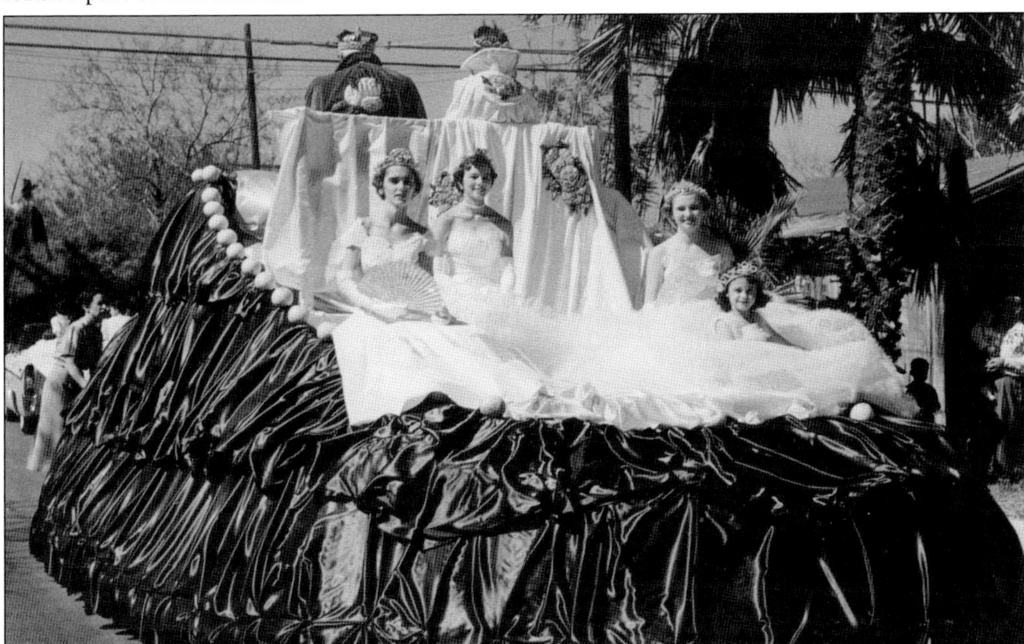

The royal float in 1956 features King Citrus XIX, Joe L. Crump (top, left), and Jeanette Waters, Queen Citrianna XIX (top, right). Seated in front are, from left to right, Sheridan Sammons, First Princess; Janis Stutz, Lady-in-Waiting; Jean Knapp, Second Princess; and Janis Billue, Princess Anna VI. Knapp became Queen Citrianna XX in 1957.

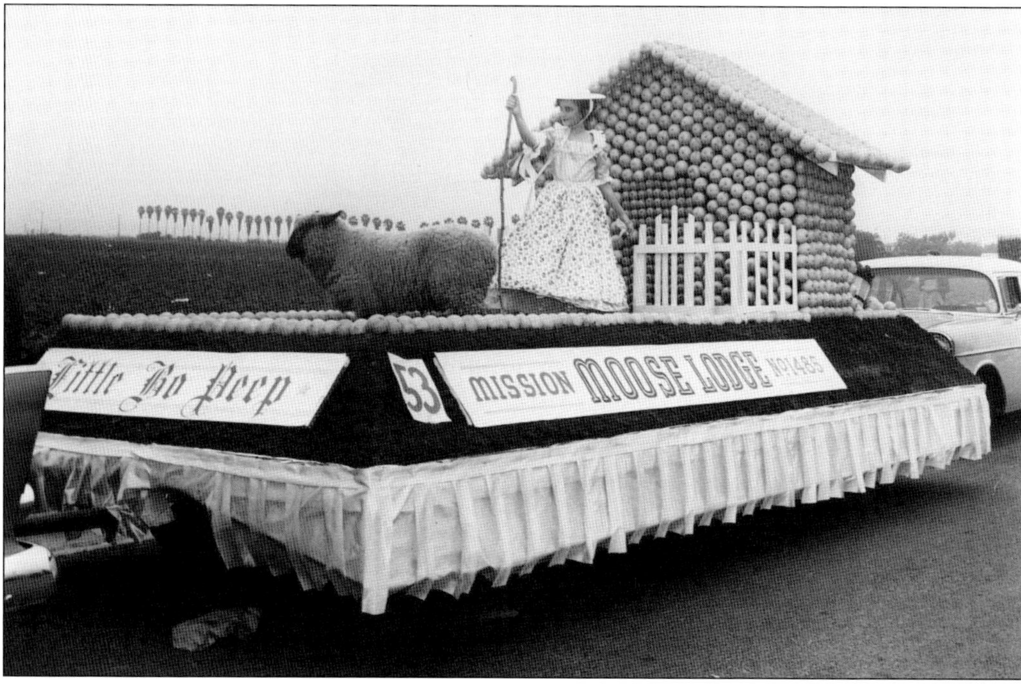

In 1957, Barbara Warbritton, as "Little Bo Peep," shares this float with a live sheep. The float was sponsored by Valley Farm Products and was constructed by the Mission Moose Lodge. The shed, made of citrus, stands on a base of cotton that was sprayed green. The float won second prize.

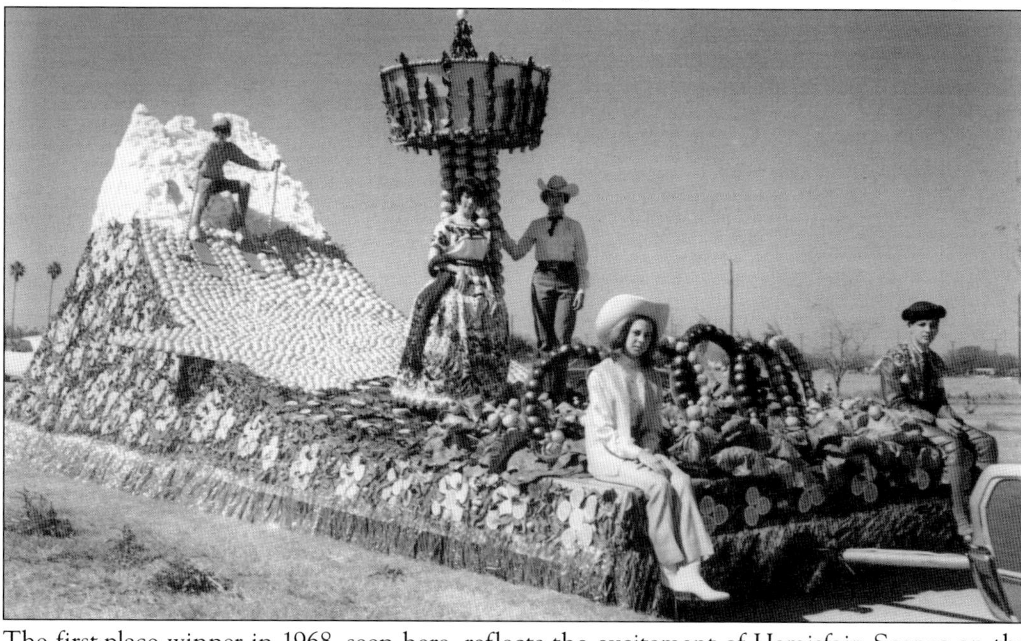

The first-place winner in 1968, seen here, reflects the excitement of Hemisfair. Scenes on the float represent the snow of Canada (left), the Hemisfair opening in San Antonio (center), and the Olympics in Mexico City (right). Willie Gossett (left) is perched on the ski lift. Cathy Canady and Jill Bodine stand beneath the abbreviated Hemisfair Tower. Cindy Doty and Javier Cantu are seated at the front of the float.

Seven

The Earliest Style Shows

Although a brief style show may have been held in 1932, the first style show to use Rio Grande Valley products for certain occurred in 1934.

Each costume began with a foundation garment, constructed before the fiesta, and sized for a specific model. Vegetables, flowers, fruit, seeds, and leaves were selected as part of the design process. The day of the style show, ladies of sponsoring organizations met at the home of a committee member to place the natural products on the costume. They used scissors, kitchen tools, glitter, thread, glue, lacquer, and cellophane. Details made from seeds, flowers, onion skins, and other small parts were carefully attached. The finished costumes were then hung in cold-storage lockers of meat markets or produce sheds until time to be worn (that day) and stored overnight for the next day's showing. The most durable costume was that of Mrs. David Smith, created in 1937 from corn husks, which she wore at several fiesta style shows. The husks did not deteriorate as rapidly as fresh produce.

Rules for the 1940 style show pageant allowed cactus, shelled corn, corncobs, corn shucks and stalks, avocados, and papayas as natural products. Popped corn was not permitted, because it was not in its natural appearance or state. Any kind of preservative was acceptable as long as it did not change the natural color or appearance of the product.

Because of national attention due to widespread publicity, the style show became a significant component of the Texas Citrus Fiesta. Joske Brothers Department Store in San Antonio invited the contestants to model their costumes for as many as 2,000 spectators at a special showing immediately after the fiesta. Other stores in New York, Houston, and Corpus Christi extended similar invitations.

Playsuits were added in 1938, and the next year, the costumes were divided into categories—evening dress, street or sport dress, playsuit, and costume.

Special mention should be made of Mrs. Raymond White, who narrated the style shows for many years.

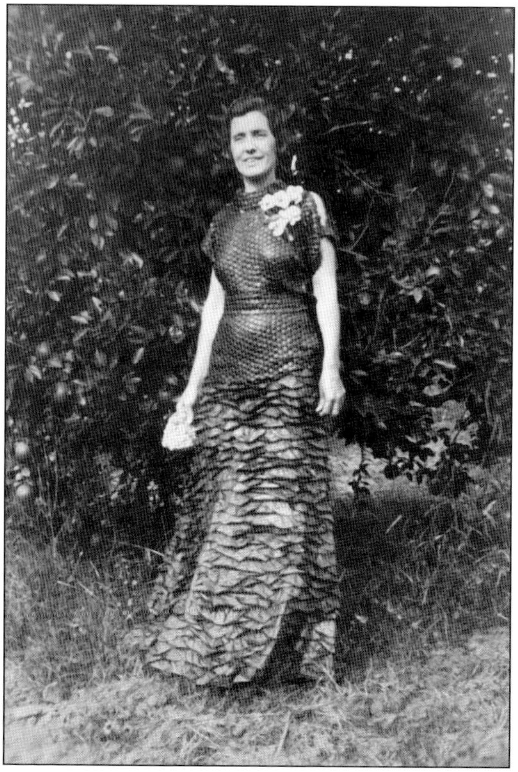

An audience of about 1,000 people attended the 1935 Citrus Style Show, with 19 entrants. Prizes for the best costumes were $25, $15, and $10. The costumes consisted of a foundation garment covered with citrus fruit and vegetables, or their parts, leaves, vines, or other natural materials grown in the Rio Grande Valley. Seen here wearing an evening dress of natural products is Mrs. Seth Barrett, sponsored by the North Mission Home Demonstration Club.

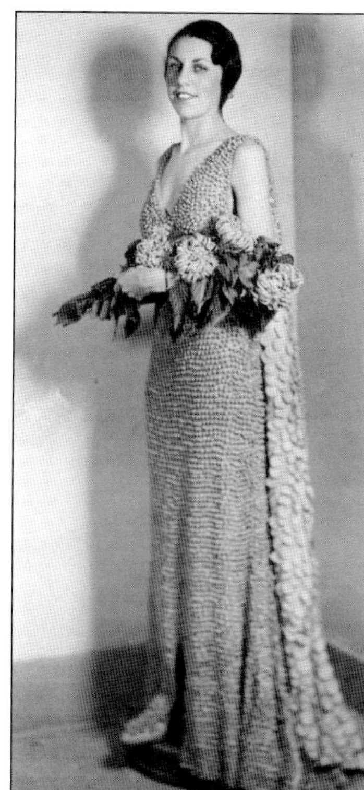

In 1937, Virginia Winn of Mercedes wears a formal evening gown of shelled English peas. The scarf that extends from her left shoulder to the hem of her skirt is lined with fresh sliced carrots. Her shoes are covered with carrots, and her arm bouquet of "chrysanthemums" is in fact carrots. The Mercedes Chamber of Commerce was her sponsor.

In 1937, the Edinburg Garden Club made this "Empress Eugenie" costume, designed by Mrs. Paul Jones, from 20 bushels of corn husks. Mrs. David Smith modeled the long-lasting dress in the 1937 competition and in 1939, 1947, and 1949 for exhibition only. She modeled it at department stores in San Antonio (1938) and Corpus Christi (1939), and at a Houston flower show (1938). The costume appeared in three national and several valley magazines.

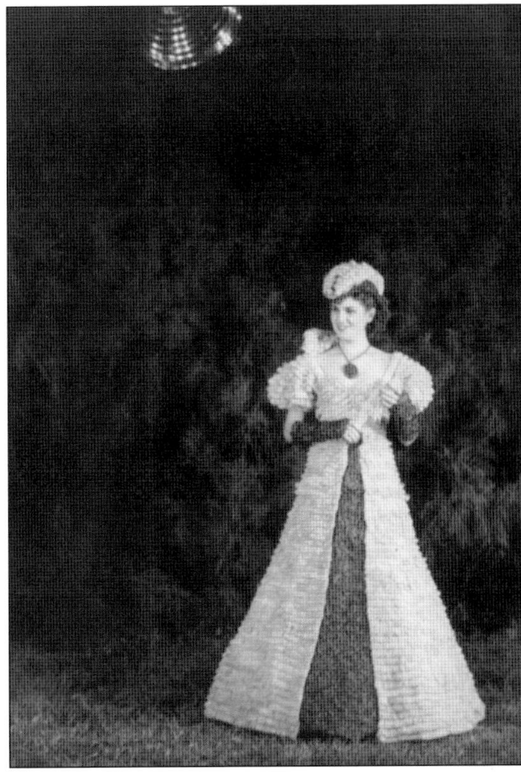

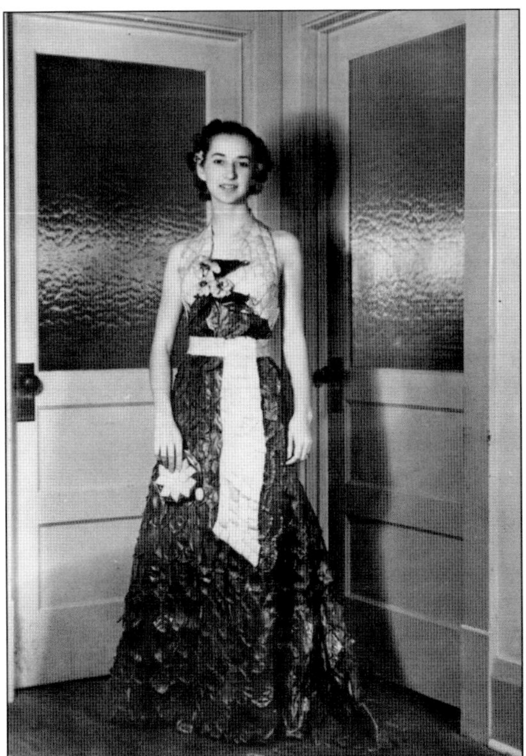

In the 1938 Citrus and Winter Vegetable Style Show, Mission High School senior Evelyn Eppright, sponsored by the Mission Garden Club, modeled an evening dress of leaves with decorations of fruit. She wore the dress again at an invitational showing of the costumes at Joske's department store in San Antonio on the Tuesday after the fiesta, at which 15 models promenaded for an audience of 2,000.

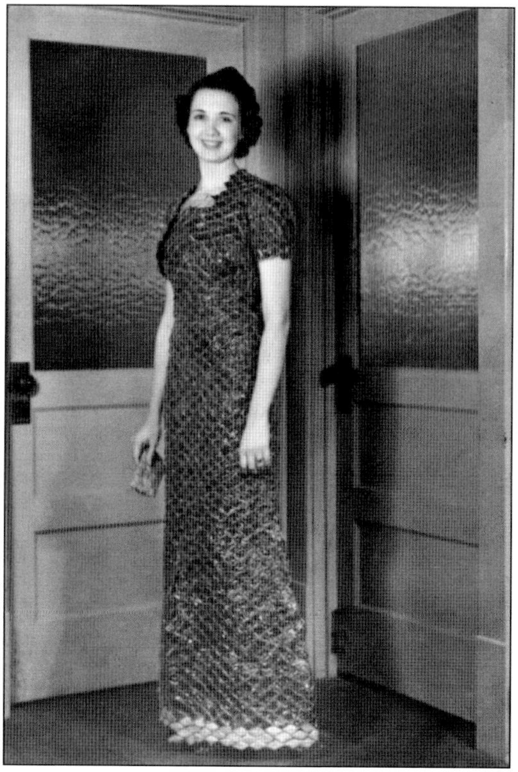

The 1938 style show attracted a crowd of about 8,000. Dorothy Hager of Weslaco, seen here, wears an evening dress of eggplant wrapped in cellophane. After the fiesta, Hager's evening dress was one of two dresses sent to New York for a showing there.

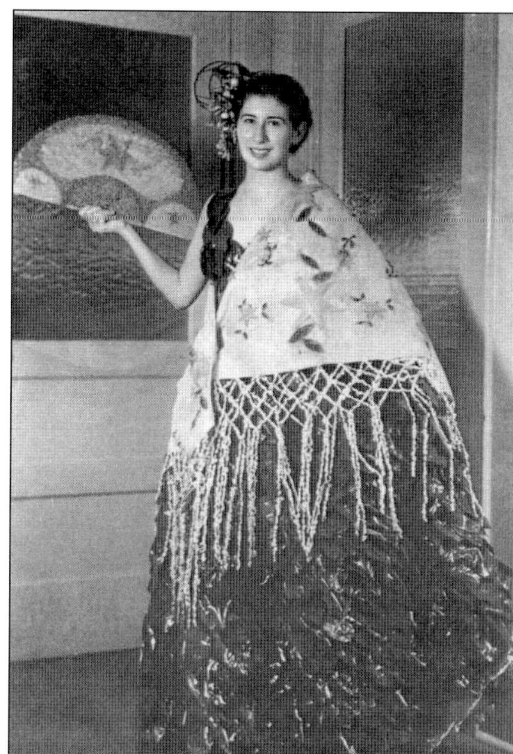

In 1938, Alicia de la Garza of Mission wears the costume of a Spanish lady. Fruit and a large comb of wood from an orange tree make up her headdress, and her dress is covered with leaves. The shawl has a base of grated citrus peel and a floral accent of tangerine and green grapefruit peel and flowers, plus a fringe of 8,000 strung seeds, tied by hand.

Lelia Flores of Mission won first place in 1938 for her colonial-themed costume. About 1,500 pieces of grapefruit peel cover the hoopskirt. The bodice is made of tree leaves, the collar of strung seeds, and the headdress of orange blossoms. She carries a "scepter" of orangewood bearing half a grapefruit and a spoon of orangewood. The costume required 1,000 hours to construct.

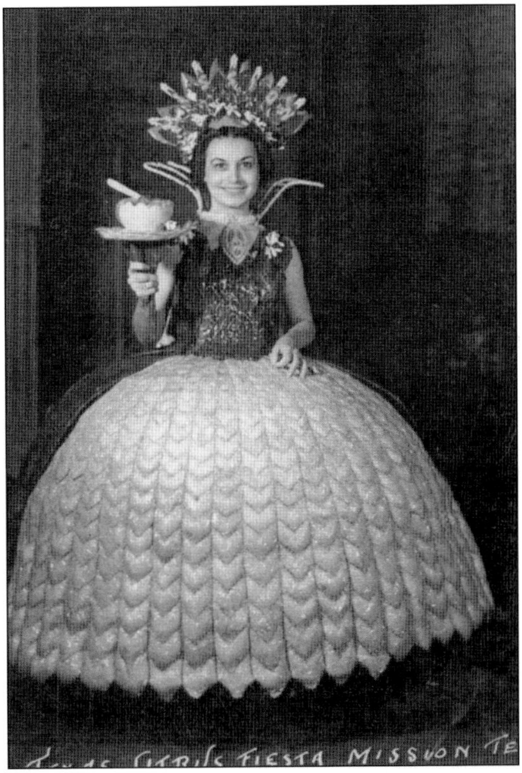

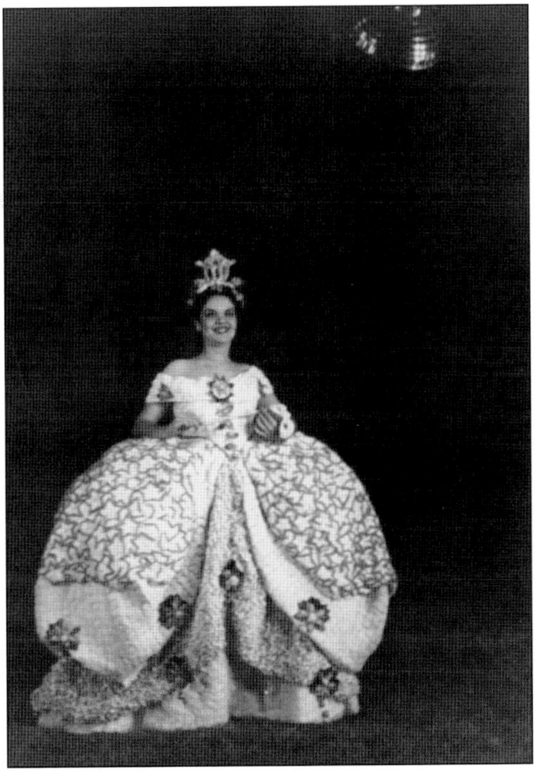

The 1939 Citrus Style Show of 30 entries was held at the Mission High School athletic field. In keeping with the theme "Pageant of Old World," Katherine Morris, sponsored by the Hayes-Sammons Hardware Company, wears a French court costume styled as Queen Marie Antoinette. Morris's costume, designed by Quita Sammons, required over 1,000 hours of work from over 45 people and weighed 27 pounds.

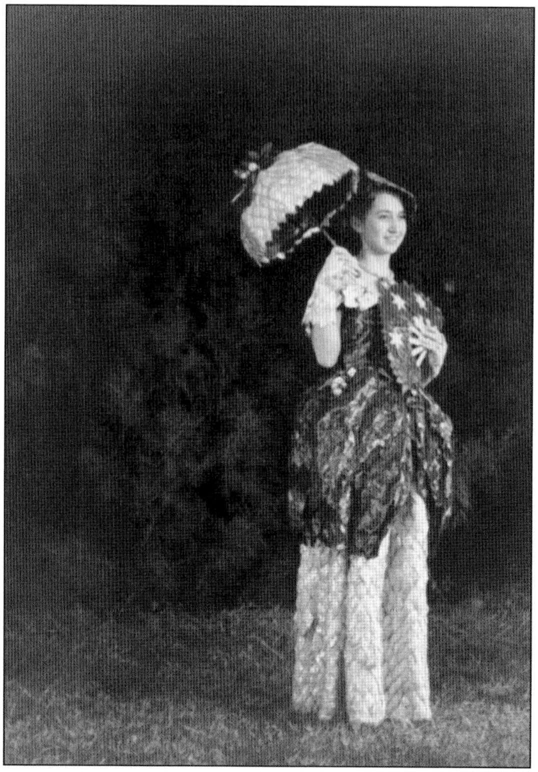

Evelyn Eppright, seen here in 1939, was sponsored by the Mission Garden Club. She models a dress made of citrus peel wrapped in cellophane. Leaves form the overskirt.

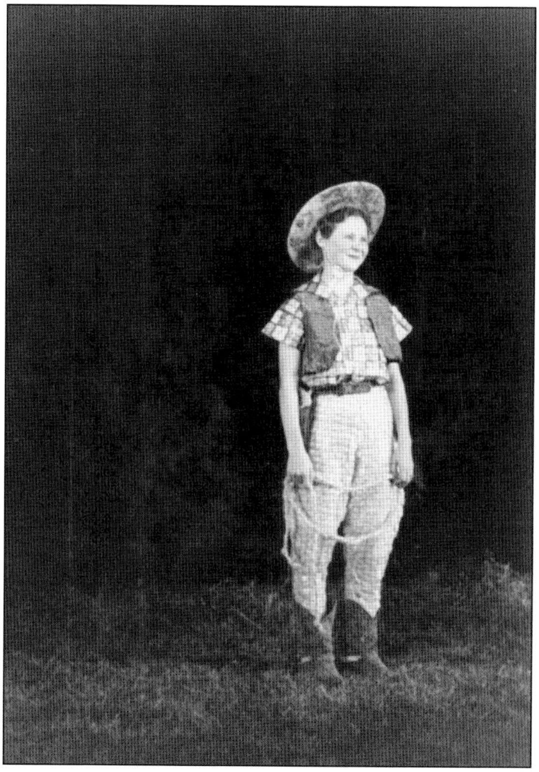

Mrs. Chester Williamson, sponsored by the North Mission Home Demonstration Club in 1939, wears a cowgirl costume made of citrus peel in several colors.

The evening dress worn by Billie Marion Parks of Weslaco won second place in 1939. Over 500 chili peppers cover her gown. Of special note is the trim of parched carrot slices shaped into tiny flowers. The Weslaco Business and Professional Women's Club sponsored her dress. The photographer is unidentified.

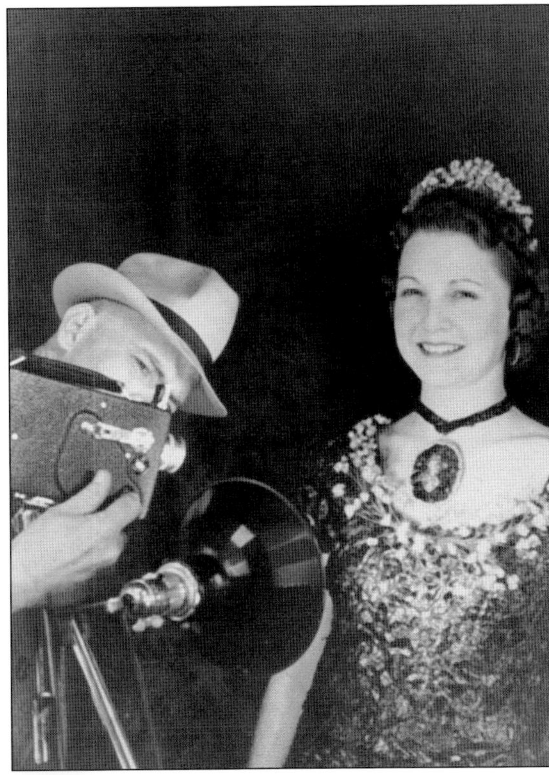

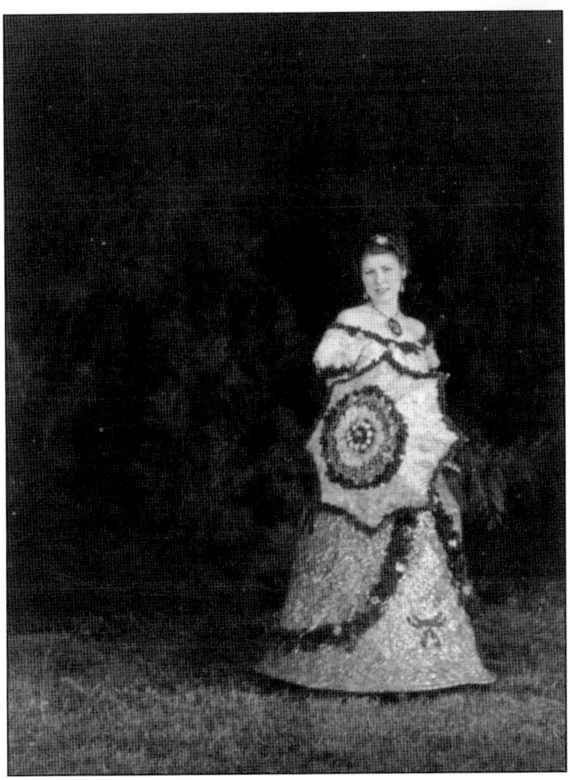

Mrs. E.M. Whitaker, sponsored by the North Pharr Home Demonstration Club, represents Scarlett O'Hara and won first place in the 1939 costume division. The dress required 10,000 pieces of cabbage shaded from dark to light green. Flowers and 10 kinds of vegetables comprised the trim. Mrs. Logan Duncan Sr. designed the dress.

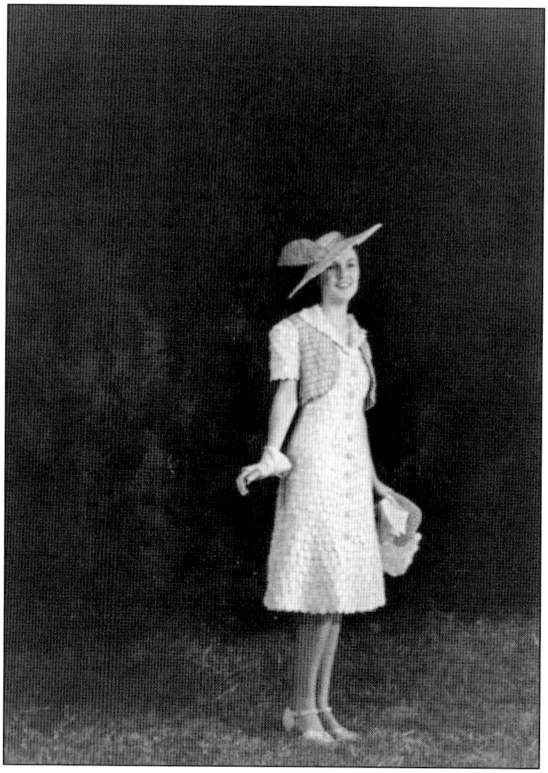

Wilma Beth Schuelke, sponsored by the Mission Dry Goods Company, won first place in 1939 for this street dress. The dress, hat, and purse are made of corncobs sliced very thin, trimmed with orange peels. She submitted this photograph of the outfit to Ripley's Believe It or Not! photograph archives in 1940, and the image appears in *Texas Highways* magazine in July 2000.

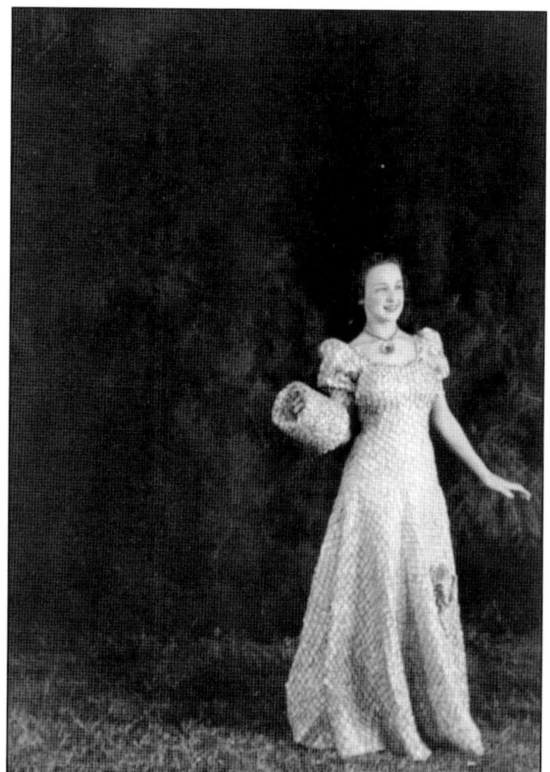

Betty Sue Robinson, sponsored by the Mercedes Garden Club, won first place in 1939 for her evening dress, which required more than 1,200 hours to complete. Tangerine peel was reversed and cut into diamond shapes, which were wrapped in cellophane, glued onto the foundation, and then trimmed with the centers of poinsettias. The muff was made of the same materials.

Mrs. Seth Barrett Jr., as "Queen of Grapefruit," wears this court costume in the 1940 style show. Her sponsor was the North Mission Home Demonstration Club.

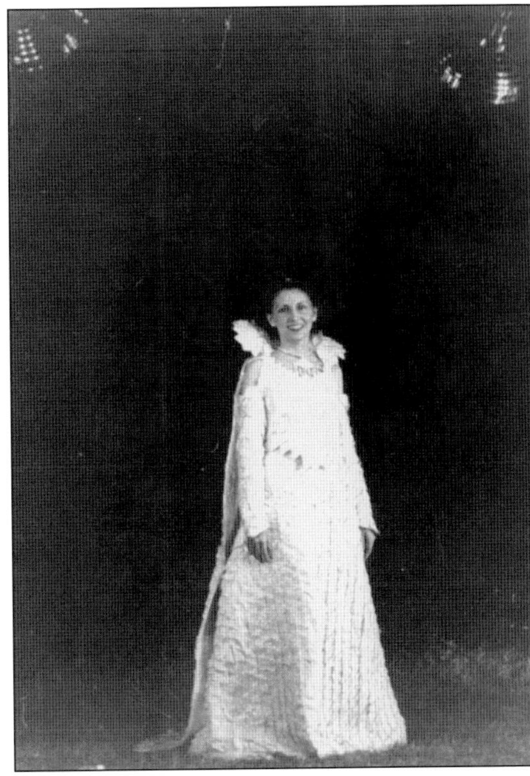

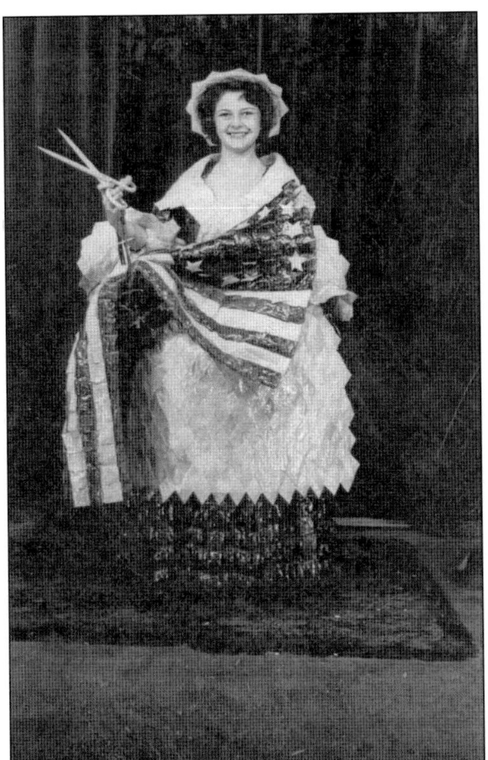

In 1941, Colleen Buescher won first place in her division with this Betsy Ross costume designed by Mrs. Emil Duensing. Details include a flag, a sewing basket, and scissors made of grapefruit wood. Green peppers cover the hoop skirt; corn shucks cover the apron, collar, cuffs, and hat; and red peppers trim the shoes and hat. Buescher became first alternate for 1942 Queen Citrianna.

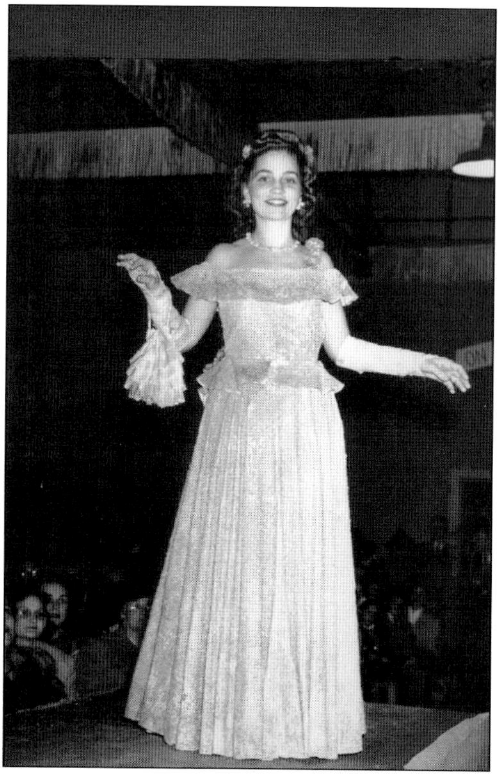

In 1948, Mrs. Magus Smith of Sharyland wears an off-the-shoulder evening dress of ground and sifted, red and white corncobs. The bertha around her shoulders and the peplum at her waist use white cobs at the top that shade into red at the bottom. She carries an evening bag made of corn shucks and wears chrysanthemums in her hair. Smith won first prize in the evening dress division.

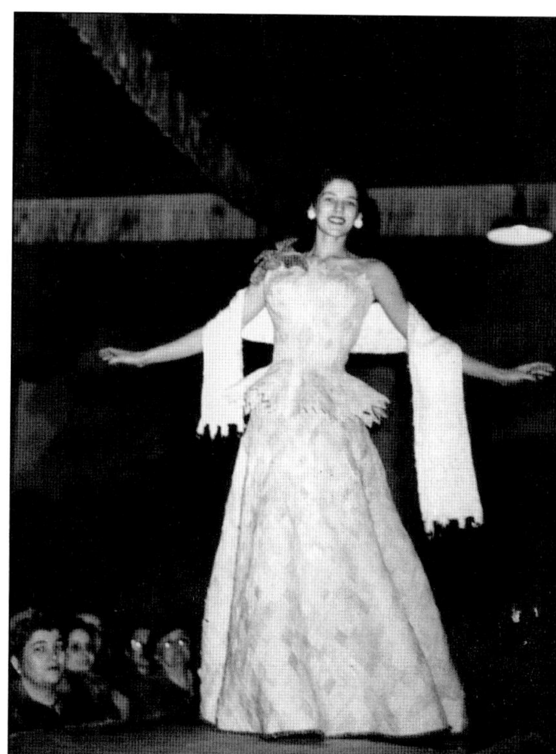

Mrs. Duane Martin, sponsored by the Donna Garden Club, wears a nonperishable evening dress of corn shucks cut into diamond shapes ranging from one to four inches long. The bodice required 1,320 diamond-shaped corn shucks and the skirt, 2,800. Each piece was sewed on by hand. Dried bachelor buttons border the hem. The ermine-like stole is made of cotton and the "ermine tails" of onion seed.

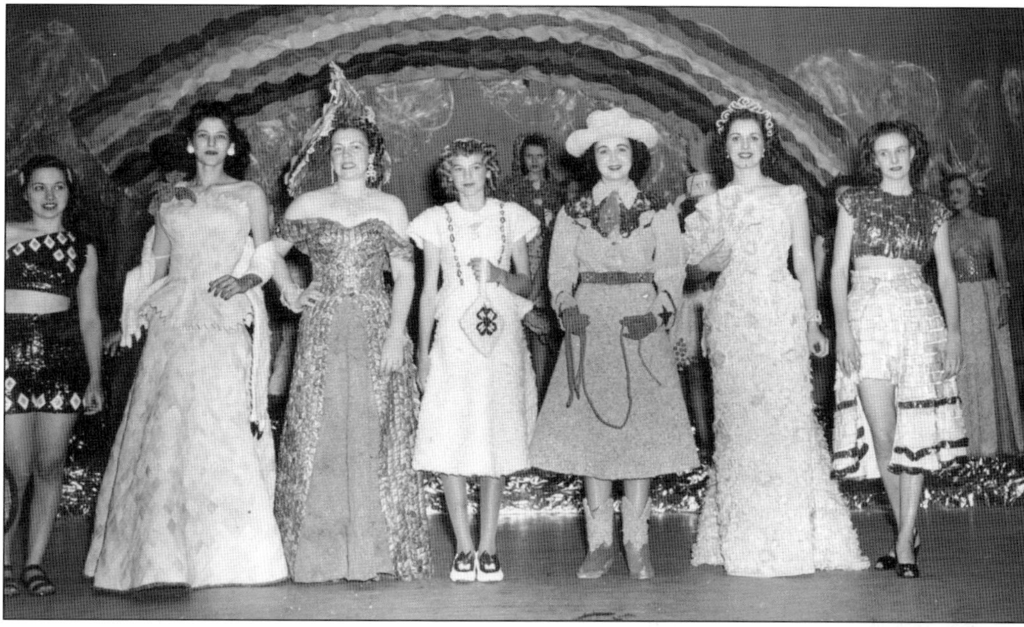

These seven ladies represent a portion of the Citrus and Vegetable Style Show winners in 1948. They are, from left to right, Tommie Sue Russell (playsuit), Mrs. Duane Martin (evening dress), Mrs. J.R. Hensley (costume), Betty Jackel (street dress), Mrs. Scott Toothaker (costume), Mrs. Robert Williams (Jean Kilgore) (evening dress), and Betty Flo Landers (playsuit). First-place winners were Hensley, Jackel, Williams, and Landers.

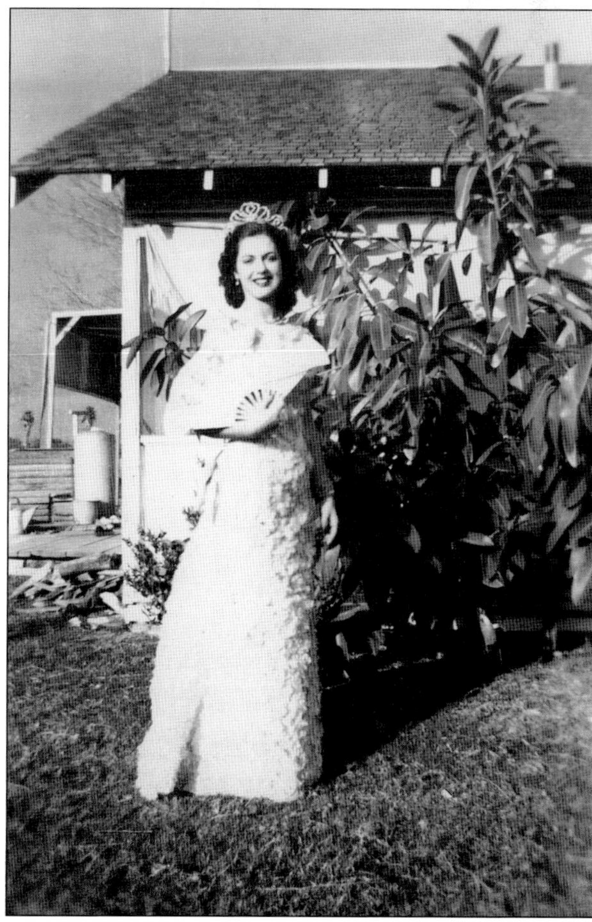

In 1948, Jean Kilgore Williams, seen here at Moore Field north of Mission, modeled this evening dress for the North Mission Home Demonstration Club. The background of finely ground corn is embroidered with membrane of ruby red and white grapefruit and seeds. Flower centers are thin slices of corncobs. The same materials cover her fan. Citrus "pearls" sealed with shellac decorate her tiara, necklace, bracelet, and earrings.

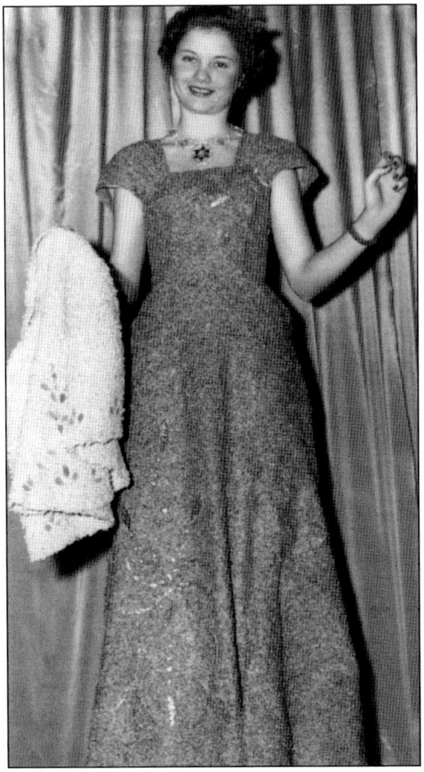

Betty Lee Smith (Queen Citrianna XVIII) won the grand prize of $150 for this evening dress at the 1949 style show held at the Mission Armory. Earlier that year, members of the sponsoring North Mission Home Demonstration Club had planted bachelor buttons specifically for this dress. Petals and seeds from bachelor buttons, candied citrus peel, citrus seeds, and ceniza leaves cover the dress, trimmed with "sequins" of candied citrus peel.

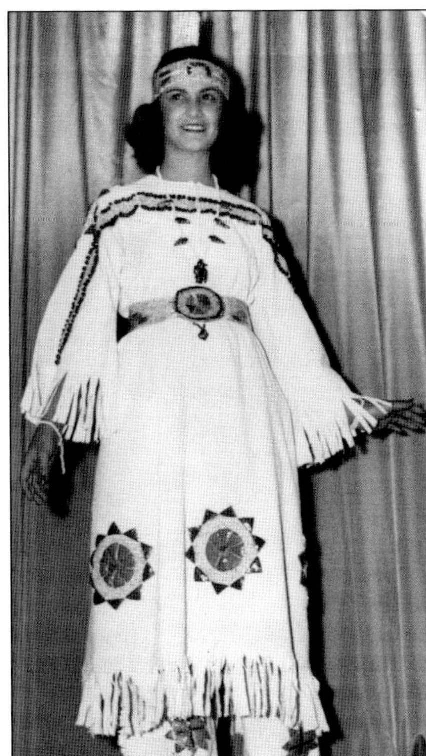

Mary Alice Longoria, sponsored by the Mission Study Club, wears this costume in the 1949 style show. The dress is made of white cornmeal, chopped corn, green grapefruit peel, tangerine peel, and red berries; the belt and leggings of bell peppers, green lemon peel, white and yellow cornmeal, eggplant, and tangerine; and the moccasins of yellow cornmeal and red berries. Corn, eggplant, orange membrane, and tangerine peel cover the headdress.

Eight

The Product Costumes

With the return of the fiesta after World War II, the product costume show reflected the latest national styles. The bertha, worn around the shoulders, was a return to past details, but the peplum softened the straight lines of the new suit and dress fashions. The first use of dehydrated materials (tomato pulp to simulate velvet) occurred in 1947.

Mrs. M.W. Held expressed concern for the preservation of the costumes, which became the property of the Texas Citrus Fiesta. Mold and mildew, mice, weevils, and other insects attacked the costumes. Most of the early costumes are gone, but several later costumes are now at the Mission Historical Museum.

Due to its popularity and growth, the product costume show had to relocate several times. In the early years, it took place at the Mission High School auditorium, but in 1940, the event moved to the Tex-Sun Building, where a circular stage for the models and grandstands for several thousand spectators had to be constructed.

In 1947 and 1948, the style show was held at the Moore Field recreation hall, where models strode a 100-foot ramp. In 1949, the style show moved to the National Guard Armory, which could accommodate up to 4,000 spectators. With the opening of Memorial Gymnasium in 1950, the coronation, children's style show, and two adult style shows enjoyed a permanent home well into the 1960s, when the events moved to the Mission Community Center (formerly the National Guard Armory). To the traditional Friday and Saturday night style shows, a third show on Sunday afternoon was added in 1968. Because of the number of models, categories, and divisions, awards were presented on Sunday afternoon.

Today, the junior and senior product costume shows are held at the Mission Community Center. They remain a delightful tradition during the Texas Citrus Fiesta.

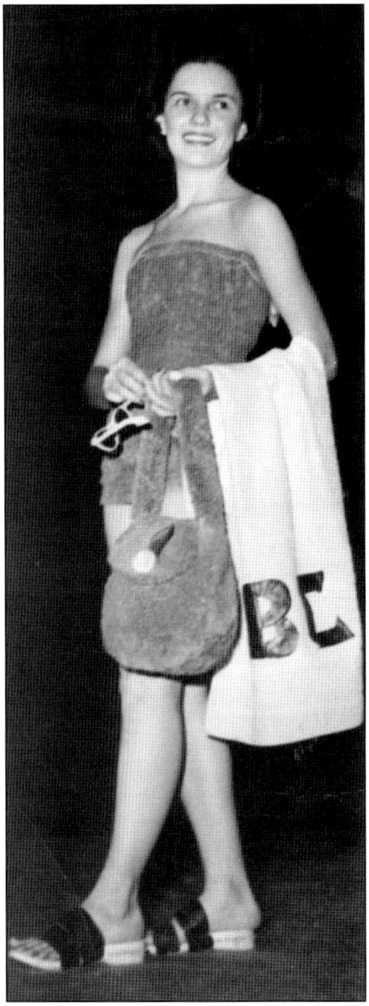

In 1949, Marianne Stutz of Mission modeled a drum major's costume made from white grapefruit pectin and tangerine peel. She wears this prizewinning playsuit and wooden sandals, and she carries a blanket and a beach bag, in the 1950 style show. A Mission duchess in 1951, she was attending Texas College of Arts and Industries in Kingsville at the time of her death in an automobile accident there in 1953.

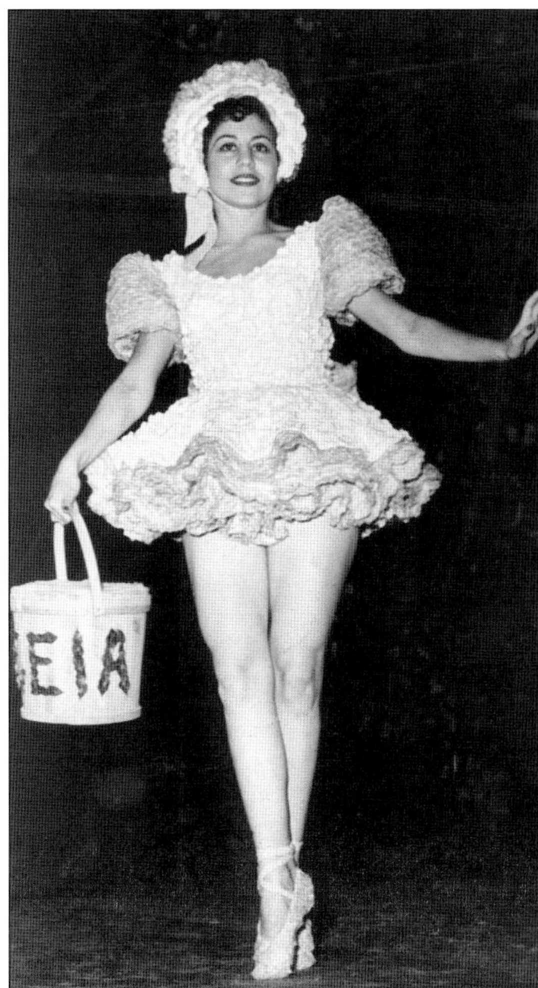

Nellie Watson of Rio Grande City wears this prizewinning milkmaid's costume at the 1950 style show, held at Memorial Gymnasium for the first time. A total of 28 models competed for prizes on Friday and Saturday nights. Judges on the first night were from department stores outside the Rio Grande Valley. On the second night, judges were valley women experienced in making product costumes.

Mrs. Robert Bentsen of McAllen wears this prizewinning evening dress in 1950. Her sponsor was the Mission American Legion Auxiliary. Prizes ranged from $75 to $35, and nonwinners received $20 to cover expenses.

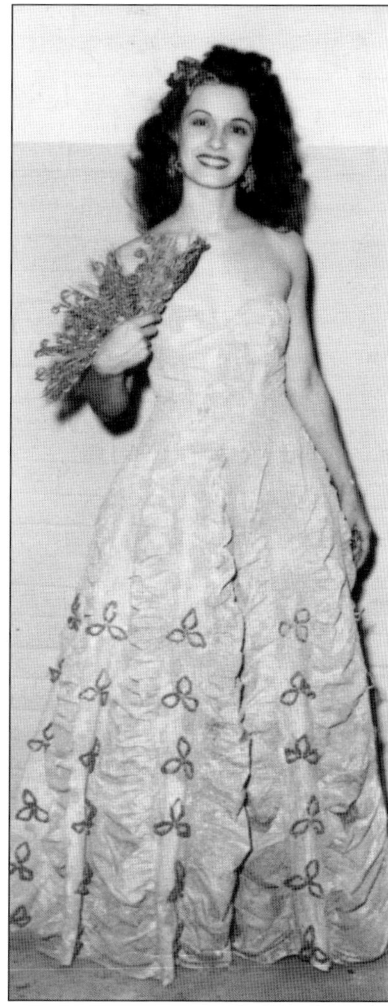

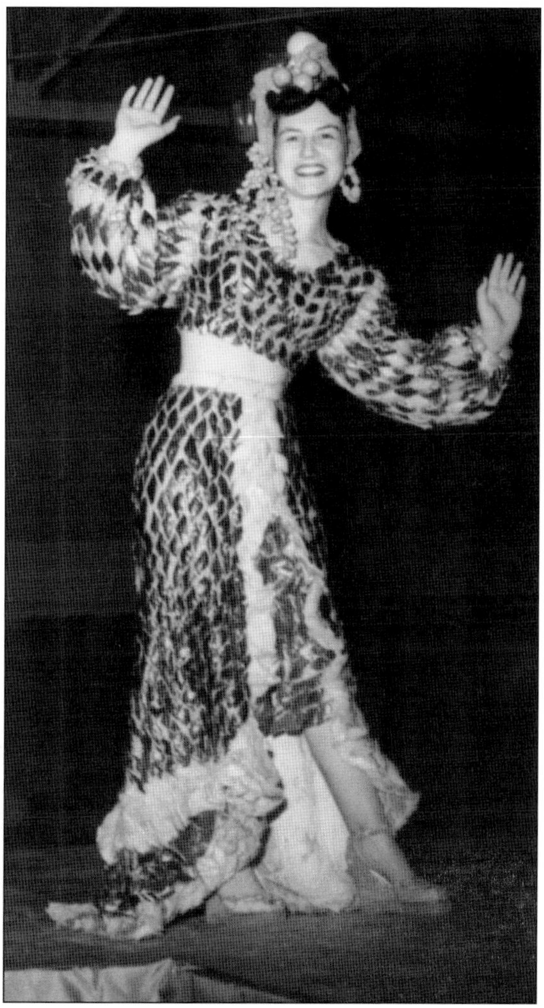

Monelle Mason of San Juan models this "Carmen Miranda" costume in 1950. She was sponsored by the San Juan Garden Club. She won first place, as did Mrs. Bentsen, on the first night of judging. Stutz and Watson won first places on the second night.

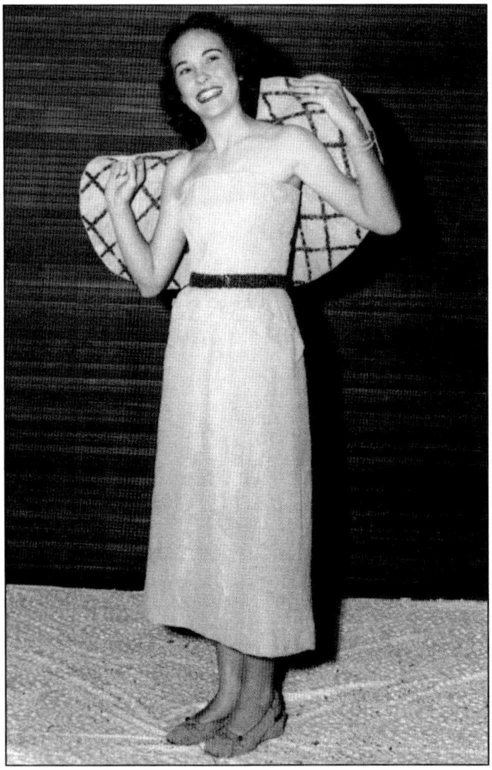

Winona Bourland, sponsored by the Atheneum Study Club of Edcouch, wears this strapless sundress and jacket made of sifted and hand-grated orange peel in the Citrus and Vegetable Style Show for 1951. Her accessories are covered with Mexican morning glory seeds.

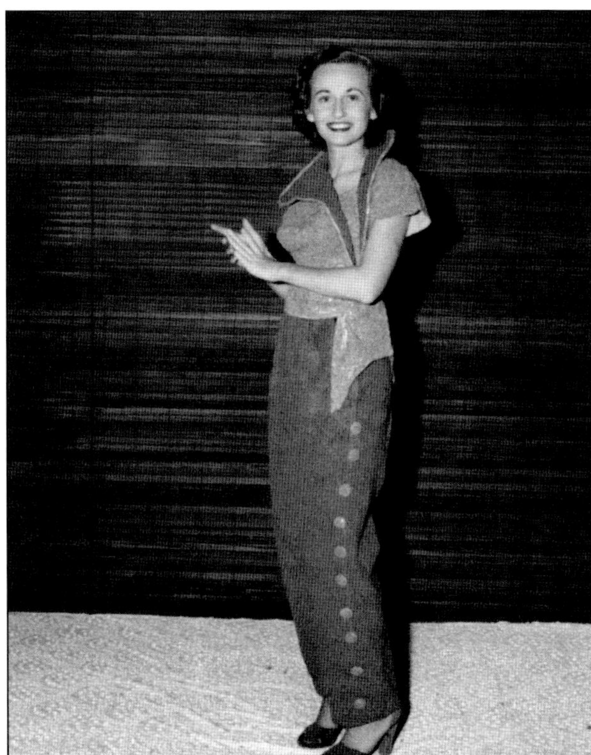

In 1951, Jackie Allen, sponsored by Danny Reed of Weslaco, wears lounging slacks of emerald green "velvet," made from ground orange leaves, and a blouse of dehydrated grapefruit pulp. Details are buttons and cord trim of dehydrated grapefruit pulp mixed with glitter; sash of glitter and orange peel; and mules covered with citrus peel.

Frances Otto of Harlingen wears a playsuit and carries fishing gear in the 1951 style show. Her top is covered with round slices of carrots, and the shorts with grapefruit leaves. Details include a billed cap of grapefruit leaves, wedge shoes covered with carrots, a bamboo fishing pole, a fishing line of palm, and sinker and hooks made from dates. Her sponsor was the Harlingen chapter of Gamma Epsilon.

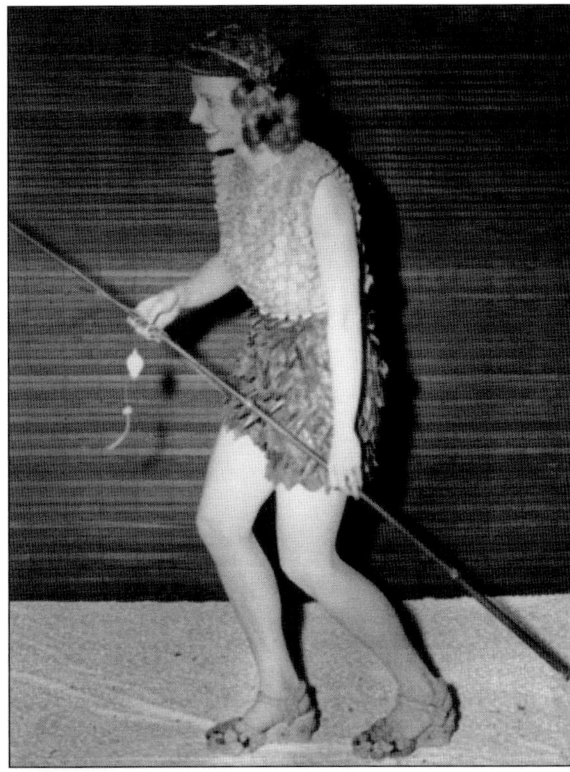

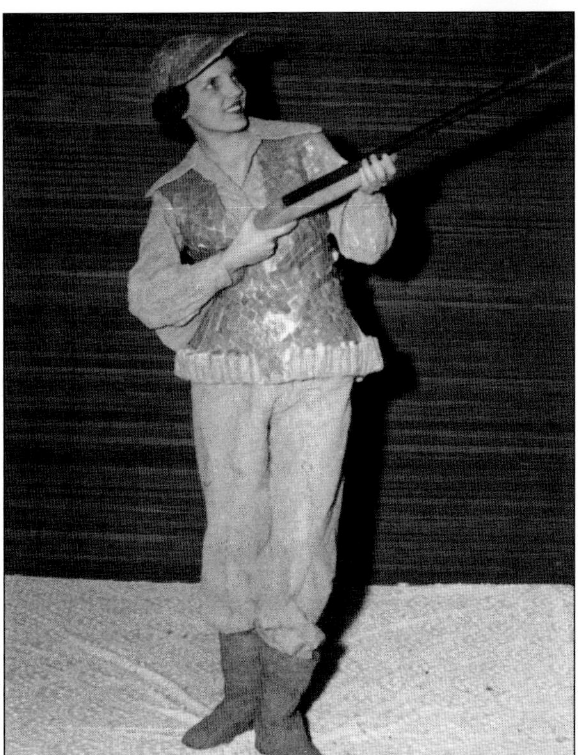

Mary Ruth Dooley of Mission won first place in both contests in 1951 with her hunting outfit of dried citrus leaves, tangerine peel, and dried avocado leaves. Her "gun" is of grapefruit wood, and the "stock" is stained with beet juice. As she modeled the outfit, she removed a "whitewing dove" made of ceniza leaves from her game bag. The Mission chapter of Texas Theta Iota sponsored her.

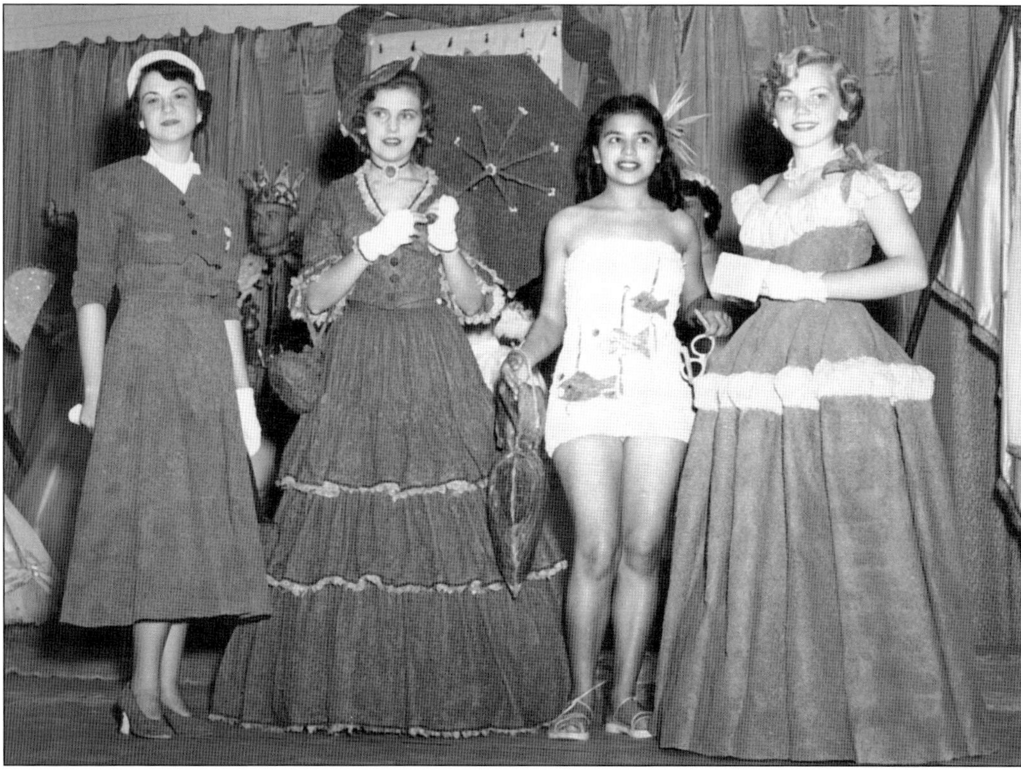

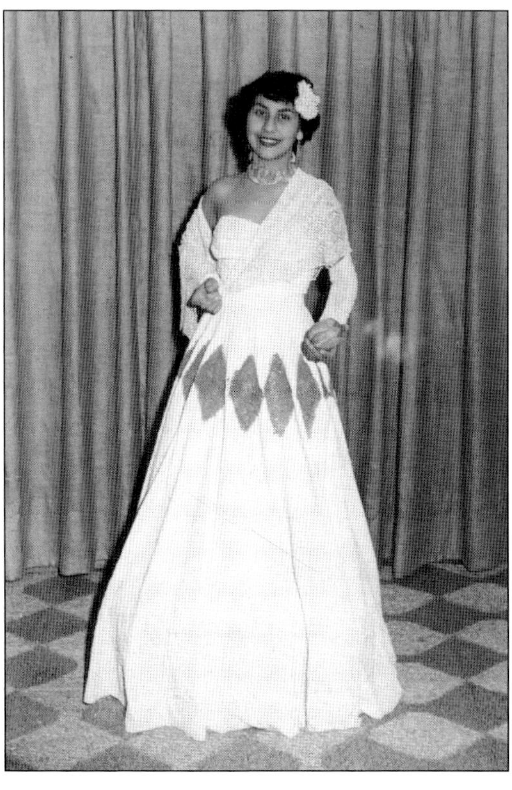

Style show prizewinners in 1952 are, from left to right, Betty Jean Daniel (Mission), Faye Maiville (Donna), Lupe Mata (Donna), and Jean Ellis (Mission). Primary ingredients in the costumes are dehydrated citrus peel and trim of ground corn (Daniel), dehydrated bougainvillea petals (Maiville), natural color corn shucks that were hand-knitted (Mata), and dehydrated leaves of the bird-of-paradise plant with trim of crushed citrus membrane (Ellis).

Claricia Ballí of Weslaco wears an evening dress of white ground corn and a diamond-shaped trim of orange rind, seen here in 1952. Her sponsor was Mrs. Marie Robinson of Weslaco, her mother, who designed and made the dress. Ballí had competed in 1951 as well.

Rose Marie Bentsen of McAllen, sponsored by the Mission Garden Club, wears this prizewinning strapless formal evening dress at the 1952 style show. The brown bodice is covered with chrysanthemum seeds and grapefruit seed "jewels" that sparkle with glitter. The skirt is styled with alternate panels of dehydrated chrysanthemum seeds and sawdust from a green grapefruit tree.

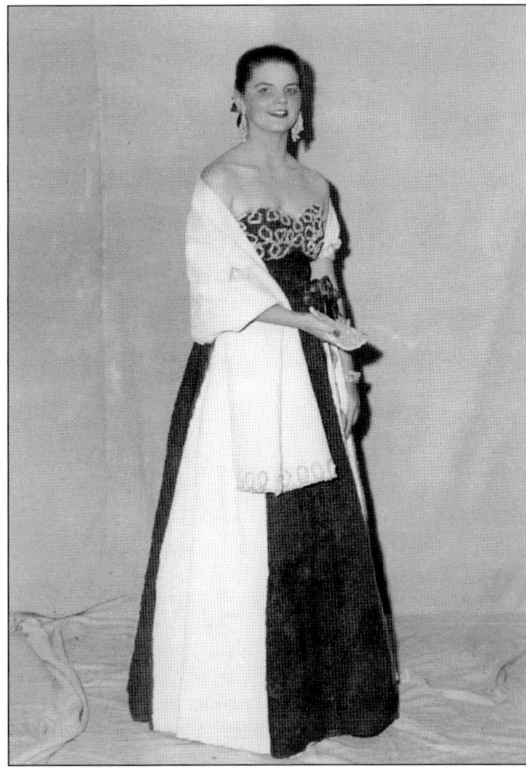

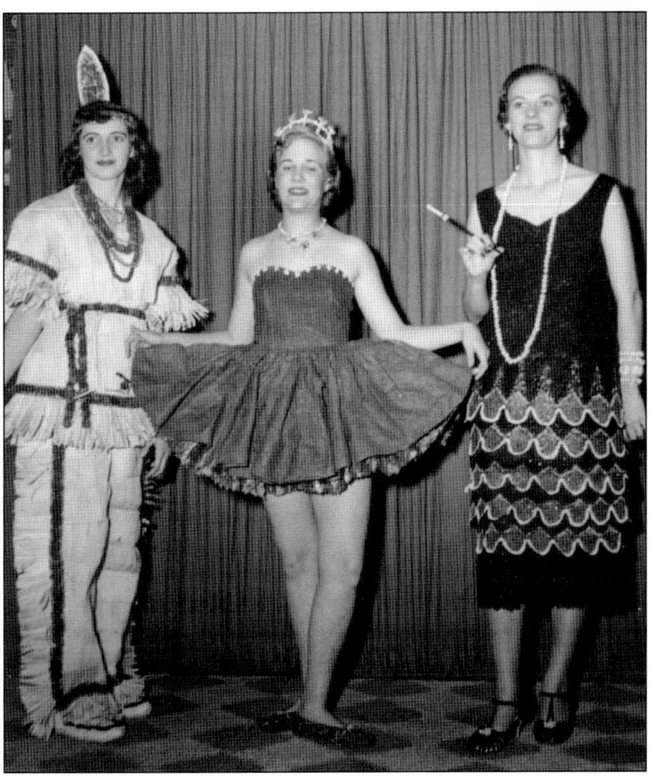

The outstanding style show for 1955 featured a variety of costumes. Posing here are, from left to right, Carol Folkerts (Indian costume), Glenda Mitchell (ballerina), and Mrs. Fred de Julio (1920s flapper). Primary ingredients are corn shucks and braid trim of pyracantha berries (Folkerts), bougainvillea (Mitchell), and onion seeds trimmed with cornmeal, cornflowers, and "bead" fringe of Anaheim peppers (de Julio).

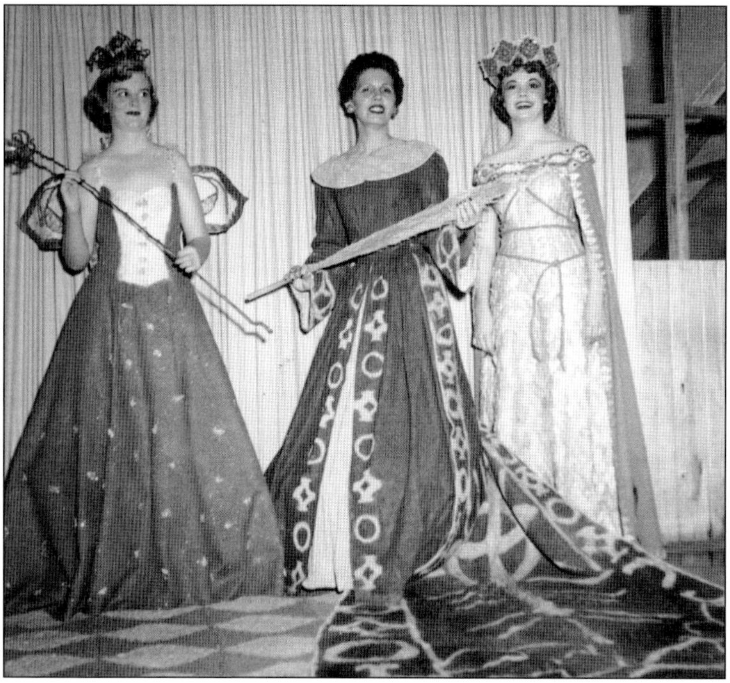

Another group of 1955 costume prizewinners includes, from left to right, Ann Ellen Armstrong ("Fairy Princess"), Mrs. Florence Park ("Duchess of the Sea of Galilee"), and Jane Mosely ("Medieval Princess"). Natural products used are dehydrated purple bougainvillea flowers and wings of milkweed down (Armstrong), dyed garnet bougainvillea flowers and "jewels" of grain (Park), and grapefruit peel with trim of poinsettia petals (Mosely).

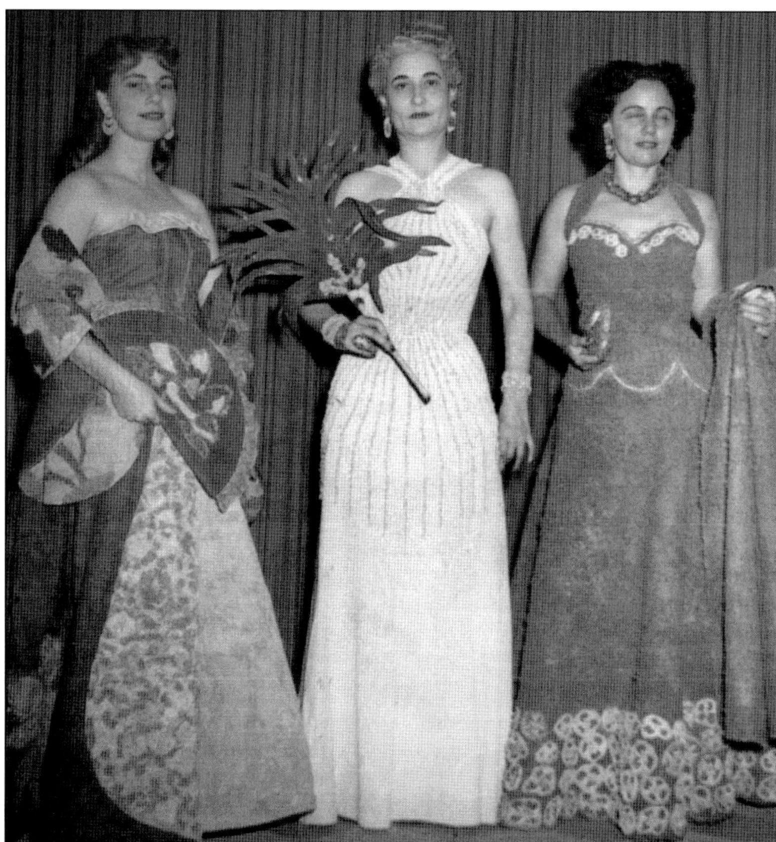

Winners in the evening dress division for 1955 are, from left to right, Mrs. G.M. Baltus, Mrs. M.R. Jennings, and Mrs. Merle Goudy. Natural products used are dehydrated red bougainvillea, orangewood dust, and dehydrated citrus peel (Baltus); ground corn, orange seeds, and the red feather fan of poinsettia petals (Jennings); and ground citrus leaves with trim of dishrag gourd (Goudy).

Winners in the street dress and sports divisions in 1955 are, from left to right, Darlene McHenry, Sheridan Sammons, Sandra Kimbriel, and Mrs. Harold Graves. Materials used are green castor bean leaves (McHenry), dehydrated carrots with a petticoat of dehydrated citrus leaves (Sammons); white cornmeal, trim of dehydrated purple bougainvillea, and map of Texas in citrus peel on the back of the vest (Kimbriel); and fresh ground citrus leaves (Graves).

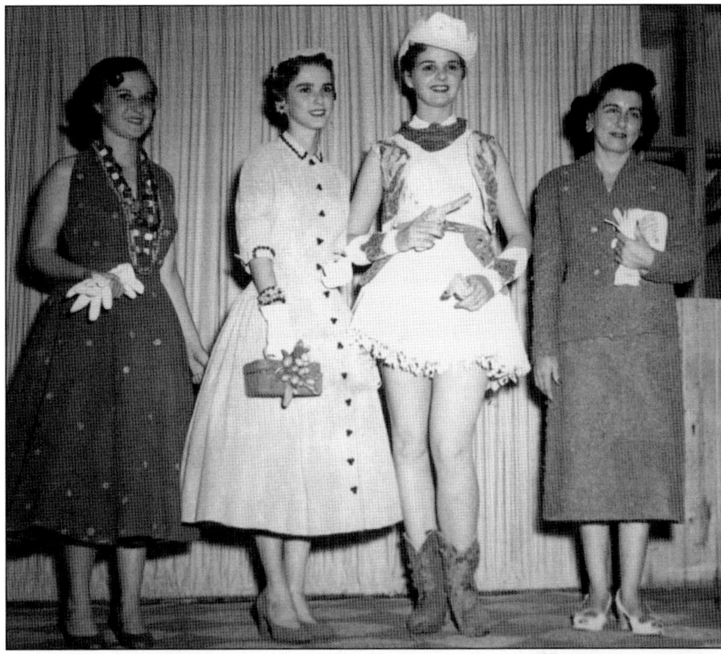

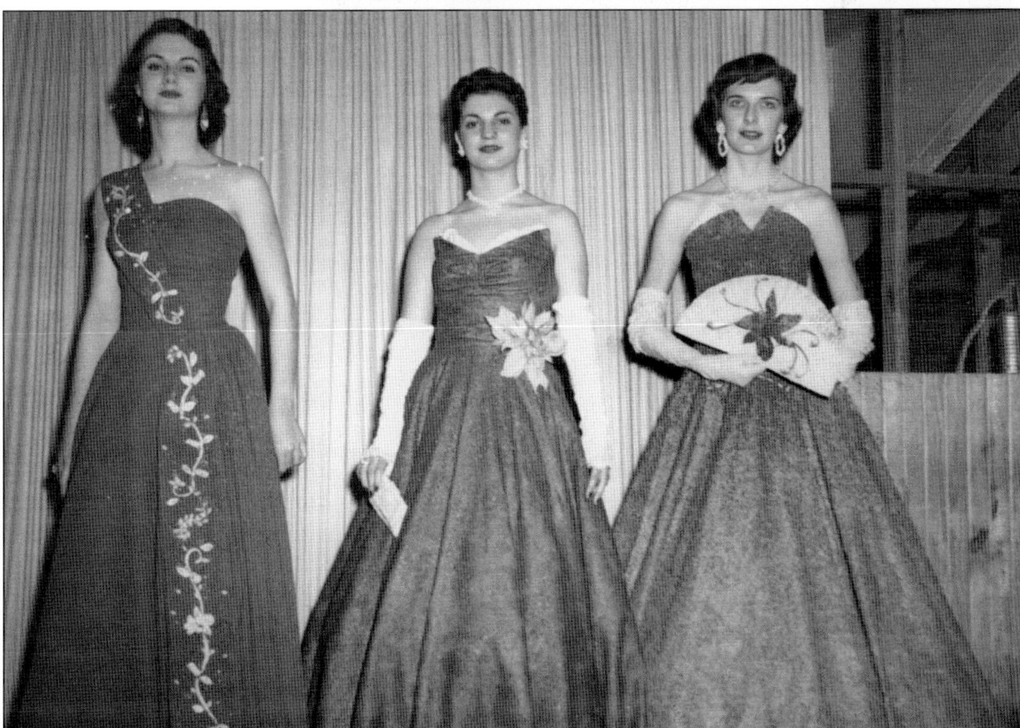

Additional winners in the 1955 evening dress division are, from left to right, Minta Curtis (first place, both nights), Sylvia Ortolan, and Ann Harrison. Natural products are dehydrated papaya leaves, trim of bronze glittered grapefruit membrane and seeds plus Bells of Ireland (Curtis); dehydrated red bougainvillea with pink "magnolia" blossom of citrus peel (Ortolan); and bachelor button flowers, dried and sifted (Harrison).

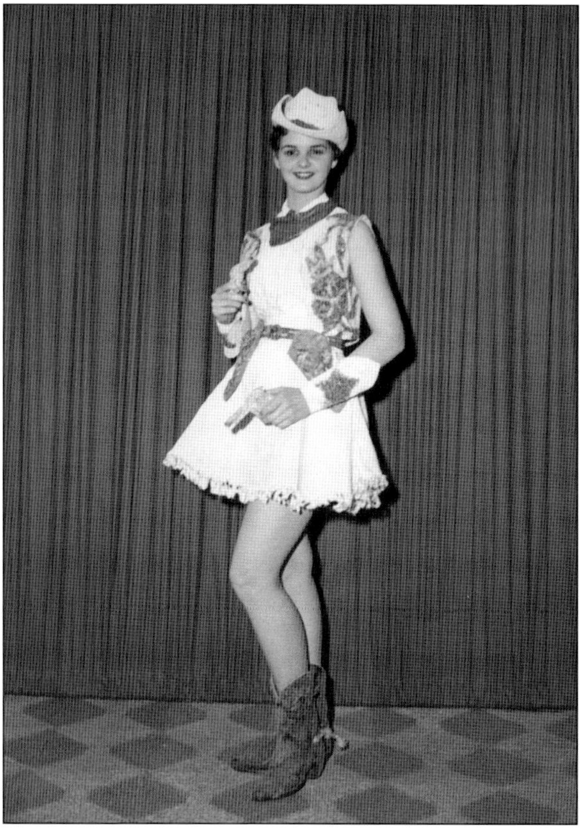

Sandra Kimbriel was attending Pharr–San Juan–Alamo High School when she modeled this cowgirl outfit in 1955. The tall, red-haired teenager represented San Juan as the Duchess of Calamondin and rode a float designed as a basket full of oranges in 1956. That year, she won prizes both nights as a costume model and was named First Princess for the 1957 court. She became Queen Citrianna XXI in 1958.

Seen here in 1956 are style show costumes made by the Pharr Garden Club. The models are, from left to right, Dixie Eubanks, Carolyn Hall, Minta Curtis, and Sandra Kimbriel. Detailed descriptions of the costumes were not available to the author.

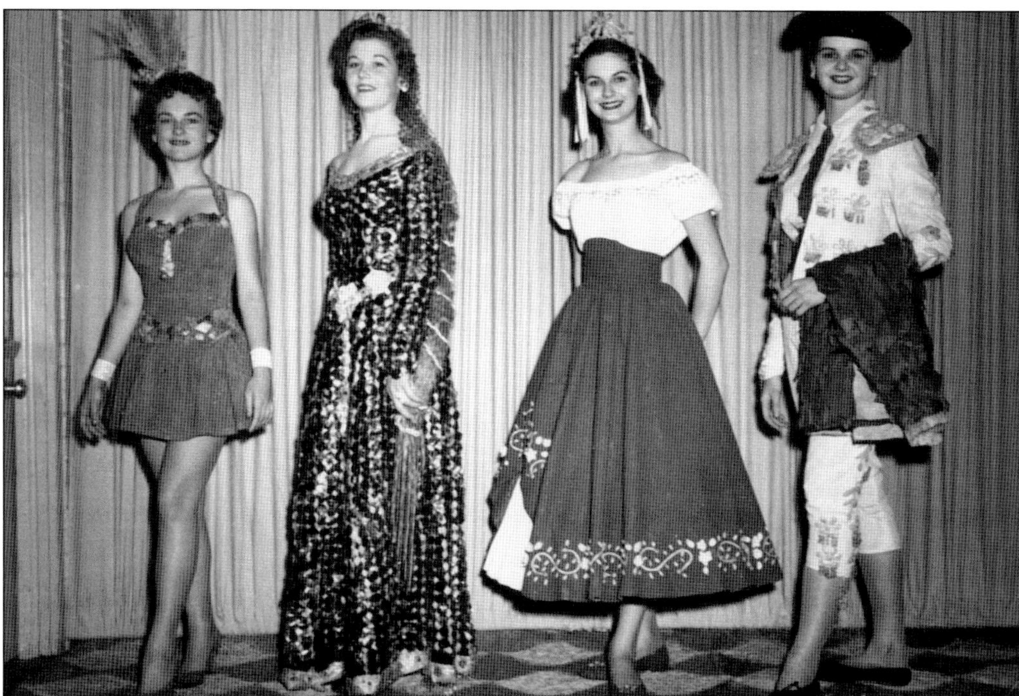

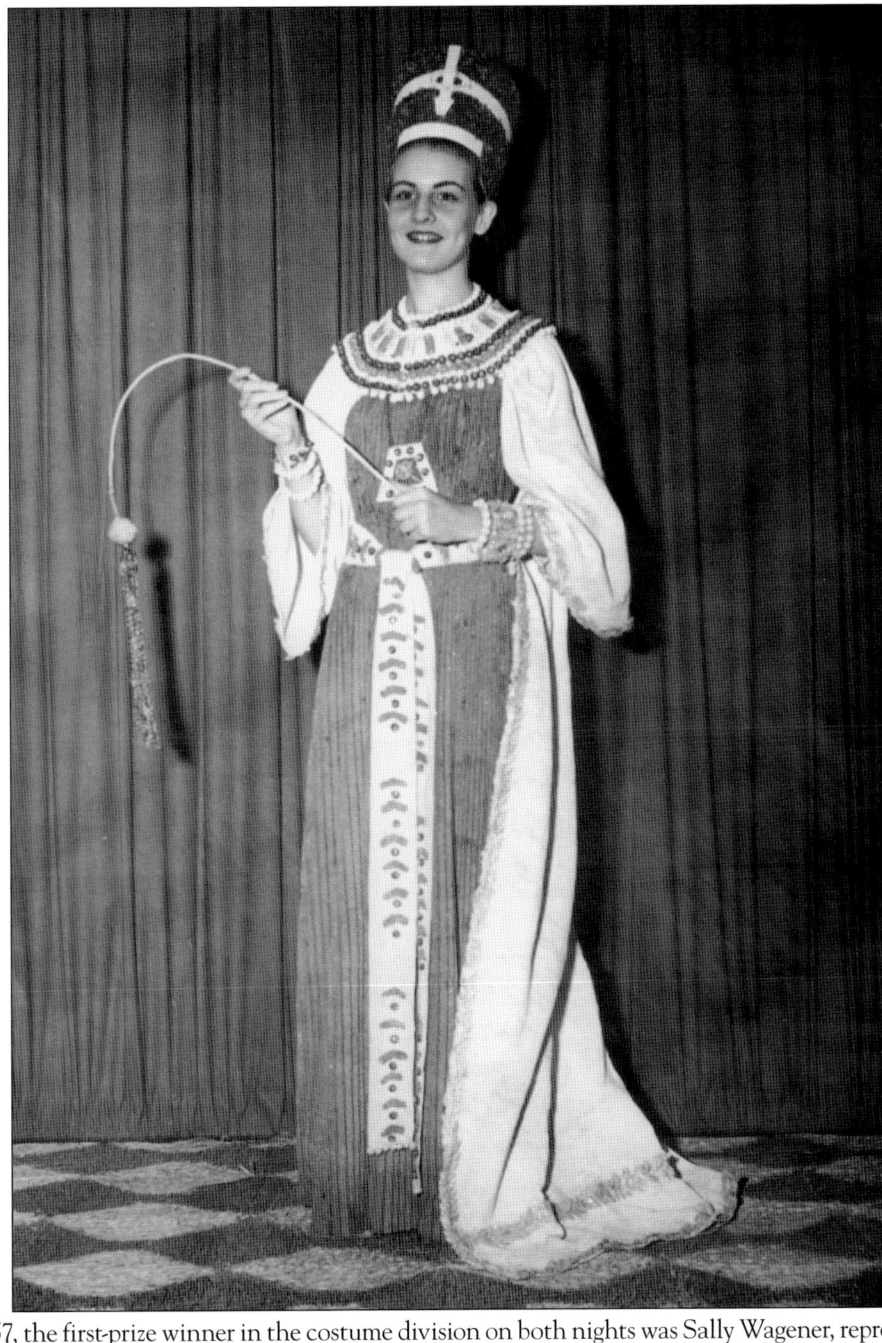

In 1957, the first-prize winner in the costume division on both nights was Sally Wagener, representing "Queen Nefertiti of Egypt." The Upper Valley Art League of Mission sponsored the costume. The front of the dress is accordion pleated and covered with four bushels of dehydrated citrus leaves. Fresh petals from bachelor buttons decorate the headdress. The veil is covered with meal from 10 ears of ground corn and some glitter, and edged with a border of the leaves from sea oats. The yoke, bracelets, and belt use green and red peppers, ripe and green berries, pyracantha berries, and citrus seed and peel. Wagener's gold sandals feature dehydrated citrus leaves and glitter. Construction of the costume took 980 hours and cost $21 in materials.

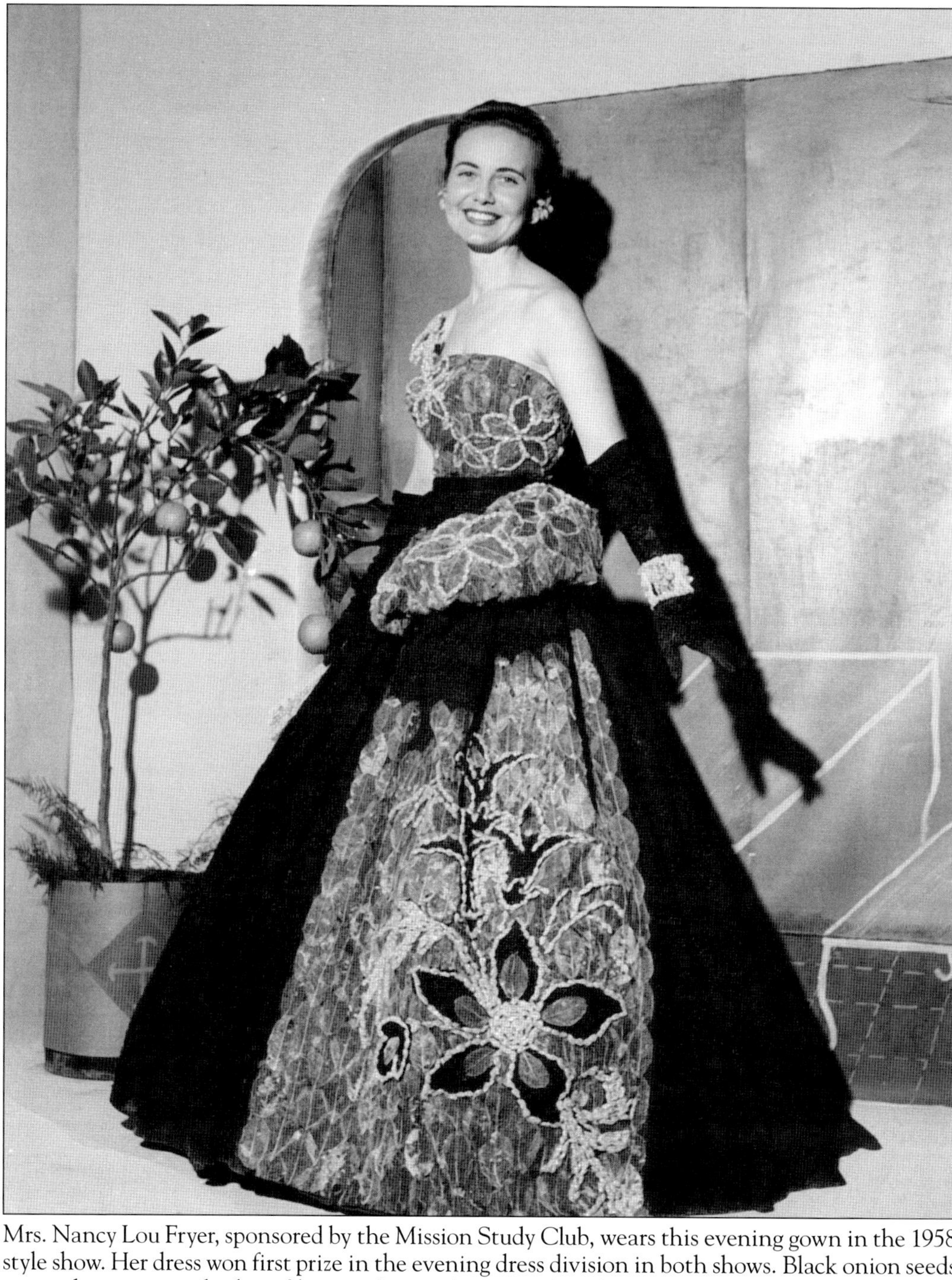

Mrs. Nancy Lou Fryer, sponsored by the Mission Study Club, wears this evening gown in the 1958 style show. Her dress won first prize in the evening dress division in both shows. Black onion seeds cover the gown, and a lacy filigree of citrus leaves outlined with glittered orange seeds covers the bodice. The skirt is accented with a side-draped pannier that repeats the filigree of citrus leaves. Onion seeds cover the gloves. Her earrings and tiara use glittered seeds, and her bracelet is made of the interior fibers of native cactus with a design of orange seeds. Also of cactus fiber, her evening bag incorporates a design of orange and grapefruit seeds. The costume required 732 hours of work and cost $26.41 in materials.

Minta Curtis Dietrich, sponsored by Mrs. C.B. Curtis, wears this "dressmaker suit" in the 1958 style show. On the dress are ground-up frostbitten bougainvillea flowers trimmed with onion seeds. Ground white corn, onion skins, and glitter cover the hatbox, and the harlequin design is styled with frostbitten bougainvillea flowers. The hatbox handle is made of braided pampas grass. Her necklace features tiny white onions alternating with cherry laurel berries.

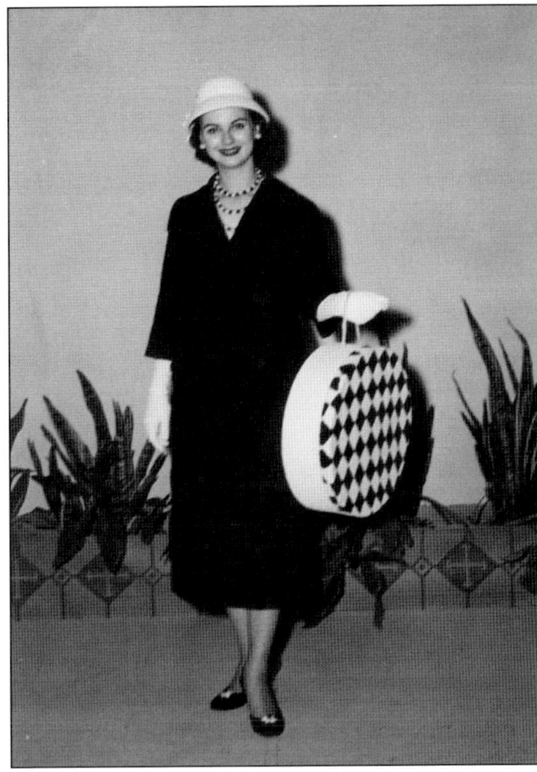

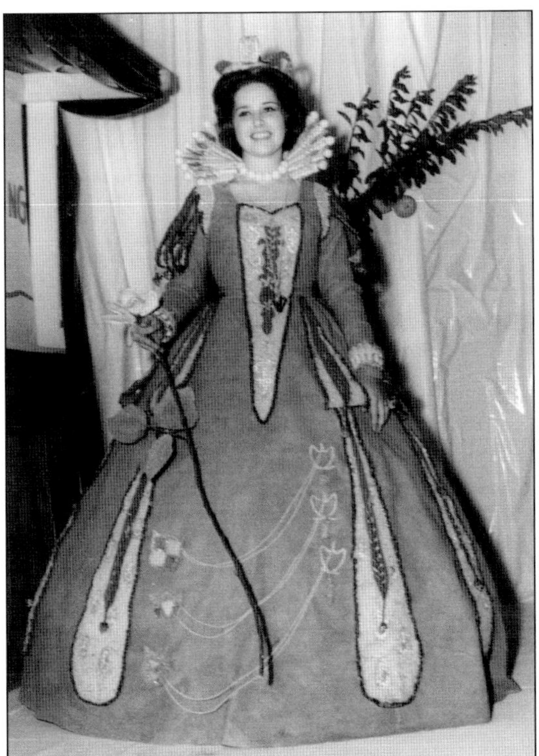

Over 1,000 hours were needed to make this Queen Elizabeth I costume, worn by Maurine Duncan's daughter Nicki in the 1963 style show. Powdered marigold petals give the dress a velvet-like quality. Seeds are used in the panels and overskirt. Other materials are squash, cantaloupe, roses, bougainvillea, fern, and Mexican morning glory. Her pearls are made from potato dipped in paraffin.

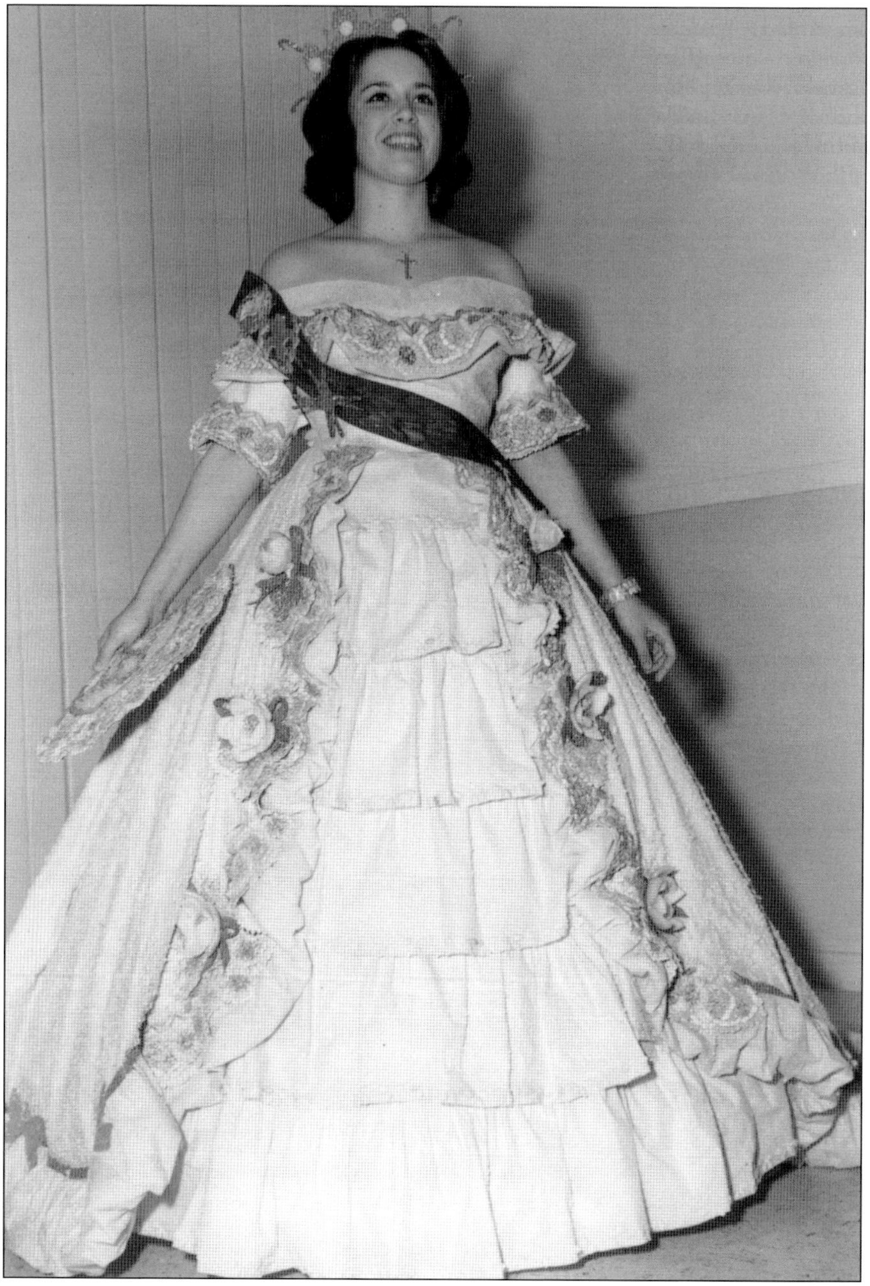

In the 1964 style show, Nicki Duncan modeled this replica of the coronation dress worn by Empress Carlota of Mexico. The Mission Garden Club sponsored the costume. Maurine Duncan, Nicki's mother, designed and made the dress, which took seven months to plan, 500 hours to construct, and $20 in materials. To simulate ivory velvet, Mrs. Duncan used flaked onions and dehydrated garlic. The large roses on the skirt are made of fresh grapefruit peel, and the sash of fresh poinsettia leaves. The badges of four countries include orange peel, congealed orange juice, sea oats, poppy seed, and poinsettias. Marigold and rose dust cover the crown, and potatoes form the jewels. The fan incorporates seeds of citrus, squash, cantaloupe, pepper, and flaked onion. The costume won the grand prize for 1964.

These 1964 prizewinners are, from left to right, Mrs. C.T. Popplewell, Mrs. J.H. Hinojosa, and Mrs. B.T. Bell. Popplewell's dress, made with thin slices of lemon and a mixture of ground corn and popcorn, weighed 14 pounds. Hinojosa's costume uses purple onion skin to simulate brocaded satin. Her "fur" stole required over 100 "old man" cacti. Dried curly parsley cover Bell's long sheath.

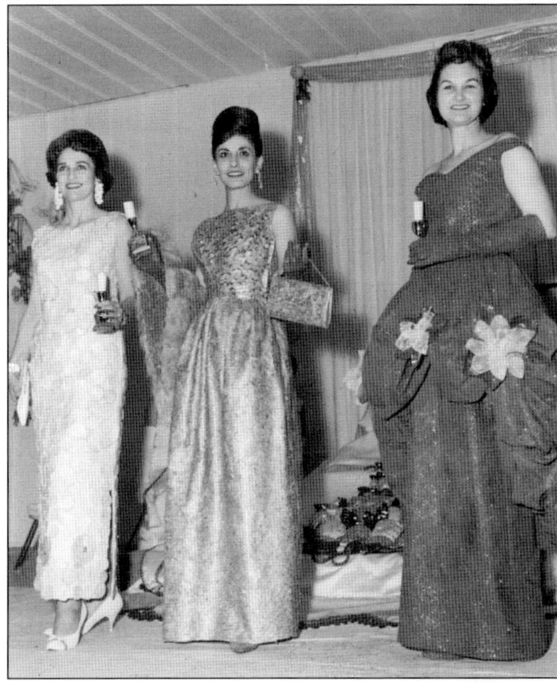

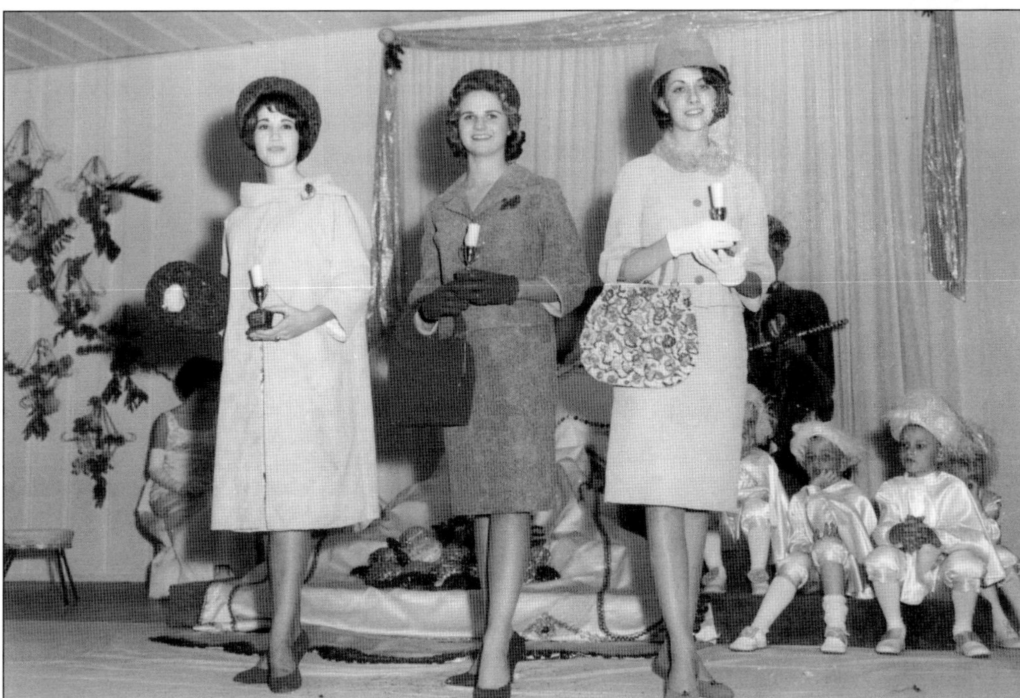

Winners in the 1964 Senior Style Show are, from left to right, Diane Birdwell, Henrieta Starnes, and Connie Lemon. Birdwell's ensemble is 90 percent citrus, with the coat the color of strawberry ice cream and the sheath a lighter color. Starnes's green "tweed" suit is a mixture of ceniza and citrus leaves. Lemon's two-piece suit uses ground popcorn and 6,160 *tepehuaje* seeds for the bag and shoes.

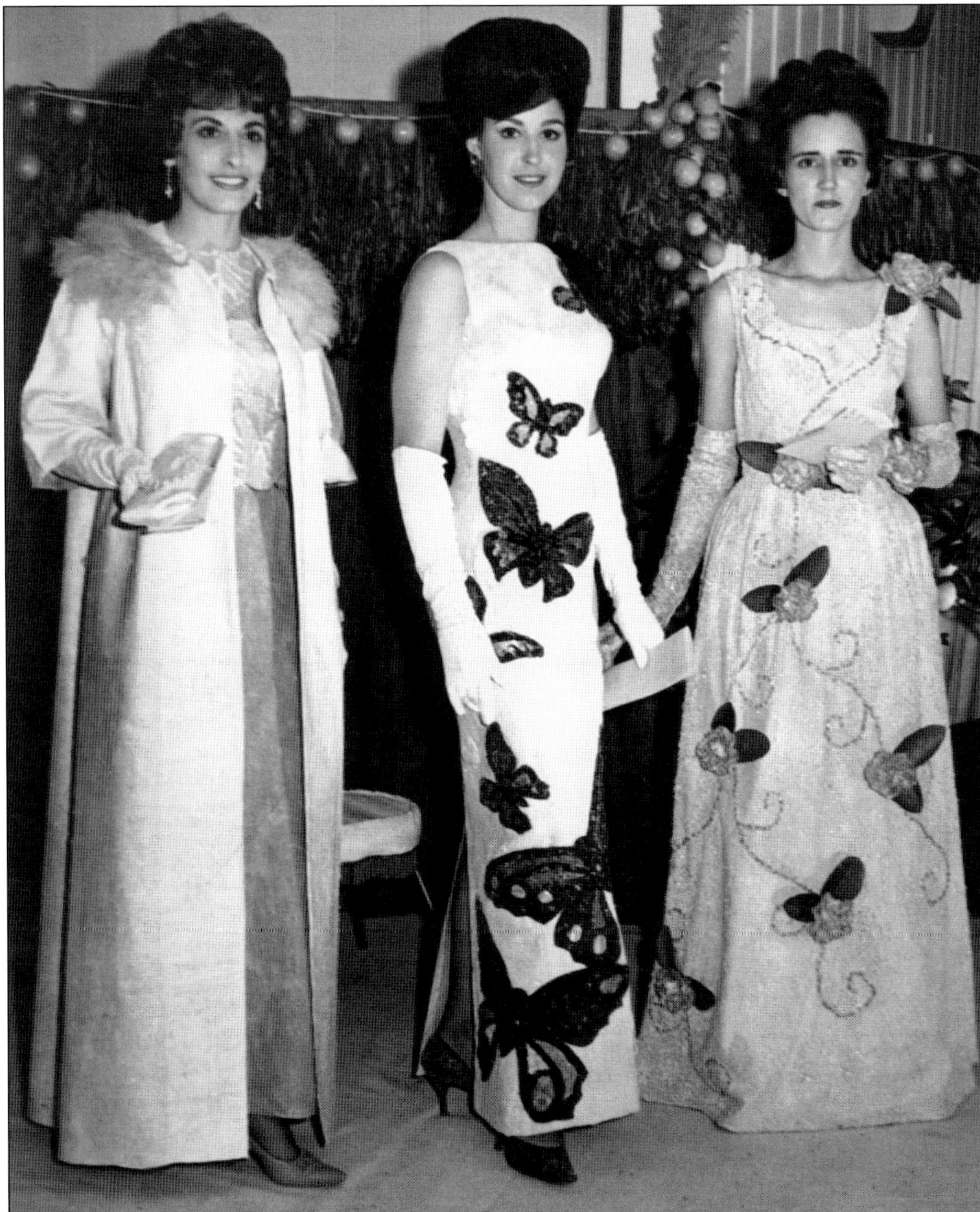

These style show winners from 1966 are, from left to right, Mrs. Norma Hinojosa, Connie Lemon, and Linda Winfrey. Hinojosa won first place both nights of the style show with her long coat and dress. Lemon wears a gown that uses design features from Hawaii and Japan. She won second place on both nights of the style show. Winfrey's dress required 16 bushels of Ruby Red grapefruit. The main material of her dress and train is the white "rag" of the grapefruit peel. The side panels are covered with chopped Ruby Red grapefruit membrane. "Rag" is the white part of the peel.

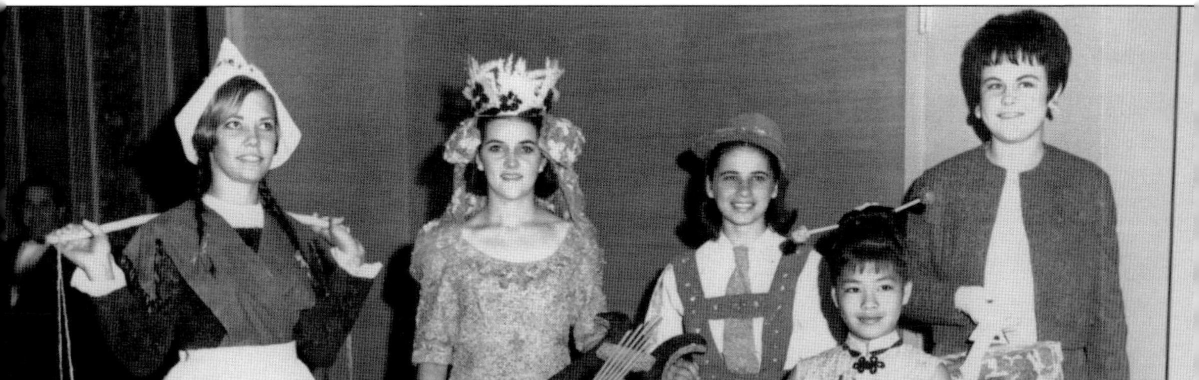

Additional costume winners in 1966 are, from left to right (first row), Natalie Gay Bruns ("Little Bo Peep") and Jo-Jo Shiba ("China Doll"); (second row) Rose Ann Eckroat ("Katrinka of Holland"), Nora Longoria ("Lady from Murcia"), and Pamela Brewer ("Bavarian Costume"). Standing at right is Linda Sanford. The main materials used are as follows: ground corn, lace made from membrane of white grapefruit, citrus and parsley leaves, seeds of citrus, squash, dates, flowers of maguey cactus, ground corn, "lace" of maguey fiber (Bruns); cantaloupe seeds in vertical and horizontal rows with a large dragon on the back (Shiba); onion seeds, dehydrated grapefruit "rag," red dehydrated bougainvillea petals, Rangoon Creeper seeds, and orange peel (Eckroat); unidentified materials (Longoria); dehydrated ceniza leaves to create the leathery texture of the lederhosen, trim of citrus and parsley leaves (Brewer); and dehydrated jasmine and citrus leaves (Sanford).

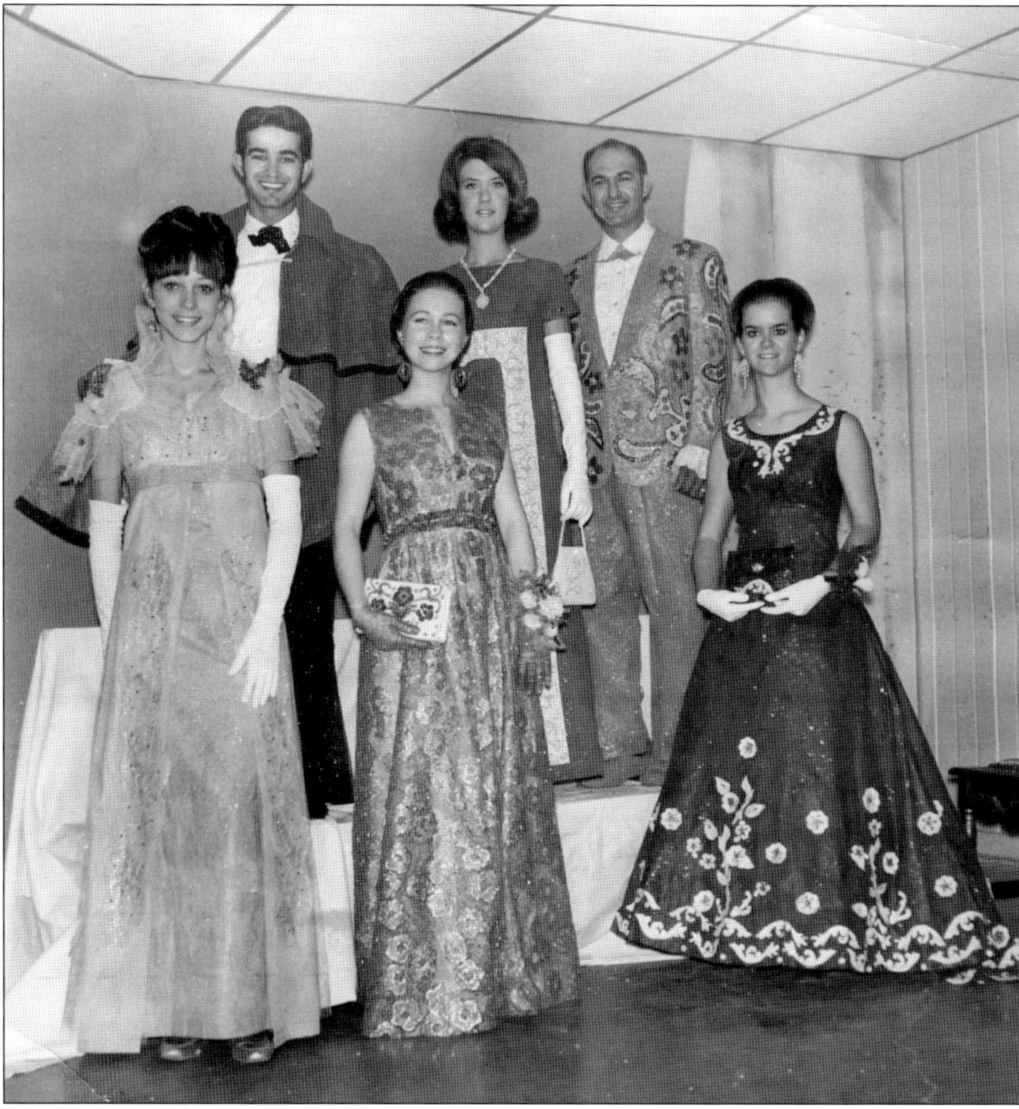

Style show winners from "An Enchanted Evening" in 1970 are, from left to right, (first row) Mrs. Jan Williamson, Twinkle Rackley (winner of the King Citrus trophy), and Kathy Miller; (second row) John Peña, Suellen Wicks, and Salomon S. Marroquín (winner of the second-place trophy). Williamson wears a yellow formal dress with an empire bodice adorned with white lace from skeletonized citrus leaves. Rackley's evening gown of gold French lace is made of onions and onion skins. Miller's gown of silk organza over taffeta is completely covered with dried, pulverized bougainvillea petals. Peña's evening costume includes a cape of bougainvillea flowers trimmed with black onion seeds, a shirt covered with white ground corn, and trousers of black onion seeds. Wicks's dress, made from lettuce, incorporates "sequins" of onion peel and "pearls" of tiny lime seeds. Marroquín dons a gold dinner jacket made with blooms from the golden showers tree. The paisley design includes wildflowers, citrus wood pulp, and handmade "sequins" (commercial sequins were not allowed).

Diane Duncan won the Queen Citrianna Trophy in 1970 for this lace overblouse and pants suit, made entirely from citrus. Four and one-half bushels of lime seed and peel, plus six bushels of Marsh Seedless white grapefruit, were needed for the costume. The lace is made from the membrane of the grapefruit. Small lime seeds were used as beads on the lace, and the banding is covered with flaked membrane.

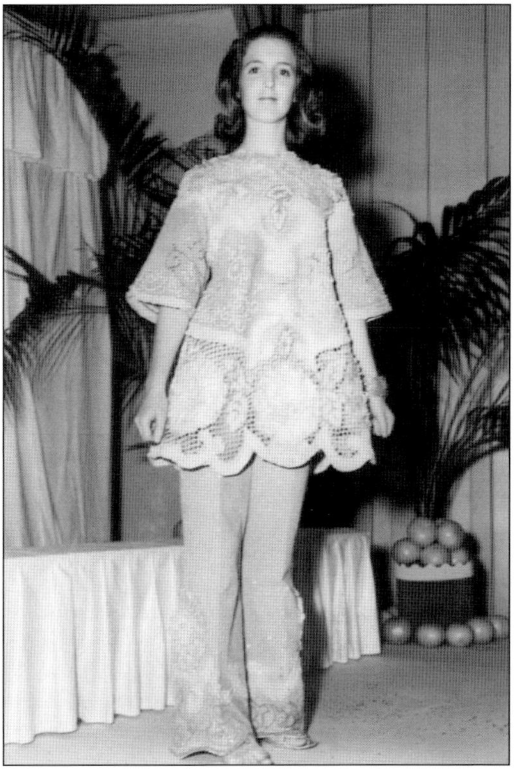

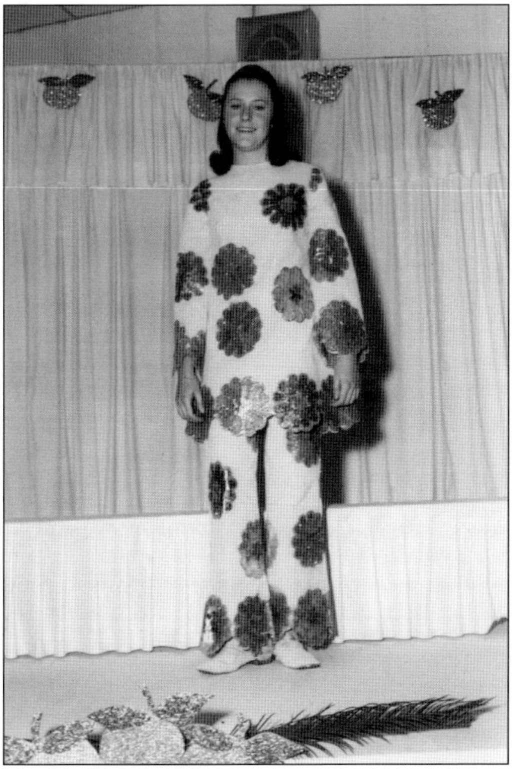

Mary Kay Thompson was a teenage style show winner in 1970. Her pants suit is covered with green citrus wood ground to sawdust to make the yellow background color. The nearly 50 flowers on her outfit are made from purple bougainvillea, red pomegranate, pink roses, green fern leaves, orange cosmos, and marigolds.

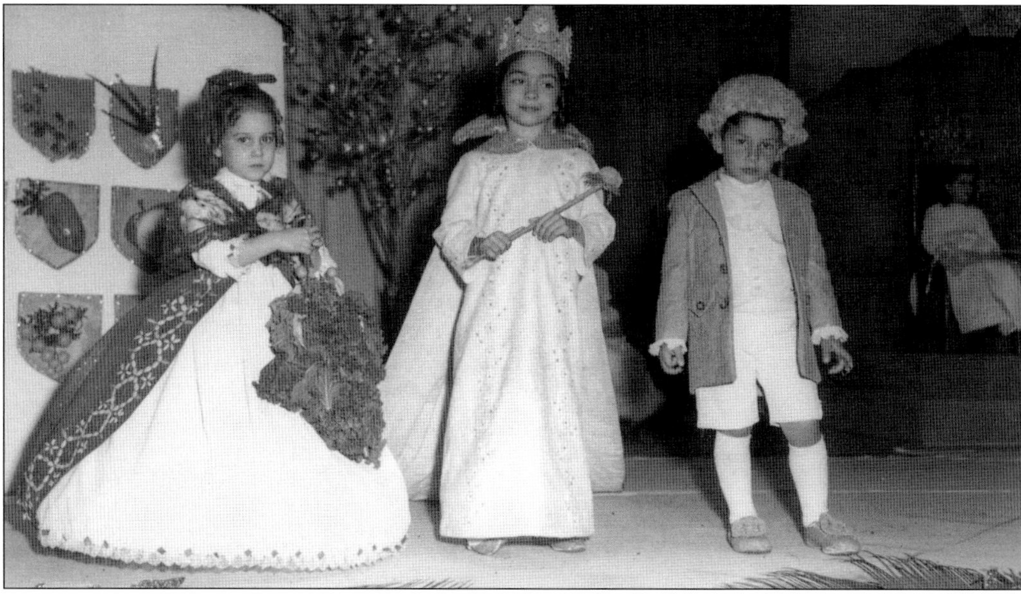

Seen here in 1970 are, from left to right, Melissa Willems, Valerie Valverde, and Marc Barrera. Willems, "Martha Washington," wears a dress of white grapefruit rag mixed with corn, a shawl trimmed with green fern, and a parasol covered with mustard greens. Barrera, "George Washington," wears a coat of onion skin and grapefruit membrane with buttons of valley pecans, plus vest, shirt, and pants of ground corn and grapefruit rag.

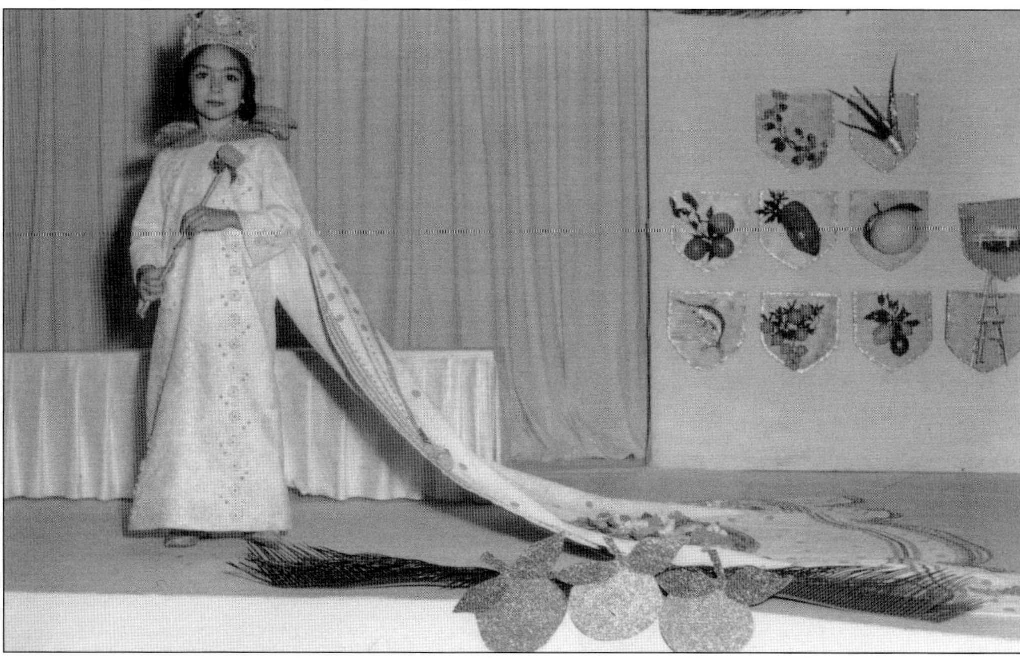

Valerie Valverde wears a costume replicating that of Queen Citrianna, with a dress of pulverized onion skin and glitter and a train of yellow cornmeal. Seeds, citrus leaves, 43 different citrus fruits, onion, orange membrane and rind, and pomegranate were needed to provide details such as "sequins" and "beads." Her crown is made of gold orange rind and membrane, citrus seeds and leaves, cantaloupe, and red pepper seeds.

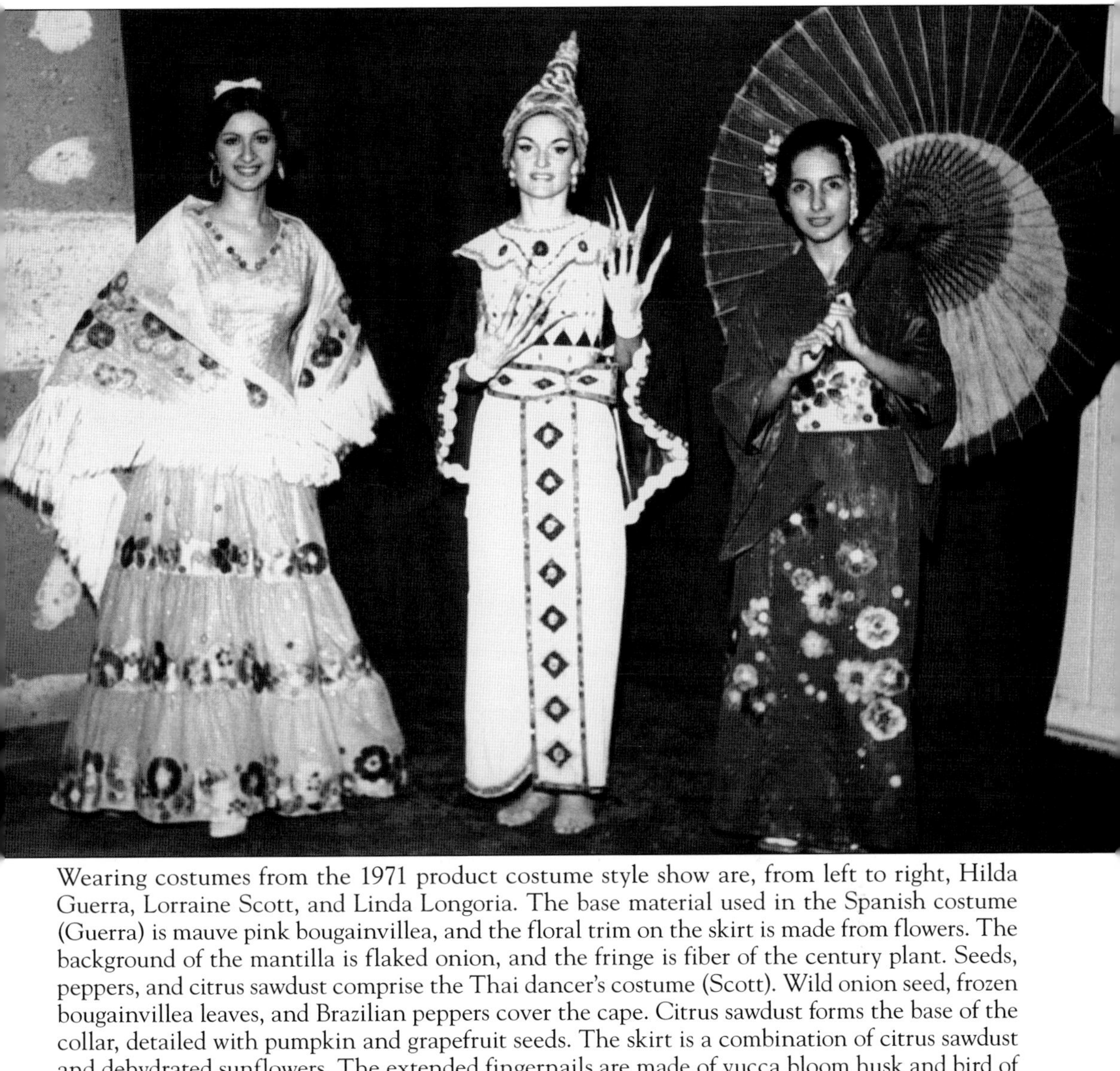

Wearing costumes from the 1971 product costume style show are, from left to right, Hilda Guerra, Lorraine Scott, and Linda Longoria. The base material used in the Spanish costume (Guerra) is mauve pink bougainvillea, and the floral trim on the skirt is made from flowers. The background of the mantilla is flaked onion, and the fringe is fiber of the century plant. Seeds, peppers, and citrus sawdust comprise the Thai dancer's costume (Scott). Wild onion seed, frozen bougainvillea leaves, and Brazilian peppers cover the cape. Citrus sawdust forms the base of the collar, detailed with pumpkin and grapefruit seeds. The skirt is a combination of citrus sawdust and dehydrated sunflowers. The extended fingernails are made of yucca bloom husk and bird of paradise. The Japanese kimono (Longoria) consists of red pomegranate with flowers made from hollyhocks, petunias, and other flowers. The obi uses the previous materials plus sunflowers, chrysanthemums, and roses. The umbrella, made in Japan for this style show, uses valley bamboo decorated with citrus leaves.

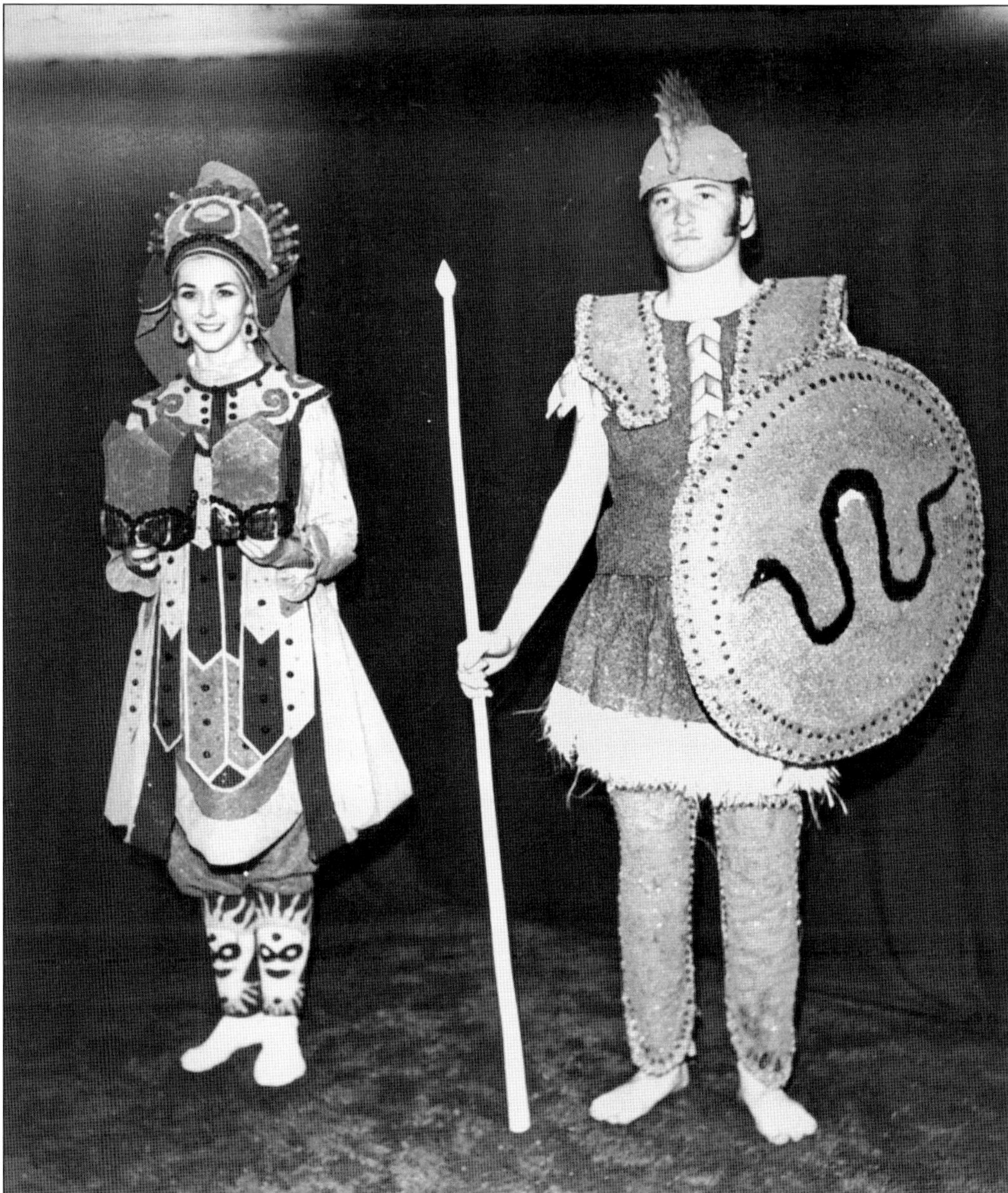

These exotic costumes are modeled in 1971 by Nita Mercantel (left) and Hollis Rutledge. The South Vietnamese ballet troupe costume (Mercantel) required a colorful array of flowers; citrus sawdust and leaves; leaves from hibiscus, carrots, bougainvillea, and Brazilian pepper; prickly pear tunas; and red and savoy cabbage. "Alexander the Great" (Rutledge) wears a helmet covered with dehydrated magnolia flower leaves, trimmed with orange and lemon peel, and a plume of pampas grass. Dehydrated magnolia blooms are used on the shoulder armor, shield, and leg coverings. The snake symbol is made with onion seeds. The tunic is covered with dehydrated carrot leaves, and the underskirt is covered with sisal from the century plant. The staff is made from sour orangewood.

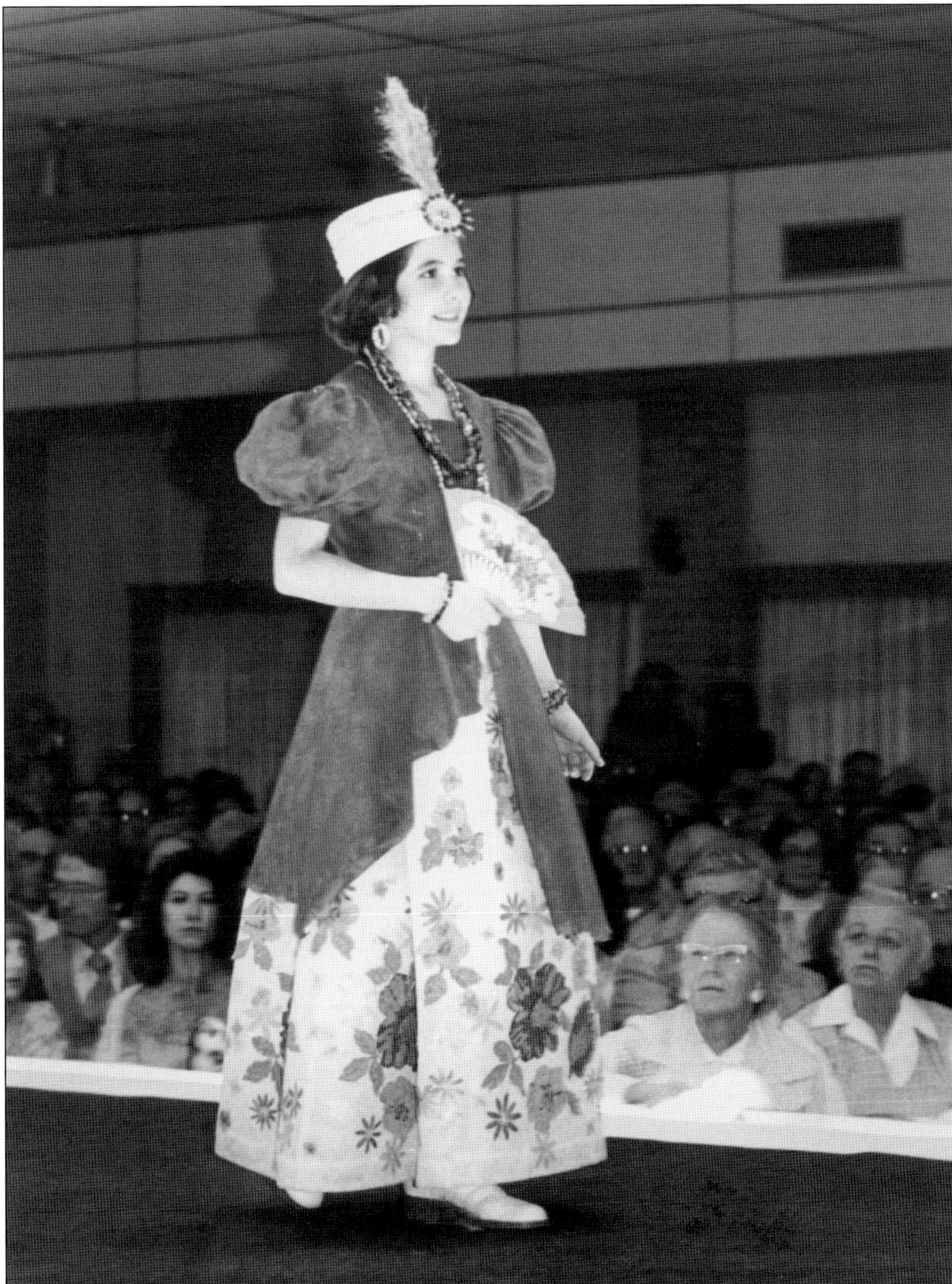

Liza Domínguez represents South America in the grade-school division of the 1979 product costume show. She won first place for her costume made from pomegranate flowers, onion skin, bougainvillea, sunflowers, and citrus leaves. The "feather" on her headdress is made from pampas grass and oleander seed pods. The 11-year-old invested many hours in helping her grandmother make the costume.

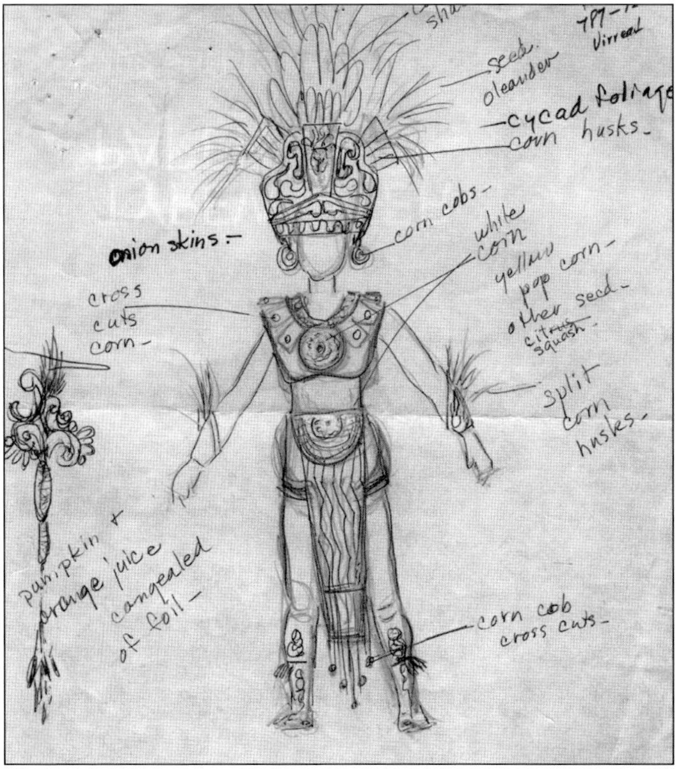

Maurine Duncan incorporated her art and fashion design skills into every costume she made. This drawing shows the planning that went into the one worn by Cruz Tijerina in 1979. Orange and pumpkin juices, congealed on kitchen foil, created "gold-leaf." Feathers were made from cycad foliage, corn husks, onion skins, and oleander seed. This degree of detail indicates why so many of her costumes were prizewinning garments.

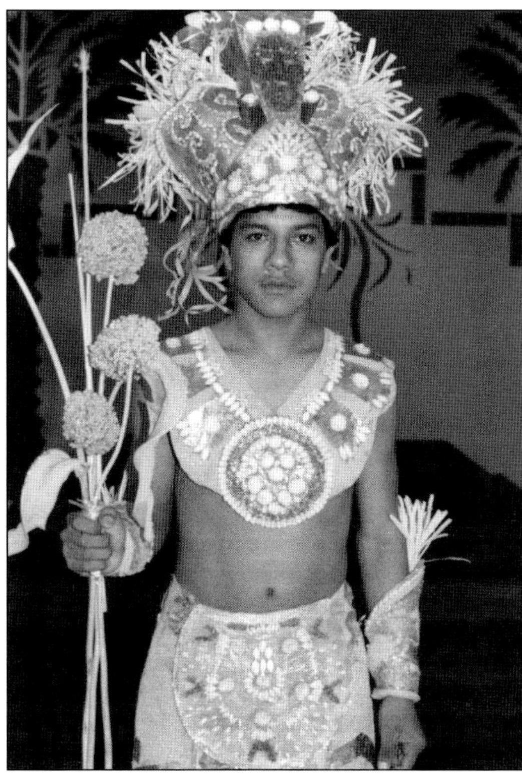

This exotic costume worn by Cruz Tijerina in 1979 represents a Mesoamerican Golden Corn God, known for happy qualities, fertility, and abundance. In keeping with history, the following materials were used: white corn kernels; yellow unpopped corn kernels; seeds of citrus, squash, and oleander; cross cuts of corncobs and popcorn cobs; and corn husks. This costume was the Judges' Choice Best-in-Show.

Javier Treviño wears a suit covered with dehydrated purple bougainvillea flowers in the 1980 product costume show. The design on the shirt is made with flowers and seeds, and he carries a lantern covered with dehydrated pomegranate petals. Letters on the lantern are formed with onion skins. His shoes are covered with charred sugarcane leaves.

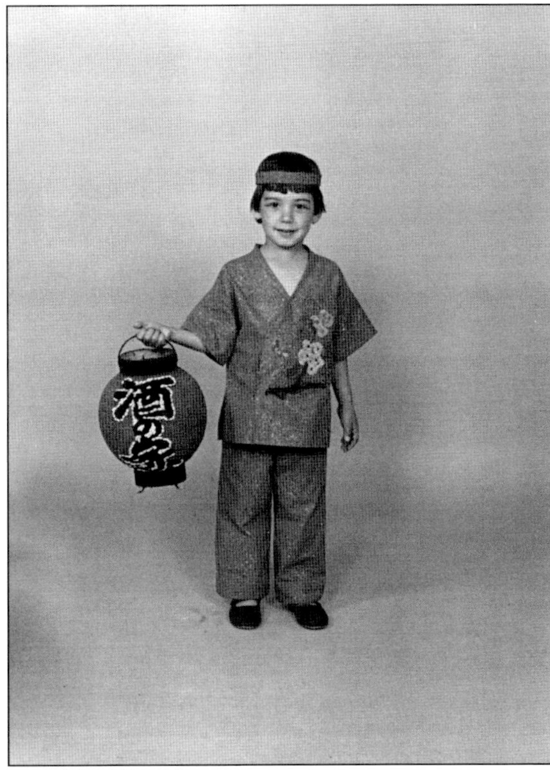

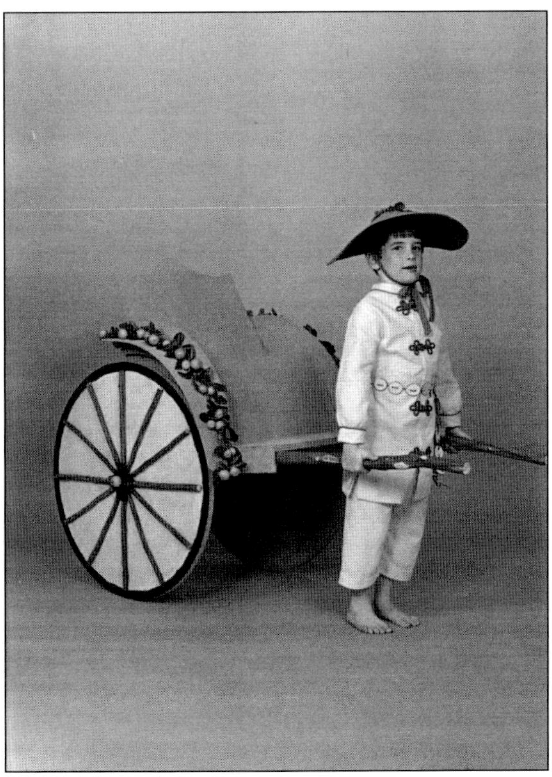

The 1980 fiesta theme, "Texas Citrus in the Orient," was expressed in elaborate product costumes. Michael Carter wears a tunic and pants of green citrus sawdust. The body of the rickshaw is covered with sawdust from dried citrus limbs, the wheels with green sawdust, and the rims with burned tangerine rind. The luggage area is filled with citrus fruit and wood.

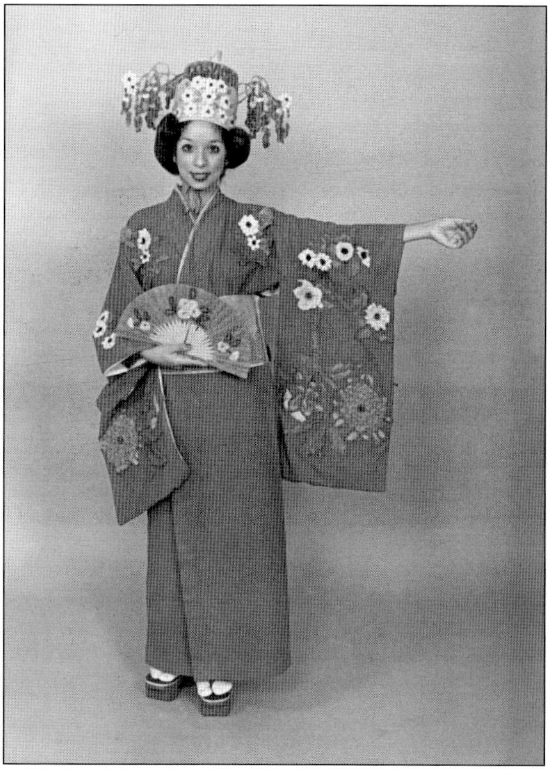

Miriam Morales represented Empress Meiji (1868–1912) and was named Judges' Favorite in 1980. The kimono is covered with citrus sawdust soaked in pulverized beets and red bougainvillea petals. The large "chrysanthemums" are pods from rain lilies. Other "flowers" are made from seeds. The crown is covered with dehydrated sunflower petals, and the fan with seeds and citrus leaves.

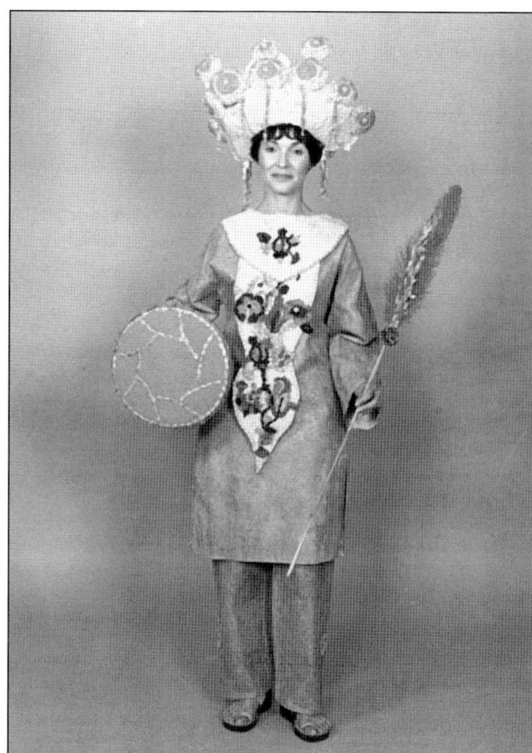

In 1980, Judy Bannworth wears this costume representing a Chinese woman warrior from Peking opera. The tunic is covered by plumbago blossoms with braid of squash and alpha seeds glued on one at a time. The shield is covered with dried flowers and decorated with sea oats. The elaborate headdress uses flowers and popcorn cob slices, the seven strings of pearls are orange seeds, and citrus bark covers her sandals.

Adolfo Huerta, sponsored by the Duncan Insurance Agency, wears this samurai warrior costume in 1980. Instead of the traditional string, leather, metals, bone, and bamboo, this armor consists of white corn, pumpkin, squash, citrus, and onion. Corn husks, pulverized avocado seed, and citrus wood pulp represent leather. The decorated sword began with a palm stem, and the helmet uses the same materials as the suit of armor.

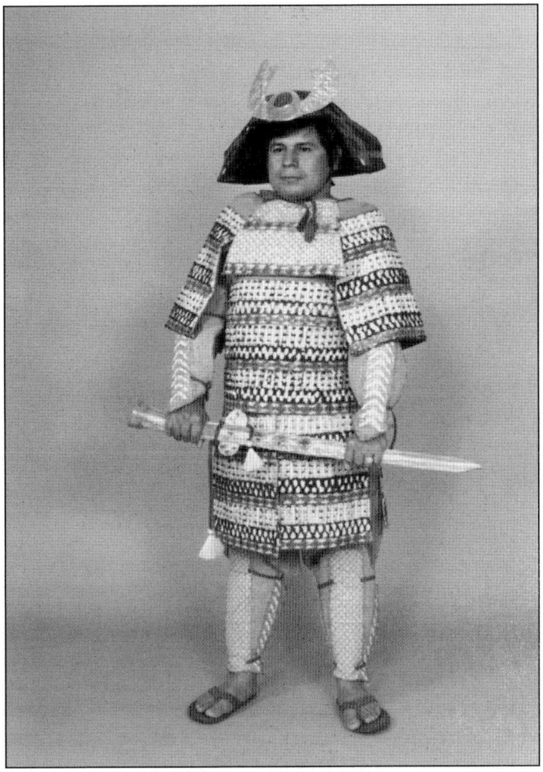

Based upon descriptions of the costumes in the narrator's script, these 1980 style show winners are believed to be, from left to right, (first row) Armando Cespedes III, Rebekah Saenz, Olivia Compton, Patricia Toothaker, and Michael Carter; (second row) Sandra Valencia, Karen Rhea Scott, Miriam Morales, Judy Bannworth, and Jamie Hess.

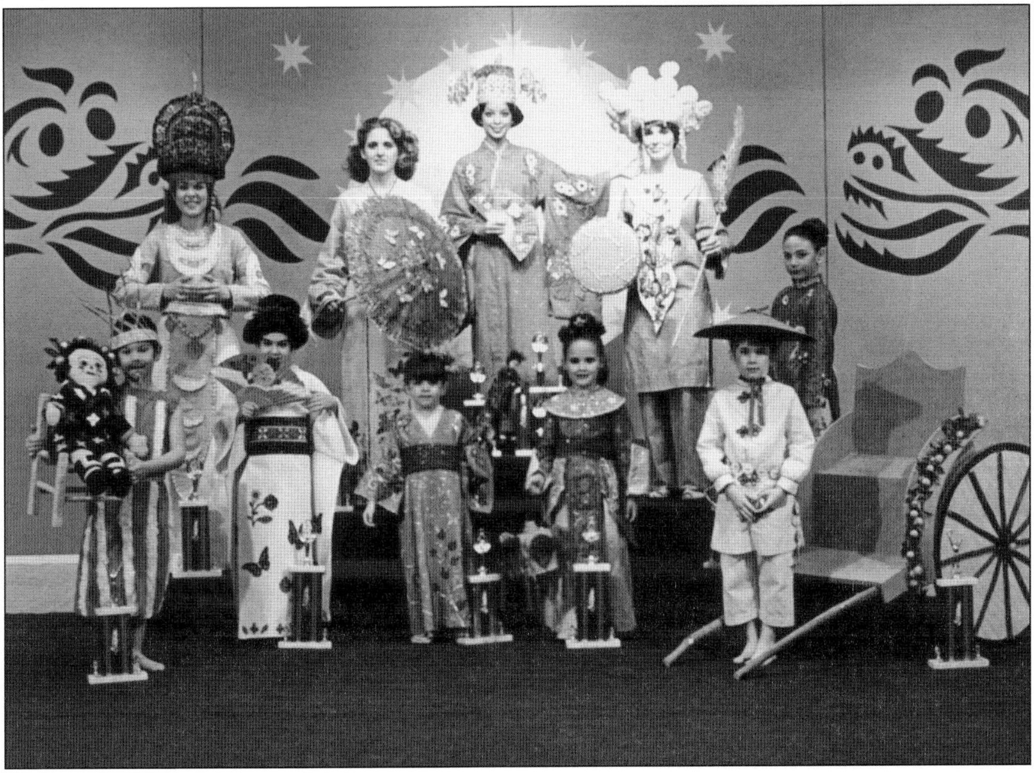

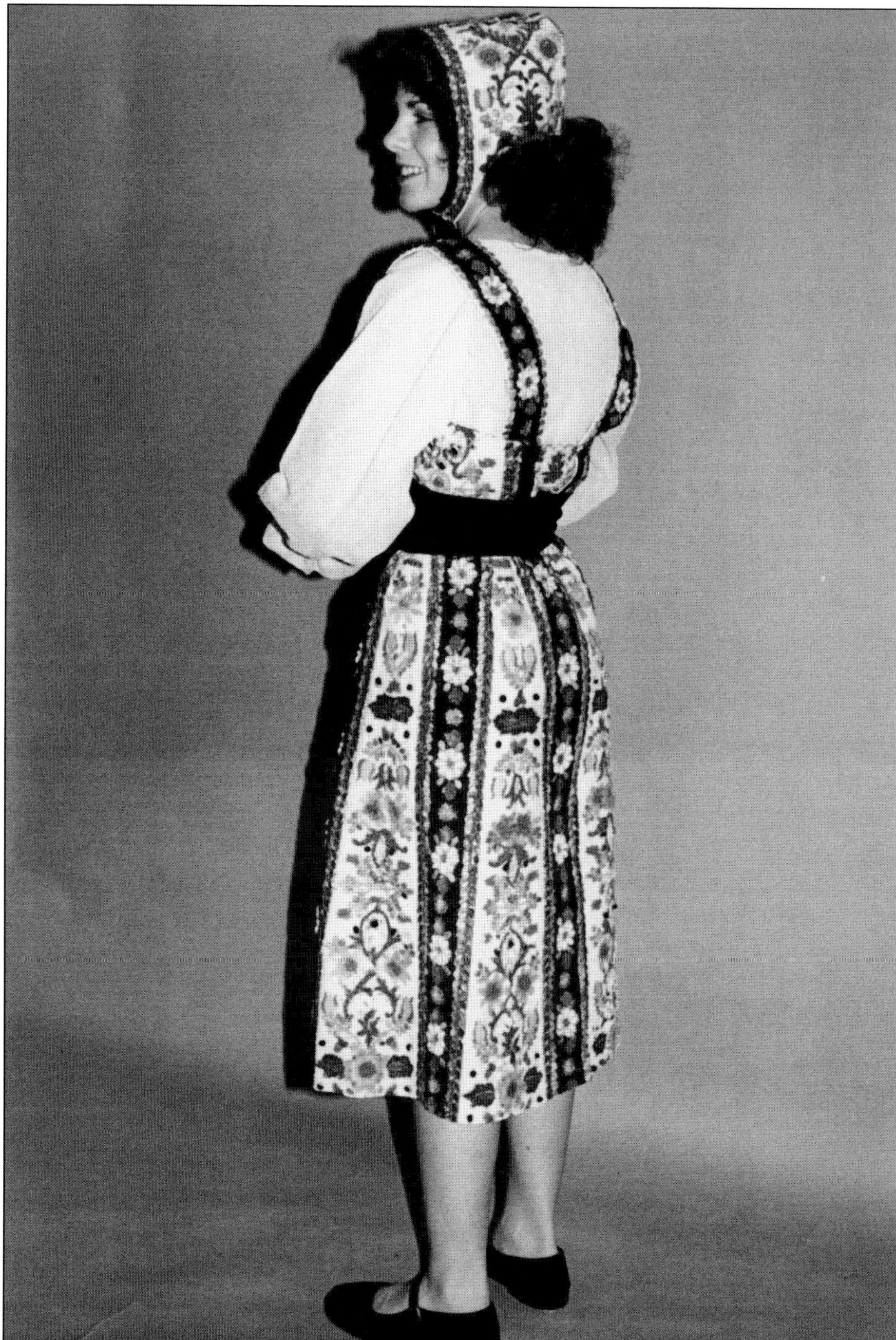

In 1981, Debbie Bannworth received the Queen Citrianna Award, teen division, for this costume inspired by the movie *The Sound of Music*. Yellow on the blouse comes from the sawdust of a green citrus tree. The dust from black onion seeds covers the black apron and slippers. Designs on the skirt use various flowers, parsley, plus seeds from watermelon, avocado, onion, sweet pea, celery, squash, and citrus in 14 layers.

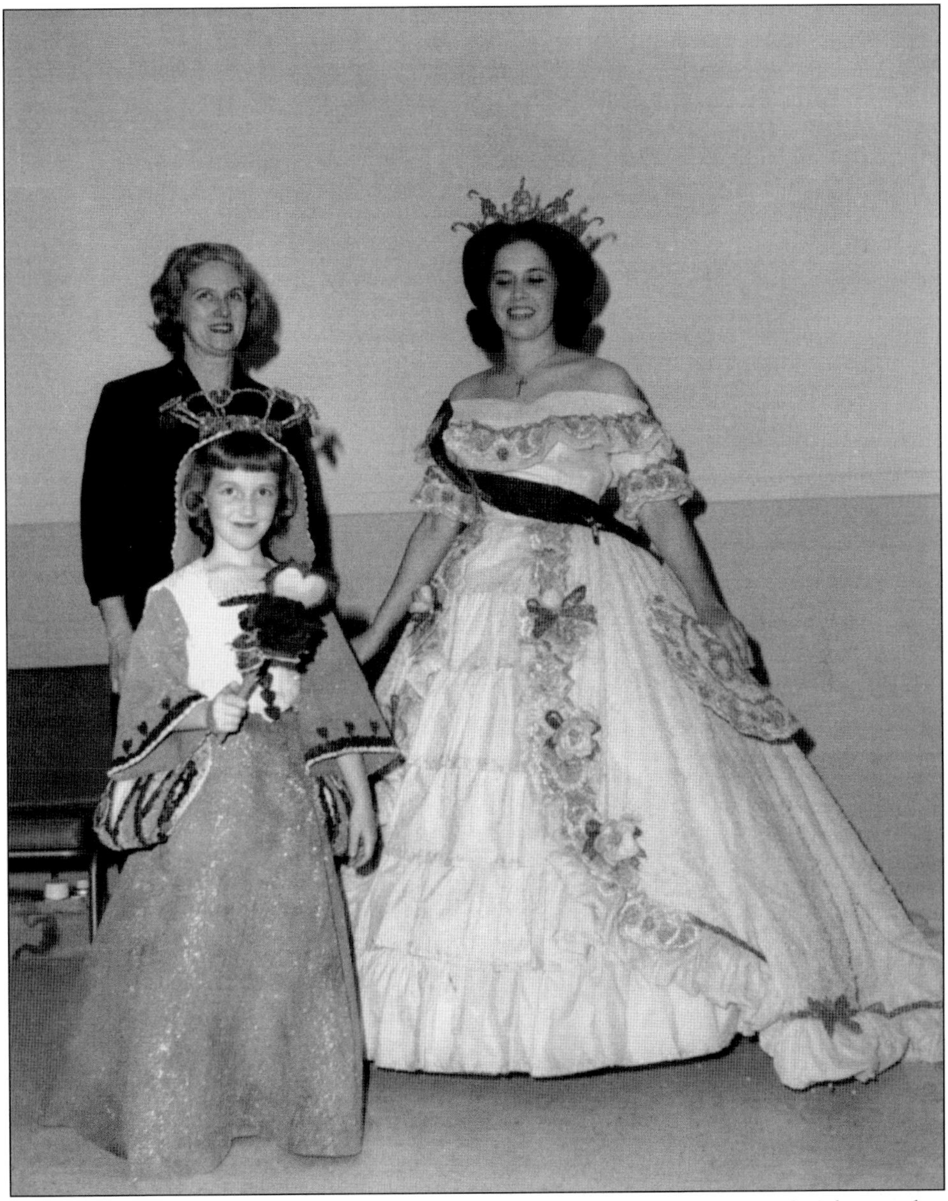

Maurine (Yarborough) Duncan Nickolaus was born in Shiner, Texas, in 1915. After graduation from Texas A&I University in Kingsville, she came to Mission in 1935 to teach fine arts. She continued teaching until 1955. In 1939, she married Thomas Logan "Billy" Duncan Jr., and they raised two daughters. Diane (left) and Nicki (right) are seen here with their mother in 1964. In addition to costume design, painting, and competing in flower shows, Maurine organized the Mission Historical Society, served on the board of the Mission Historical Museum, and received special recognition, including First Lady of Mission (1967), for numerous civic activities. Elected to the city council in 1977—the first council position held by a woman—she served until 1983. Billy died in 1979, and Maurine operated the Duncan Insurance Agency until it was sold in 1981. She married William Leonard "Nick" Nickolaus in 1988, and he passed away in 2002. Mrs. Nickolaus died in 2009 at the age of 93. The Maurine Duncan Award is given to those who contribute years of talent to the Texas Citrus Fiesta style show.

Consistent with our mission to preserve history on a local level, this book was printed in South Carolina on American-made paper and manufactured entirely in the United States. Products carrying the accredited Forest Stewardship Council (FSC) label are printed on 100 percent FSC-certified paper.

MADE IN THE USA